Cost Accounting for Financial Institutions

The Complete Desktop
Reference Guide

Revised Edition

Leonard P. Cole

A BankLine Publication

PROBUS
PUBLISHING

Chicago, Illinois
Cambridge, England

A BankLine Publication

ISBN 1-55738-739-7

Printed in the United States of America

BB

1 2 3 4 5 6 7 8 9 0

D&G

I would like to give special thanks and recognition to my wife Lynn, who devoted many hours of her time toward the completion of this book.

Contents

Preface

This book was designed as a practical and informative daily reference guide for cost analysis and control in financial institutions. It should also be useful to chief financial officers, controllers, asset/liability managers, product managers, management information systems analysts, as well as personnel engaged in marketing, strategic planning, pricing, financial planning, budgeting, profit improvement, students enrolled in cost accounting, and consultants.

The ever-changing marketplace for financial institutions today requires management to act, not just react. The competitiveness of the modern marketplace presents many challenges that did not exist before. In the past management could afford to wait and see what would happen in the marketplace before making changes in services offered; they could count on a reasonable return given a large deposit base of low-cost funds. Today, with many regulatory controls lifted, financial institutions find themselves competing for funds in the marketplace and having to pay higher costs for funds. The pricing pressures are double-sided. In addition to asset pricing, management must now concentrate on liability pricing. Optimal attraction of funds is key to maintaining a well-managed deposit base. The pressures of developing new products and reacting to new business opportunities are great.

The nature and style of management in financial institutions has changed. The style, though still prudent and conservative, is innovative, creative, and ever vigilant for new opportunities in the marketplace. The "will to manage" requires that an increased emphasis be placed on controlling noninterest expenses. This is one area that, in the past, was often ignored. Ignoring such costs was possible because the business of banking contained enough spread in interest margins to compensate for areas with unfavorable expense variances. Today's management sees controlling expenses as an opportunity for increasing profit margins. Profitability depends on knowing the costs of doing business and being able to contain and control them.

As business in financial institutions becomes more diverse in nature and in geographic position, managing becomes more challenging. Good managers know that survival in a competitive environment depends on access to early and accurate information. This need is compelling to those whose job it is to provide information to management. With this sharpened focus on decision information, it is not surprising that cost analysis and control has emerged as a profession in financial institutions. In every profession there is usually one person who stands out as a pioneer in advancing that profession. In financial services cost analysis Terence A. Quinlan, president of Financial Management for Data Processing, is that person. He had the vision to form two organizations to further cost analysis in the services industry and thereby recognize it as a profession. I attended his organizing meeting of the National Association for Bank Cost and Management Accounting (aka NABCA) in 1980. Later on Mr. Quinlan founded Financial Management for Data Processing. These associations provide important forums for the exchange of ideas. They have added much to the awareness of the importance and necessity of cost analysis as a function in the service industry. Many small and large organizations have benefited from the collective thoughts of others. As the synergism increases among those who share their ideas, the profession will benefit further.

Clearly today's management needs to know the cost of doing business. The nature of profitability sources must be more precisely known in order to make sound business decisions. The ever-changing structure of financial institutions demands a three-dimensional view of profitability, a view that includes organizational profitability, product profitability, and customer profitability. Cost analysis is the means of achieving this multidimensional understanding. Performing cost analysis requires good judgment and objectivity. Sometimes good judgment prevails and subjectivity is necessary in place of objectivity, if all the necessary information is not completely available. This book presents the techniques and methods that are the essential tools for sound cost analysis.

The format of this book is such that each chapter stands alone. The reader should be able to read a chapter anywhere in the book and understand it without having read the other chapters. Nonetheless, the reader will find the chapters complement one another.

Chapter 1 introduces cost analysis in financial institutions and explains how it differs from cost analysis in manufacturing industries. Chapter 2, on costing concepts, should stimulate thinking on how to approach a given project. It provides a host of concepts and practical usage ideas.

Work measurement techniques and their practical usage are covered in chapter 3, which gives a step-by-step approach to the use of relative values.

In chapter 4 the concept of average item costing is dealt with in detail. The reader will become familiar with all the aspects and considerations involved in doing a cost study with this approach.

The standard costing approach is covered in chapter 5. Again, much detail is provided. Explanations, examples, and diagram are generously given. Variations to the standard costing approach are also presented. The material should be sufficiently thought provoking to stimulate new ideas.

Data processing is covered from the cost analyst's point of view in chapter 6. The complexities of data processing are broken down in simple and easy-to-understand explanations. Cost pools, transfers, and product allocations are covered in a "how to" format.

Chapter 7 covers expense allocations. The concepts, methodologies, formats, and psychology of this process are explained. The necessary ingredients to any allocation system are covered from the standpoint of what to consider when developing or improving such a system. Suggested report format are included as an aid toward establishing a usable system with readable reports.

The first of the profitability triad—organizational profitability—is covered in chapter 8. The elements to report are discussed. Success factors to effective reporting are indicated.

The second area of the profitability triad—product profitability—is covered in chapter 9. This is by far the most important chapter in this book. It covers the essential elements of a product-profitability reporting system, listing the core items to include in such a system. Cogent examples from the experience of several financial institutions in establishing cost effective and efficient systems are given. Suggested reports formats are included as well as many diagrams showing the possibilities of such a system.

To complete the profitability triad, chapter 10 is devoted to customer profitability, an area that has experienced much pressure for change over the past few years.

Chapter 11 focuses on the need for decision information. How to establish an effective reporting and analysis system is the topic. Which areas to emphasize and which to deemphasize are listed. Cost analysts will find many valuable suggestions in this chapter for strengthening their role as providers of decision information.

A cost study is covered from start to finish in chapter 12. This chapter should be especially helpful to those who are just becoming familiar with the cost analysis function. It brings much of the previous material together. Each step is covered with a checklist of items to consider. Several diagrams and work flow descriptions are included to simplify understanding of the process. The end product—a completed cost study—is then explained in terms of its usefulness and significance to management. Readers should gain appreciation of what cost analysts can do in their role as providers of information on the cost and profitability of doing business in a financial institution.

In chapter 13 the fundamentals of cost control are covered. This chapter is useful in establishing a cost control function. Care has been taken to provide sufficient tools in this chapter to help the reader establish an effective cost control program.

The conceptual approach to the process of administrative expense plan analyses is explained in the chapter, and framework and formulas for sorting out necessary costs from inflated costs are presented.

The benefits of product management and the need for consistent pricing are covered in chapter 14. The role of product management is explained. Tactical and strategic considerations are covered. How to set up and conduct a pricing committee is explained in detail.

There is a time for managers and supervisors to consider changes in the way things are done. This may be due to a change in technology, senior management, business emphasis, or all three. The cost analysis function must keep pace with technological, managerial, and business changes.

Chapter 15 deals with issues to consider in evaluating a new cost accounting system. It is also an appropriate chapter to read for starting a costing program. Such decisions as whether to bring in consultants or embark on an internal projects are covered. The factors to consider in such a venture are set forth in a checklist. A self-analysis is included to aid the manager in determining where possible change is needed.

Chapter 16 is written as an aid to those managers and supervisors who must organize a cost analysis function and manage it. This chapter also provides insight on the dimensions of the costing environment to those involved in cost analysis.

The concepts, ideas, and relevancy of cost analysis are summarized in chapter 17. It is a chapter that brings together many of the things that are mentioned throughout this book.

A glossary of terms and definitions follows chapter 17. The definitions are general, and some vary from definitions used in the manufacturing industries. The reason is that financial institutions are in a service industry.

It is with the intent of providing a useful desk reference that I have written this book. I hope you will find it both useful in practice and stimulating in thought.

Cost Analysis in Financial Institutions

UNIQUENESS OF COST ANALYSIS IN FINANCIAL INSTITUTIONS

Costing in financial institutions is unique. The raw materials of funds and services being provided are looked upon differently than are goods being manufactured. In service industries the set of criteria for costing differs from those used for costing in manufacturing industries. Most of the costing process centers around period costs. The inventory of period costs is the value added to the delivery of a service. Essentially there are no "goods in process." The instantaneous nature of providing services realizes a finished product within seconds, minutes, or hours from the beginning of the process. The raw materials in a service organization are whatever supports the service being offered. The intangible nature of services presents a challenge in cost analysis in a financial institution.

The essential ingredients to be considered in costing for a financial institution are money, people, processing equipment, and facilities. It is the significant utilization of human resources of this business and the commodities of money and service that are provided as products. They set the stage for cost accounting. All service activities are consummated in a relatively short time. (One exception is the probate activity in trusts, a process that may take months or even years.) The analyst must have adequate measuring devices to capture these fast-moving costs. The need for activity and volume measurement is concomitant with the need for good cost data.

Obviously in a manufacturing environment there are raw materials, goods in process, and finished goods. In financial institutions, the raw materials are money and the capacity or energy to produce services. Any physical raw materials, such as brochures, computer runs, and the like, all support some kind of service.

One of the big items that may be viewed as raw material is money. This factor is unique in that the financial institution uses money belonging to someone else (depositors) to loan to someone else (borrowers). In effect the financial institution is borrowing its main raw material and attaching a carrying cost on top of it. The financial institution is effectively acting as a clearing agent for the taking and placing of money. When a financial institution is short on money, it borrows. When it has excess funds, it places them on the market. Therefore, the inventory is quite fluid save for reserves, correspondent accounts, operating capital, and the like.

DESCRIPTION OF A FINANCIAL INSTITUTION

From the perspective of costing it may be said the delivery of financial products falls into the following categories:

- Deposit services

- Loan Services

- Clearing or processing services

- Brokerage services

- Financial services

- Miscellaneous

Since deregulation, the list has been growing as a result of perceived demand. Some financial institutions are leaders in offering new services, reacting quickly and aggressively to changes. Many financial institutions have managers who take an active role in maintaining the quality and life cycle of these services. Many of the services are considered to be *fee based*—that is, a fee is charged to the customer for using the service. Most financial institutions that have commercial (corporate) customers use *analysis* charges to charge them for some of the services they utilize. In lieu of paying a fee for service, the customer is required to maintain a minimum balance to support the cost of the service. (More discussion on this topic occurs in chapter 10, on customer profitability reporting.)

A financial institution may have some or all of the following organizations and their complement of services:

Consumer (retail) banking

Deposit services

Loan services

Financial services

Trust services

Information services

Commercial (corporate) banking

Domestic and international

Deposit services

Loan services

Financial services

Correspondent services

Clearing services

Processing services

Trust services

These may be further expanded as follows:

Consumer

Deposit services

   Checking accounts (demand deposit)

   Saving accounts

Loan services

   Credit cards

   Unsecured loans

   Secured loans

     (automobiles, boats, and real estate)

   Lease financing

Commercial (corporate) banking

Domestic and international

Deposit services

   Business services

   Business savings

Loan services

   Syndications

   Credit lines

   Direct loans

   Acceptances

Consumer (continued)	*Commercial (corporate) (continued)*
Financial services	Financial services
Stock brokerage	Acceptances
Income tax preparation	Remittances
Escrow	Payments
Appraisal	Letters of credit
Investment	Collections
Trust services	Securities brokerage
Pensions	Correspondent services
Estate planning	Placements
Financial management	Information
Probate	Clearing
Information services	Paying
Economic studies	Receiving
	Cash
	Processing
	Data processing
	Trust services
	Business
	Employee benefits

Financial institutions are widening their scope of activity. Many are adding subsidiary companies with diverse activities. As they grow so does the need for cost information. As financial institutions venture into new areas as a result of deregulation and as management seeks to control these activities, they look to cost analysis for cost and profitability measurement and reporting, and particularly for reporting of relevant information.

THE NEED FOR COST ANALYSIS IN FINANCIAL INSTITUTIONS

Many financial institutions find that on a daily basis they need reliable data on costs and profitability. This information is necessary for effective management.

Higher levels, or hierarchical summaries, of cost data often are the most difficult to produce because of organizational allocations, departmental transfers, and the like. However, the cost analysis profession in financial institutions emerged as a result of the need for decision information at *all* levels.

The cost analysis function is usually placed within the controller's office or the finance department. Exceptions to this are decentralized functions serving such organizations as data processing and the line functions (income centers). A good analysis program permeates the entire financial institution. It covers the essential areas for decision making.

A good cost study is founded on consistency—consistency in methodology, procedure, approach, and presentation. Management likes to compare current data with previous cost data. The more explanation required, the less credible the information.

The nature of cost analysis assignments is similar to that of consulting; it requires the same objectivity and broad overview. This is particularly true in the more complex and unstructured areas of cost analysis. The variety of assignments ranges from routine to complex, and from structured to unstructured. Some of the accountabilities are:

- Income and expense reporting

- Overhead allocations development

- Transfer rate development

- Organizational costing

- Product line costing

- Customer costing

The ideal cost accounting system for a financial institution reconciles organizational profitability, product profitability, and customer profitability. All three bottom lines of this triad are the same or at least their differences are explainable. This triad must be kept in mind as one begins a cost study, for it will surface as an issue during the course of presentation to users. Frequent recipients of cost data usually have a reservoir of previous cost studies and may query the comparability of one study to another. Double counting must be avoided. If the triad has been well thought out and the costs appropriately identified, the problem should be minimal. As shown in table 1-1, the three areas are traditionally compartmentalized, tracking essentially the same activity in three different dimensions of profitability. Organizational profitability measures the profits of an income-producing group such as a commercial or corporate group. Product profitability measures the profit of the product lines, the various services offered, grouped according to similarity. An example of product line would be deposit services. (More will be said about this in chapter 2, which treats costing concepts in detail.) Customer profitability is the tracking of composite activity on a per customer or per industry basis. At a minimum the commercial customers of a financial institution are tracked for activity, income, and balances. Many customer reporting systems include cost data for internal use only.

TABLE 1-1 The Profitability Triad

Organizational Profitability	Product Profitability	Customer Profitability
The total income of the financial institution is listed by organization by product.	The total income of the financial institution is listed by product.	The total income of the financial institution is listed by customer by product.
The total costs in the financial institution are listed by organization by product.	The total costs in the financial institution are listed by product.	The total costs in the financial institution are listed by customer by product.
The total profitability of the financial institution is listed by organization and sometimes a subset by product.	The total profitability of the financial institution is listed by product.	The total profitability of the financial institution is listed by customer by product.

The burden of proof is usually placed on the cost analyst to show how these three aspects of profitability tie in or reconcile. In some financial institutions that lack even the reconcilability feature, the request is reduced to proving the compilation of data is conforming to an equitable distribution within each area of the triad.

Integration of information is important. That is, the capturing, transferring, and allocation of costs to organizations, products, and customers must be logical and done with a global view of the entire institution. This requires research so as to document the flow of work and processing.

In order for the cost information to be accepted by the users, it must be clearly presented and simple to understand. Numerical accuracy is essential of course, and the data must be accumulated in an orderly and logical manner. The question "How did you arrive at this number?" must be readily answerable. The analyst must be prepared for questions—bundle of folders and several schedules will not help. The preparation must include editorial notes, formulas, arithmetic computations, and other simple supporting data on the analyst's copy of the memorandum or report. The more probes that are answerable, the more credible the analysis. The integrity of the numbers is of paramount importance. The decision makers need to feel assured that they are working in the proper information quadrant. The processing center managers need to feel they are being represented accurately.

Because financial institutions operate in such a highly competitive environment there is a need for timely and appropriate information. Management may need to know both historical and anticipated costs. This requires identifying past, current, and normative costs. The broader picture such identification affords can be useful for decision making and helpful at times when it seems necessary to take a fresh look at improving the efficiency of certain operations.

A hybrid background in cost analysis and industrial engineering can pay dividends. The analyst can propose a more efficient work flow. Reorganizing work flow should be done with two purpose in mind: efficiency of the work flow and convenience of tracking it. Volume count and cost accumulation could fold together for management reporting given such an arrangement. In smaller financial institutions this hybrid approach is most feasible and can result in cost savings.

The need for current data is important. Managers need data to interpret daily business activity in both financial and operational terms. Decisions must be made quickly. To act, rather than merely react, executives need "here and now" information as well as "what if" information.

Because the trends for financial institutions have been toward more competition, higher costs for deposits and funding, market pressure for additional services, and higher operating costs, a wider array of information is needed for analysis for intelligent decisions. Narrower profit margins have made operating costs an obvious target for cost reduction and control. Some financial institutions have effectively implemented cost management systems to control costs. As a consequence, the cost analyst may be asked the following questions.

- What does it cost the financial institution to open and maintain a checking account?

- What does it cost the financial institution to accept and process a debit item?

- What does it cost to process a cash withdrawal from an electronic teller?

- If we no longer offer the XYZ product, what will it save or cost the financial institution?

- What is the profitability of the consumer automobile loan product line?

- What are the overhead costs for the commercial lending group?

- What is the incremental cost of adding a night shift in Unit A?

- What is the potential profit of a new product in consumer lending?

- If we raise checking account fees to level x, what is the expected drop in balances? Will we effectively come out with more profits?

- What is the average amount and percentage increase per equivalent staff in next year's plan?

- Do we have more than necessary staff in Department C?

- What is the profitability of our relationship with the AB Company?

- Are we making a profit with Industry E?

- Are debit cards cost justified?

These are just a few of the questions one typically receives in the course of performing cost analyses. Some of these questions are relatively easy to answer if a good information system is in place. Others are difficult and may tax the creative skills of the analyst.

There are many issues to be considered in the area of cost analysis. One of the most frequently discussed is the approach to developing an adequate and useful product-profitability reporting system. This in itself has an abundance of underlying issues. The aggregation of data for a product-profitability report takes many factors into consideration.

The cost system methodology needs to be decided. The question of whether to base it on standard costs or actual costs has to be resolved. Either method or a hybrid of both has its advantages. There are also decision issues regarding cost analysis philosophy. One issue pertains to the worth of data and the level of information needed for decision making.

Another issue has to do with the sequential flow of data. Decisions on the level of tracking, the combination of data, and the aggregate of cost pools become points for consideration.

The major issues facing those whose manage, supervise, and practice cost analysis today include

- Whether to expense or amortize research and development costs for new systems and products

- How best to report product profitability and hence develop a reporting system
- Whether to use standard, actual, or a hybrid cost system
- Whether to have a complex or simple reporting system
- Whether to bring in outside consultants for development of a new system
- Whether to centralize or decentralize the cost function
- What roles and accountabilities cost analysts should have in a changing banking environment

These are ongoing dilemmas in financial institutions. The changing environment necessitates an alertness and vigilance toward the institution's accountabilities. Cost analysis is certain to be important in helping to maintain a healthy posture in terms of financial management in the years to come.

BASIC CONCEPTS OF COST ANALYSIS

Let us now begin with some of the basics of cost analysis. In reporting the revenue of a financial institution for management information purposes there are three dimensions to consider: organizational, product line, and customer. Ideally the bottom lime of each one of these should be reconcilable with the others. In performing cost analyses one strives to identify properly and align the revenue with each of these dimensions and its components. The dimensions of total financial institution revenue are shown in table 1-2.

TABLE 1-2 Total Revenue

Organizational	Produce Line	Customer
Commercial	Loans	Wholesale
Consumer	Deposits	Retail
Trust	Services	Other
International	Other	
Other		

Next we have what is referred to as the "other operating expenses." The same concept of bottom-line comparability holds true with this reporting category. In this case one tries to identify and align expenses to each dimension and its components. (See table 1.3.)

TABLE 1-3 Total Operating Expenses

Organizational	Produce Line	Customer
Commercial	Loans	Wholesale
Consumer	Deposits	Retail
Trust	Services	Other
Headquarters	Other	
(overhead)		
Branches		
Service centers		
Remote facilities		
Other		

The last concept that is important to understand in this introductory chapter is the difference between expense and cost. Expenses aggregate to costs when there is a value buildup and a cost object identification. An expense alone does not hold a value. However, a collective set of expenses can equal a cost when there appears to be a discernible value or worth.

Expense versus *cost*
Expense = Amount actually paid.
Cost   = Value or worth. (Cost object)

The expense incurred for a product may differ from the calculated standard cost of the same service as a result of efficiency, volume and capacity, or spending considerations.

The Concept of Standard Costing

Standard costing is prescriptive in nature. That is, it prescribes what the cost *should be*. The standard is benchmark, a basis for comparison. It may be viewed as a criterion for what the value of an activity or product should be and a guide for attaining uniformity.

Standard costing has been in existence for many years. Various forms of standard costing that are unique to the financial industry have come to fruition over the past three decades. Recently some interesting variations have been proffered from the ranks of creative cost analysts.

All variations of standard costing rely on some form of consistent measurement work or activity. This measurement is akin to industrial engineering in seeking to establish a reference point for gauging what the unit timing should be. Industrial engineers measure tasks for two basic purposes: staffing levels and costing. An institution's measurement program for establishing standards must capture both of these factors. (Standard costing will be dealt with in greater detail in chapters 2 and 5.)

AVERAGE ITEM COSTING

The concept of average item costing is based on the premise of finding the actual costs at a given point in time. Simply stated, it looks at the cost of an activity based on the total applicable expenses divided by the total applicable volume.

The method has some drawbacks. Costs in this method are subject to wide variations when there are significant volume changes. It also relies more heavily on subjective evaluations than does standard costing. The cost levels become somewhat unpredictable and therefore do not remain consistent. However, average item costing does let management see what the real costs are without much technical rearrangement of the data.

It is often quicker to produce an average item cost study than a standard costing study, but the procedure does have its complexities. Such considerations as allocations may need to be aligned to activities and products.

This approach assumes a cost structure given a certain volume level. It assumes the cost, as developed, is an average based on that volume level. This approach is quite useful if it is not possible to apply some form of standard costing in one's financial institution. (Average item costing is covered in more detail in chapters 2 and 4.)

Consistency in Costing and Tracking

As stressed before, an aspect essential to any good costing program is consistency, mainly consistency in methodology. The analyst must be able to show the comparative changes in costs from one period to another based on similar assumptions and methodologies. If there are frequent changes in assumptions and methodology, the usefulness of the data deteriorates. Management is usually conditioned to expect data that is comparative. This is not to say that changes should not be made, but that changes should be judicious and infrequent.

If changes in data categories are frequent, users will perceive a decrease in data integrity. Changes in operations, organizations, and the general environment are beyond the control of the cost analyst, however.

The tracking of information entails the same criterion of consistency. Tracking mechanisms must be stable in order to be useful. The construct must be continuous so that new data can be compared with previously tracked data. Again, changes must be infrequent.

The following should be considered in maintaining the integrity of cost accounting through consistency. The assumptions and methodology should be well researched and thought out in advance of a study. This is especially important when there are periodic updates to previous studies of the same subject. The format and structure should be arranged so that a comparable analysis to previous periods can be made. An audit trail of explanation that shows a consistent and logical approach is necessary in providing an understanding of the data being presented.

THE ROLE OF COST ANALYSIS IN COST CONTROL

In understanding the effectiveness and efficiency of an organization, management must focus on its cost data. Usually some alignment to organizations (departments), functions, or products is made with the cost data. This is a result of having to understand the application of costs before one can control them.

The forces of lower interest margins, more intense competition, and the staffing levels all add to the need for cost control. Cost control is a continuous process. It may begin with the planning process, when actuals are compared to plan. Or it may entail obtaining top management's approval on discretionary and major item expenditures. Certainly one of the biggest areas for cost control is staffing. (This is covered in detail in chapter 13.)

For many years financial institutions did not need to concern themselves with a rigid cost control system, although surely many have always been judicious in their control of costs. But the more recent environment has caused financial institutions to look even a closer and to glean further on cost containment and reductions. This requires a degree of sophistication that essentially was not necessary for maintaining a healthy profitability posture in the past. The accomplishment of cost control is vital to the success of profitable and well-run organizations.

The importance of cost analysis is in the function of providing a multiplicity of decision makers with reliable information. The data must be timely, consistent, logical, and accurate.

Depending upon the size of the institution and the interest of senior management, the role of cost analysis can very. It can range from a perfunctory reporting function, all the way to an integrated and analytically charged group of analysts. Therefore, the role of cost analysis may involve some or all of the following:

- Organizational profitability reporting
- Product profitability reporting
- Customer profitability reporting
- Profit plan monitoring and analysis
- Work measurement
- Pricing committee administration and support
- Cost analysis
- Financial analysis
- Litigation cost analysis
- Organizational effectiveness analysis
- Internal funds transfer reporting (development and maintenance)
- Cost transfer rate development and maintenance
- Cost control (profit improvement)

This list is vast but not all inclusive. This is because the cost analyst fills the role of being an internal consultant to management in some organizations.

Cost Analyst as a Clearinghouse

As a staff function, cost analysis serves as a clearinghouse for cost and profitability information, as well as for volume statistics, balances, and data on organizational effectiveness.

Depending on the size of the institution the following departments may look to the cost analysis department for meaningful information:

- Product management
- Marketing
- Pricing committee

- Income organizations

- Data processing

- Asset/liability management

- Legal

- Customer management

- Strategic planning

- Project management

- Financial planning

- Senior management committee

- Operations

The list goes on further. However, the important thing to highlight is the web of complexity that one must experience in the course of serving an institution's needs. The manager of a cost analysis function must balance the requests of such a diverse and active group of departments such as those listed.

Often it becomes a matter of allocating resources according to a predetermined priority or perceived importance. The prospect of serving virtually a whole institution brings to light the need for a comprehensive perspective on the needs of the institution in total. Needed even more is an integrated approach to information gathering.

PRODUCTION FLOW

As a financial institution operates from day to day there are many activities that take on the characteristics of a production shop. This is particularly true in the operations and data processing areas. A good portion of their functions are given to essentially repetitive and routine kinds of activities. Assuming that a certain product's activities remain within the confines of an operations or data processing department from start to finish, the flow is somewhat straightforward. However, if a product is produced by more than one department, then the flow takes on more complex dimensions.

The cost analysis process involves tracing the product from one activity to another, step by step. The important elements of information to gather are obviously volume data, machine time, work measurement data, and expenses. One should try to sort out the relevant factors. Only to count those things that apply is a discipline in itself. Sometimes there is too much data. Discussions with departmental management and supervision hopefully affords some enlightenment in situations like this.

Finding a common volume denominator and staying with it is essential to production flow analysis. Some people call these common denominators *natural value units* (NVUs). They are common units of measurement for an activity or product.

The idea is to focus on the relevant aspects of production flow as they apply to the present cost analysis assignment. One must obviously be careful not to double count elements as the production flow focuses on a particular product or group of products to the exclusion of others. When there is a mutual exclusion for costing purposes, the rule is that the sum of the parts is not to exceed the value of its whole. This is particularly important when a production area is studied in parts and at staggered intervals. The preferable way to approach a production area is to treat it as a whole entity and cost it at one time. The integrity of proper activity flow thereby has a better chance of being maintained.

PRODUCT IDENTIFICATION

Before discussing product identification it is probably a good idea to define what a product is. The generally accepted hierarchy is as shown in table 1-4.

TABLE 1-4 Product Identification Hierarchy

Term	Definition	Example
Product group	A group of related product lines	Depository products
Product line	A group of products	Demand deposits
Product	The lowest level for which revenues are attached	Business checking
Activity	The level at which a unit cost is developed	Process a deposit
Task	The level at which a unit time is developed; in average item costing often the lowest level at which a unit cost is developed	Verify item count

There are many variations to the nomenclature of this hierarchy. The important thing is to define a hierarchy and be consistent with its usage.

The hierarchy at the product level is the one that is emphasized by product management or marketing, customers, and the pricing committee. It is the level where cost data is aligned to revenue data.

It is obvious that the construct of costs at the product level involves some from of measurement. It begins with tasks, which build up to activities, which in turn are folded into products. The integrity of product identification goes back to common volume denominators, or the natural value unit.

For example, we have eight tasks building into four activities. The four activities then fold into one product. This of course assumes there are no other products in the area being costed. Often what happens is that tasks and activities are shared with other products. This complicates the analysis. The section that follows deals with these aspects.

Identifying Multiple Products

In processing areas that have multiple products the tasks and activities need to be sorted out. In some instances some products weave in and out of the processing area in an unusual way. The flow may have breaks in it as regards to how the shared tasks and activities of multiple products are configured. Each then needs to be tracked separately.

There are some interesting challenges to discovering multiple products in a processing area. The processing center's manager and supervisors should be able to identify most products flowing through their respective area. They may identify them in somewhat different terms than would, say a marketing person.

The cost analyst will find that a schematic of the center's tasks and how they flow to activities is a good start. The next step is to show how the activities flow into a product. Volume counts, expense information, and processing time would be the next items to contend with.

Process Flow Analysis

By following the steps of processing for a product the analyst gains insight into all the factors that are to be considered in building costs. The usual procedure is to make a sketch of the work area and draw simple diagrams of the process flow. Names of work stations, equipment, and key contacts become useful in doing a cost study. A sketch of the process also serves as documentation in substantiating the cost buildup to those who may be curious regarding what factors were considered.

The interview process seems to be most helpful in gathering data. Specific information that is useful includes (1) an up-to-date organization chart with names, functions, and phone numbers; (2) a simple diagram showing the work flow for each product; and (3) a brief description of what each function does.

Once you are acquainted with the area the next step is to start gathering volume data. If the volume data is associated with work measurement data, it must be checked for an ultimate product alignment.

You will find it most helpful to next prepare an organizational expense spreadsheet. This will be used for capturing expenses and spreading them to organizations such as departments.

The organizational data is then spread to functions that have specific activities or products that are to be costed. It is particularly important to exclude unusual expenses and to list them as exceptions. Usually the supervisor or manager of the area being studied will bring this up in discussion.

The costs are then aligned based on the completed process flow analysis. At this juncture, the documentation should be thorough, easy to understand, and appropriate.

THE ESSENTIALS OF DATA GATHERING

The analyst should prepare a list of items to cover in the early meetings with the supervisor or manager. A checklist is suggested. The following items may be helpful as a starter:

- Organization chart with names, functions, and staff
- Work measurement data (if available)
- Volume data
- Applicable volume weights (factors that indicate how long one task takes to perform relative to others)
- Cost center expense reports
- Responsibility center expense plan
- Functional descriptions of organizational units
- Items to be excluded (unusual expenses)
- Tasks, activities, and products in the center
- Unusual specialized activity
- Allocations and transfers (both outgoing and incoming)

On salaries it is usually best not to push the issue of exact data. Clerical salary data often is easier to obtain than is exempt and officer data. A good hedge is to resort to midpoint salaries. These can be checked later for a total theoretical recovery. If they are not fully accounted for, then a check with the processing center's manager for "approximations" should help to smooth out the data.

There are a number of phases to go through in gathering information. Assuming for a moment the assignment is to do a cost study for a significant processing center, you will probably have to sort through volumes of information in order to obtain what is relevant.

In performing a cost study there are several steps to go through from start to finish. A project begins when it is assigned. Assuming a typical assignment for a processing center, the sequence of activities generally should parallel the following:

1. Inform staff of the cost center.	Send a memo announcing the cost analyst's arrival and clearly stating the central purpose of the study, to help the recipients to prepare and to defuse apprehension.
2. Establish ground rules.	Hold an initial meeting with the center's manager to discuss the project, its scope, purpose, and benefit and to give an overview of what is and what is not being done.

3. Meet with the center's key staff.	In a brief reconnaissance with key staff members, with the approval of center's manager, seek out more information.
4. Define specific functional alignments.	In initial one-to-one meetings with supervisors, gather specific data on tasks, activities, their flow to products.
5. Put the pieces together.	Gather data on volume, revenue, expenses, and other relevant details.

Align data by task, activity, product, or organization.

Delete irrelevant data—that is, data that has no bearing on the study.

Calculate the data that is gathered to transform expenses into costs.

Analyze the results, determining relationships.

Review preliminary findings with cost center's staff, supervisors, and management.

Make adjustments based on feedback.

Present preliminary findings both orally and in writing.

Review findings with cost analysis supervisors and management for consistency, accuracy, and procedural integrity.

Circulate final draft to cost center's management so they have another opportunity to suggest changes.

Make changes based on feedback.

Distribute the final draft after obtaining the necessary approvals.

Present final results.

Apply the new cost data to organizational, product, and customer profitability reporting, analysis, and decision making.

The cost analysis process can be summarized as a cycle of events—reconnaissance, research, analysis, and presentation. One step builds upon another as this sequence is followed in each phase of a study. The cost manager or supervisor monitors the analyst's progress throughout the course of the project.

TRACKING COSTS FOR CONTROL

Cost control is important to any organization that wishes to optimize its cost effectiveness. It is particularly important during the planning, or budgeting, cycle.

Costs should be compared to units of output or perceived worth. In other words, what is the organization getting for its money? There are several ways to isolate cost data for analysis in an effort to control costs. The idea is to focus on those items that are controllable and also account for a significant part of the budget. They should then be reviewed for necessity and reasonableness.

In chapter 13, which covers cost control and budgeting, you will become acquainted with formulas that will assist you in determining discretionary expenses. Staff compensation is one of the most difficult to deal with. Therefore, a comprehensive presentation that simplifies the process is presented.

In analyzing costs the information should first be broken down and compartmentalized by category and significance. For example, consider the costs of a data processing facility, which are generally quite high. At the first glance you may wonder where to begin. There are three general first cuts at a data processing organization's costs: (1) compensation expense and equivalent staff count, and other operating expenses; (2) a cross matrix of live "projects"; and (3) what products/organizations/functions they support.

By taking a multidimensional view of the same costs you should be able to sort them out according to a hierarchy of value to the institution. The values could be arranged as follows:

1. Obvious errors and redundancies

2. Items of questionable value

3. Items that could be reduced without any adverse effect to the organization (nonessentials but nice to have)

4. Items that have obvious value and merit

This hierarchy could be brought to senior management's attention for them to decide how far they want to go in terms of reductions.

PRODUCT ALLOCATIONS

In building expenses into a value, which we will call *costs*, the expected result is usually something that can be viewed as a product. As the processing and value building toward a product's delivery occurs, it may possibly flow from one organization to another. It may pick up direct overhead burdens as well as indirect allocations along the way. The final burden is corporate overhead. All products must share this. If one's "system" or "procedure" for capturing these allocations is correct, there will be no redundancies. Management has a vested interest in making sure there are no double charges. This places the burden of proof on cost analysis. For overhead allocations to products to be fair and equitable, they must have a sound concept or basis and be reasonable.

Overhead falls into three general categories; general administration, support center, and service center. General and administrative (G&A) overhead is the corporate headquarters kind of burden. Support centers are those that provide some indirect support to a given processing center. Service center overhead is an allocation based on some type of direct support. (These will be explained further in chapter 7.)

DECISION INFORMATION—THE FINAL REPORT

Cost data is generated for one primary reason: decision making. Cost analysis is thus both a tremendous responsibility and an opportunity for its practitioners. It requires a high degree of accuracy and research integrity.

The information must be collected, analyzed, and presented with its eventual application to decision making in mind. Because there is often a backlog of projects competing for the cost analysis staff's attention, it is important to find out what areas are of the highest priority for the decision makers.

The analyst should aim for a useful final report. The decision makers need to have the data presented in a clear and concise manner. The best memoranda or reports are those that summarize the essence of the project by means of tables, relegating detail schedules to an appendix where the usage and meaning of each schedule is explained. Thus for each table there should be a supporting schedule with the same data in greater detail. The final page in a project write-up should be a schedule of detailed assumptions.

Costing Concepts in Financial Institutions

Costing terminology for financial institutions differs from the costing terminology of manufacturing because financial institutions do not have an inventory base. This chapter presents the basic concepts of costing. The concepts of direct, indirect, and incremental costs are defined. The notion of hard versus soft dollars is explained and illustrated with an example.

Tracking the flow of costs from one work station to another is covered. The buildup of expenses into costs within an organization is an important concept to understand.

DETERMINING COSTS FROM EXPENSES

Expenses are incurred in order to produce something of value. Each time we spend money we expect some value in return, whether it is goods or services. Cost analysts look upon expenses as short-term expenditures. In service organizations some expenses by themselves do not reflect a value for delivery to a customer, becoming an element of value only when a product is identified or delivered. Therefore, cost is counted as an element of the value of the product. We see expenses building into costs at the point where value or worth becomes definable. This is when an expense is identified with a cost object. Graphically this concept appears as follows:

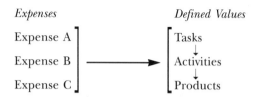

Expenses are temporary until they become task, activity, or product costs. Costs hold a value or worth, hence the difference between expenses and costs.

Consider the following example. A particular department has an information service it provides to other organizations. Its expenses have been isolated as shown in table 2-1.

The information service has a *defined value*, or developed cost, of $47,475. The $47,475 is the total of the set of expenses accumulated to defining the value or worth of this service. Since it is a defined value toward a product delivery it is considered a cost. The remaining $142,425 has not been identified with a product at this time, so it is considered an organizational expense. The next step would be to develop some form of unit cost. This could be based on time, materials, or a combination.

Assume for a moment the information service we are talking about produces a pamphlet as its product. Assume 100,000 of these pamphlets were published during the period being measured. Determining the unit cost then is a matter of arithmetic division.

$$\$47,475 \div 100,000 = \$0.47475 \text{ each}$$

The basic unit cost is therefore $0.47475. This is a simple approach to average item costing.

TABLE 2-1 Cost Assessment for a Department

Expenses	Department Total	=	(Product Costs) Information Service	+	(Organizational Expense) Other
Salaries	$100,000		$25,000		$ 75,000
Fringe	25,000		6,250		18,750
Marketing	15,000		3,750		11,250
Premises	7,500		1,875		5,625
Entertainment	8,000		2,000		6,000
Stationary and supplies	33,000		8,250		24,750
Telephone	1,400		350		1,050
Total	$189,900		$47,475		$142,425

THE NEED FOR VALIDATION AND RECONCILIATION TO ACCOUNTING REPORTS

Cost analysis delivers information within the confines of management information. The data worked with is a derivation of general ledger type accounting. Cost analysis data should be off-line in a sense. It should be in a data base that is subordinate to or apart from the general ledger. In this way one can move data about without disturbing the integrity of the general ledger. Allocations and transfers not of a general ledger nature can be made throughout this king of management information system without disturbing the general ledger. Management information systems used for cost analysis rely on the general ledger and other systems as feeders or providers of information. The link is one way from the general ledger to the management information system.

**Figure 2-1. The Flow from General Ledger
Accounting to Management Information**

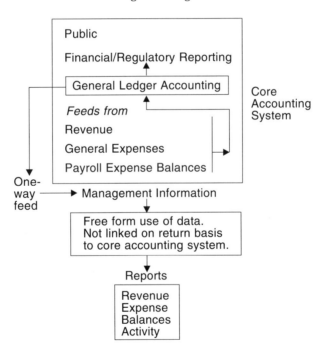

Figure 2-1 shows the difference between general ledger accounting and management information. The figure presents one concept of how a management information system can link to a core accounting system. The idea is to understand the volatility of data integrity once it leaves the core system. Because the potential arrangements of management information data are infinite, the cost analyst must take precautions to ensure an adequate audit trail has been recorded. It is essential to be in a position to reconcile management information data to the core accounting system. This is necessary as a test for validity. If the data is not reconcilable, then it must be explainable. The less specific one can be in reconciling a management information system to the core accounting system, the less credibility there is in that management information system.

Any differences need to be explained for each category. To this end a good understanding of the core accounting system is needed by those involved in management information reporting. For purposes of this book we will consider cost analysis or cost accounting data as part of a management information system.

IDENTIFICATION OF COST FLOWS

Identifying and tracking the flow of costs from one organization to another provides an interesting challenge. It entails researching the inputs to a particular organization. It also involves following the output from that same organization. Tracking cost flows requires an understanding of volume measurements. A first step in this process is the preparation of flow diagrams. Preparing flowcharts helps one gain an understanding of what is to be tracked. To identify and track cost flows from one organization to another first identify common units of measurement for a particular activity, and then decide which level is most appropriate in identifying and tracking an activity (some levels of detail are too minute and their tracking adds unnecessary and confusing complexity).

Obviously there are changes as an element flows into an organization and comes out as something greater. What flowed in as element A may come out as element AB. Becoming knowledgeable about the process that is occurring will enable you to track the flow correctly from one organization to another.

At this point it is appropriate to mention responsibility center reporting. Responsibility center reporting plays a major part in tracking expenses for costing purposes. (More will be said about this in chapter 8.) Responsibility center reporting is the process of tracking data by organization. Reporting includes revenue, expense, and activity information and is essential in the accumulation of cost information.

DIRECT VERSUS INDIRECT COSTS

Direct costs are costs that are integral to the process being measured. They are identified on an immediate basis. Direct costs are usually not allocated. Their assignment is usually determined as they are incurred. They are in the closest accountability proximity to what is being costed. Many organizations track their direct costs with little or no difficulty. They assign accountability codes to track and apply costs to appropriate departments with relative ease.

Direct costs can be captured for organizations, products, and customers. Of these three, the first is probably the easiest. Costs are usually identified with an organization by category. Invoices and other supporting documents make it relatively easy to find the benefactor of direct organizational costs. Where these costs become a matter of judgment is in product and customer alignment. Once the costs leave the primary organizational domain, tracking becomes a matter of applying them to products or customers. An example of a direct cost is the salary of a paying and receiving clerk. This person's salary is directly related to the function of paying and receiving and hence to certain products within that function. There may, however, be an allocation of this direct cost to the various products within the function of paying and receiving.

Indirect costs are those that are not in direct support of a process, organization, products, customer, or activity being costed. They must be aligned or allocated by use of a concept or basis. They are indirectly in support of a product or activity. Some can specifically be identified with a product or activity. They are called indirect specific costs. Others cannot be specifically identified with a product or activity. They are referred to as indirect nonspecific costs. Good judgment and research are needed to develop a logical and equitable basis for applying each indirect cost.

Indirect costs are therefore allocated in some form to processes, organizations, products. customers, or activities. Sometimes indirect costs are first allocated to an organization and then applied to products or processes on a secondary basis.

These costs may be referred to as *matrix costs*. They usually have a widespread effect on multiple organizations, crossing organizational lines. They may be identified as coming from a support function and be remotely related to the production and delivery of certain activities or products.

An example of such matrix costing is a marketing department that may indirectly support a paying and received function. It is a support function remote from paying and receiving. Hence its costs are indirect to the production and delivery of paying and receiving services.

It is important to note that the distinction between direct and indirect costs varies with the level of organizational hierarchy being studied.

INCREMENTAL COST

An incremental cost is the cost of additional activity. It is sensitive to activity or occurrence. Incremental costs are usually a direct function of some activity or occurrence. An incremental cost is also defined as the net difference in cost between two alternatives. This is one category that causes much debate between cost analysis and product management or marketing. Product management or marketing may be inclined to use incremental costs as a basis for bringing in new business to a processing center during periods of low activity. This may be an acceptable approach at times. However, if an area is saturated with much discounted, off-peak business, the activity will attract more than just incremental costs. Incremental and variable costs are close to being the same in a nonmanufacturing definition. When the net difference between two alternatives is being compared, then the variable cost becomes a subset of the incremental cost and the whole comparison is under the definition of incremental.

HARD DOLLARS VERSUS SOFT DOLLARS

"Hard dollar" costs may be defined as those that are incurred on a paid invoice basis. That is, a cash flow occurs as a result of the cost. The same holds true for hard dollar revenue. It would be revenue counted or collected funds received. Again, it requires a cash flow or accrual in order to be counted as hard dollars and to have hard dollar savings.

The most frequent instance of hard dollar savings is as a result of staff reductions.

"Soft dollar" costs represent allocations that are indirect in nature, such as overhead. General, administrative, and other indirect expenses fall into this category.

Soft dollar revenue is not accrued or collected as cash. Analysis charges may be considered soft dollar revenue for a financial institution. Analysis charges may be accrued for service performed on behalf of a customer. They are a levy against an earnings allowance for a customer's deposited funds.

For example, a customer may have a deposit large enough to attract an earnings credit of $1,000. The $1,000 allowance is a synthetic amount to be applied against service rendered to the customer by the financial institution. There is no movement of funds, hence the soft dollar designation. (See chapter 11.)

Soft dollar savings are fixed to the extent that they are reallocated when an activity is deleted. For example, a savings of 15 minutes per day in office operations usually translates into a soft dollar savings. Generally, no one's pay will be reduced because of 15 minutes less work to do. Rather, the staff will fill the time with other duties. That is, the savings will be realized through reallocation of resources. An aggregate of 15-minute segments in one office may accumulate to a determinable staff reduction. If the reduction occurs, then a soft dollar savings has been converted into a hard dollar savings.

CONSERVATIVE APPROACH TO REVENUE AND EXPENSE IDENTIFICATION

The conservative approach to revenue identification requires that skepticism be applied when deciding what is to be counted as revenue. It entails minimizing one's projections by counting only those items that can be substantiated and omitting doubtful items from the count. If one is to err, it should be on the side of understating revenue.

On the expense side the conservative approach is to identify all relevant expenses and overhead. This approach requires a more encompassing definition of what is to be counted and entails counting all possible relevant items. It is full absorption to the limit. If one is to err, it should be on the side of overstating expenses.

This conservative approach looks toward potentially understanding projected profits on an analytical basis. It emphasizes practicality in lieu of overestimation of projected profits. This is especially true given a high degree of risk. In applying this concept, the higher the risk and uncertainty, the more conservative one should be.

CONTROLLABLE VERSUS NONCONTROLLABLE EXPENSES

Controllable expenses are those over which a manager has discretion. They are expenses that can be either incurred or terminated by the manager of the cost or responsibility center. Examples of this would be staff salaries, travel, entertainment, and community activities expenses. The manager essentially has control of these expenses. In most organizations the manager must approve such expenses before they can be incurred . If the budget gets right, the manager can cut back on these expenses or eliminate some of them altogether.

Noncontrollable expenses are of a different nature. They are to a degree forced on the cost center manager. They are usually incurred at other levels or on an institutional basis. For example, an overhead allocation to each cost center is a noncontrollable institutional expense.

Consider a manager receiving an allocation for the activities of a cafeteria's operation. He or she usually has no leverage over this expense. The allocation usually is taken at face value, though perhaps not readily. There may be some complaining about the equity of the allocation basis, the quality of the food, the cafeteria's lack of profitability, and other such diversions. However, the manager usually ends up having to accept the allocation. It is the cost center's share of "beneficial" institutional activities.

Another example is the employee benefits allocation. The manager could state a case for having the benefits rate lowered. He or she might suggest the age group of the staff is such that a lower benefits rate should be used. For example, persons in a lower age group may not be interested in being vested in retirement pensions and hence they may not stay with the institution long enough to accrue any benefits. However, benefits are spread on an average basis. The cost of spreading benefits on an exact basis would be cost prohibitive. That is, the cost of creating an information file for the exact distribution of benefits expenses may exceed the value obtained as a result of having that information. Whatever the case, the manager once again must accept the allocation as a noncontrollable expense. Of course it could be argued that benefits are quasi-controllable (no staff, no fringe). However, it would be rare indeed for a manager to cut productive staff in order to save on benefits allocations.

Fixed Costs

Many processing centers have a fixed base of costs. These are costs that remain even if there is no processing activity occurring. Fixed costs are active even when the organization or facility is inactive. No doubt we have all seen boarded up facilities that have been vacated and placed in a dormant mode. They must represent some sort of fixed cost in the form of taxed, insurance, and protection. Sometimes owners find it is less costly to board up facilities than to continue to use them for commercial purposes. In these cases there is an economic decision in favor of incurring fixed costs in a nonproductive mode.

In a processing center the prudent manager strives to keep down fixed commitments. The more fixed costs there are, the less leverage the manager has in terms of operating decisions regarding change.

Fixed costs become variable when capacity is exceeded due to volume increases. The fixed costs may step up to increase the capacity. This means a new threshold of fixed costs is in place. For example, the processing center was at 100% capacity and was producing 100 volume. The volume increases to 125. This necessitates management to expand its processing capacity. Additional costs—fixed and variable—may occur.

Variable Costs

Variable costs are those that vary with activity. If there is no activity, there are no variable costs. For costs to be variable they must be incurred only as a result of activity.

An example of a variable cost would be computer paper. If there is no activity, the paper is not being used. But once printing reports or some form of output begins, the paper is consumed as part of the production process. The total cost varies with production.

Fixed unit costs change with volume. On a per unit basis they decrease as volume increases. On the other side, variable unit costs remain the same regardless of volume levels. This of course assumes the variable costs are within the framework of existing production capacity. (For more on fixed versus variable costs, see chapter 4.)

The Long-Run Variability of Costs

All costs become variable in the long run. Today's fixed costs may represent something that will become obsolete in future years. Hence, in the long run all costs are defined as variable. That is, they are variable within a given time frame. Factors of change measured by months or years are the determinants. What is a fixed cost today will become a variable cost over the long run. This is attributable to change. Organizations and things do change with time.

Total Costs

Fixed costs plus variable costs equal total costs. This formula represents the total capturing of all costs. This means that allocations, direct, indirect and other such categories are a subset of this formula. Knowing the total costs of doing business is important to those who manage a business. The cost analyst uses this as an objective in determining the parameters of an entity to be costed.

Unit Cost Identification

In arriving at a unit cost the analyst looks for common units of volume measurement. This is usually expressed as a common denominator. Some call these *natural value units*. They form a basis for identification of costs with an activity and ultimately a product.

It is the bringing together of all relevant costs toward an activity and then a product on a unit basis that is important. This process involves good research, interaction, and judgment.

Amortization and Depreciation

There are certain startup costs of a new operation that are expensed for financial reporting purposes but may be amortized for management reporting. Such costs represent a challenge to the cost analyst. First, the analyst must decide on where to capitalize and amortize items for management reporting. Then one must decide how long—two years,five years, or ten years—the period of amortization must be. The higher the risk and the technology, the shorter the amortization period should be. Another consideration pertains to recordkeeping. It an expenditure is being tracked outside of the general ledger system, who will remember the specifics if staff turnover occurs a few times over the next year or two? Proper documentation needs to be posted and filed so that successors can adequately amortize off-line capitalized expenditures.

DIRECT COSTING

In doing an assignment that requires direct costing, the analyst captures only those costs that are directly linked to production and delivery of the product or activity. Identification and alignment to direct expenses becomes the focus. The expense buildup must match the definition of a direct cost. All tasks and activities flowing to a product must be directly linked to that product. There can be no indirect allocations. This means that by definition indirect support cannot be counted as part of the cost. We then see and arrangement as follows:

Direct labor cost	x x x
Direct materials costs	x x x
Direct other operating costs	x x x
Total direct costs	x x x

If direct costs are properly identified and frequencied there should be little room for questions as to their appropriateness.

In summary, direct costs carry no excess. They only account for what is incurred as a direct result of the process or entity which is being costed.

INCREMENTAL COSTING

Out-of-pocket expenses for each unit of additional activity are counted as incremental costs. An *incremental cost* is the cost of an additional unit of production. There are usually no fixed costs to be counted. Often out-of-pocket variable costs related to excess capacity are the universe of incremental costs.

The costs may be captured as follows:

Processing during a relatively low activity shift

Direct labor

Direct materials

Direct other operating expenses

Some may argue that if there is excess capacity that can absorb the additional activity with no additional cost, then the incremental cost is zero. However, this approach is difficult to justify in a profit-oriented organization.

As mentioned earlier, incremental costs may also be viewed as the net difference between two alternatives being compared. It is within this context that fixed costs can be considered for comparative purposes.

FULL ABSORPTION COSTING

Under the concept of full absorption costing all fixed and variable costs are counted. This includes both direct and indirect costs. In fact, all the costs in the financial institution are accounted for. This means there may be substantial allocations of general and administrative expenses to be absorbed in the unit costs.

Some call this the "sponge approach" to costing. All possible costs are absorbed into unit costs. This means the total financial institution's expenses can be accounted for on a closeout basis with no residuals. A word of caution: It also means there is no double counting.

This costing concept takes with it the conservative approach. It assumes that bank overhead must be covered by apportioning it to profit centers, or the products being offered. The format then appears as follows:

Direct costs	x x x
Indirect costs	x x x
General and administrative overhead	x x x
Residuals	x x x
Total costs (fully absorbed)	x x x

For this format to be accurate and equitable the financial institution must have an operational allocation method that includes an explainable audit trail.

In most management information systems, period costs are defined as the expenses being closed out on a monthly basis. Because financial institutions do not hold inventories as do manufacturing enterprises, most if not all expenses are closed out as period costs on a monthly basis.

CONTRIBUTION MARGIN

The contribution margin is defined as what remains after direct costs have been subtracted from revenue. It is usually referred to as the contribution toward overhead and profits. The format is as follows:

	Revenue	x x x
	less	
	Direct costs	x x x
=	Contribution to overhead and profit	x x x

It is a way to look at organizations, product lines, or customers and quantify their contribution to the bank in total. This is often used when a decision is being made as to acquisition, continuance, retention, or termination of an entity.

The Use of Holidays, Vacations, and Absences Factors

In conducting a cost project there are times when a holidays, vacations, and absences (HVA) factor should be applied. Generally an HVA factor is applied to a per unit labor time on individual projects. This occurs when a special costing project is being done, and the cost analyst is not working with net available hours, such as is computed when doing a processing center. Another way of saying this is that the analyst is working with time factors that are being developed for a particular task, activity, product, or entity on a stand-alone basis.

HVA factors are not applied to net available hours. They are, however, applied to time estimates and standards that are part of the gross paid hours of a worker. Let's take an example that will show how this works.

Assume there is a personal financial service being provided. The product is called "Personal Financial Planning." The department that provides this service has many other products. The decision is made to charge the customers on a per hour basis for this service. Therefore, the cost analyst must develop a per hour cost rate so the service can be priced for profitability.

Assume the following:

- The HVA rate has been determined by a separate study to be 16 percent.

- A trust officer with an annual salary of $22,000 will be providing the service.

- The benefits rate as determined by a separate study is 20 percent.

- There are no special other operating expenses in providing this service. However, a ratio of other operating expenses to compensation has been calculated and determined to be 10 percent.

The study proceeds as follows:

$$\begin{array}{r r l}
& 60 & \text{minutes} \\
\times & .16 & \text{HVA factor} \\
\hline
& 9.6 & \text{minutes HVA allowance}
\end{array}$$

The 9.6 minutes is additional time to add to the 60 minutes of direct time. It is a way of recovering "nonproductive time" the officer is being paid for. In other words it factors in the cost of holidays, vacations, and absences. It becomes part of the direct chargeable time of the officer. This does not take into account any idle time on the job. Idle time will show up as nonbillable hours.

We add this 9.6 minutes of HVA to the 60 minutes.

$$\begin{array}{r r l}
& 60.0 & \text{minutes direct time} \\
+ & 9.6 & \text{minutes HVA} \\
\hline
& 69.6 & \text{total minutes to be recouped for each hour of direct time}
\end{array}$$

Next we will derive an hourly rate for the trust officer's time. Let's assume a 40-hour week and multiply it against 52 weeks in a year. The calculation is

$$40 \text{ hours} \times 52 \text{ weeks} = 2,080 \text{ annual hours.}$$

An annual salary of $22,000 has a 20 percent benefits factor on top of it. Therefore, we need to determine the total compensation for this officer. The calculation is as follows:

$$\begin{array}{r r l}
& \$22,000 & \text{annual salary} \\
\times & .20 & \text{benefits factor} \\
\hline
& \$ 4,400 & \text{benefits amount}
\end{array}$$

We next add the salary and the benefits together.

$22,000   annual salary
+   4,400   benefits amount
$26,400   total annual compensation

We are now ready to develop the hourly rate. We take the annual compensation and divide it by the annual gross available hours to arrive at an hourly rate. The calculation is thus

$26,400 annual compensation ÷ 2,080 gross available hours
= $12.6923 per hour.

For purposes of explanation let us further divide the hourly rate by 60 so that we will have a way of attaching a cost to the 9.6 minutes of HVA.

$12.6923 compensation per hour ÷ 60 minutes
= $0.2115383 compensation per minute.

We can now multiply the 69.6 minutes times the per minute compensation rate of $0.2115383.
The calculation is

69.6 × $0.2115383 = $14.7231 compensation cost per chargeable hour.

To this we add the 10 percent for other operating expenses. The calculation is

$14.7231   compensation cost per chargeable hour
×   .10   other operating expense factor
$ 1.4723   other operating expense allocation

We now have the cost per chargeable hour. The calculation is

$ 1.4723   other operating expense allocation
+ 14.7231   compensation
$16.1954   total cost per chargeable hour

Another way of using the HVA factor is to wait until the hourly rate is developed before applying it. That is, the 9.6 minutes calculation would not be used. The sequence would be as follows:

$12.6923   compensation per hour
×   .16   HVA factor
$ 2.0308   HVA allowance

$12.6923   compensation per hour
+   2.0308   HVA allowance
$14.7231   compensation per chargeable hour

To this we would add the other operating expenses as was done before, calculating

$14.7231   compensation per chargeable hour
×   .10   other operating expense factor
$ 1.4723   other operating expense allocation

We then combine the two as before

$ 1.4723   other operating expense allocation
+ 14.7231   compensation per chargeable hour
$16.1954   total cost per chargeable hour

You can see there are variations in the application of HVA factors. The main point to remember is that HVA factors are used as a means to recoup the time used for holidays, vacations, and absences by factoring it into costs. Many of the examples throughout this text will be using net available processing hours. When they are used, there is no need for applying HVA factors.

HIERARCHICAL COSTS

In some organizations there are hierarchies of cost accumulation. A basic general expense system is usually established to accommodate organizational cost tracking by hierarchy. The cost analyst can take advantage of this. The cost hierarchy becomes the analyst's map in researching the relevant costs. An example of an organizational hierarchy is as follows

Corporation
↑
Group
↑
Division
↑
Department

For costing purposes it is best to accumulate data down to the lowest working group, which in this example is a department. It allows for proper accumulation of labor and other operating expenses. However, at the lowest level it may not be cost justified to track other operating expenses at that level. In some instances, however, it is prudent to track labor costs down to the lowest level.

The cost accumulation is such that administrative allocations usually begin at the department level and work their way up. We then see the hierarchy as follows:

Corporation	General and administrative
Group	Operational and administrative
Division	Operational and administrative
Department	Operational and administrative

A common definition of cost hierarchies is important in maintaining consistency.

Figure 2-2 depicts the various costing concepts in relation to one another. What follows, is a series of charts of illustrations that depict the various costing concepts that will be presented throughout this book. Each one shows the uniqueness of costing in the financial services environment.

Figure 2-2. Relations among the Various Costing Concepts

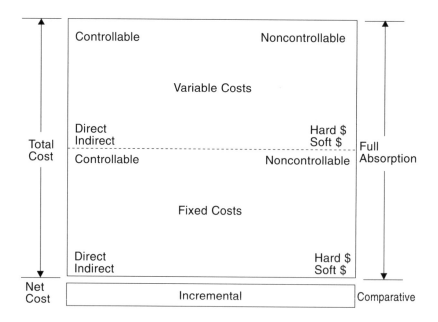

Figure 2-3 is a product flow guide. It depicts tasks building into activities, activities building into products, products building into product lines, and, last, product lines building into product groups.

Figure 2-3. Product Flow Guide

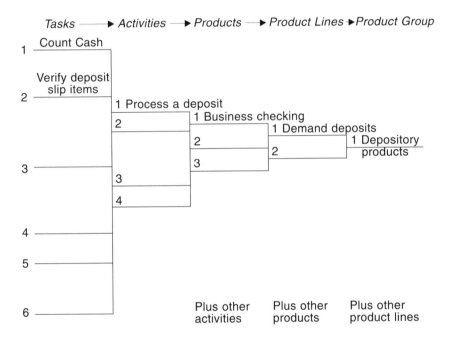

The hierarchy is somewhat simplified in this illustration and is partial. The real flow isn't always so unified. Often there are feeds from other organizations or processing centers. These feeds could be other activities, products, and product lines as they build in hierarchy to a product group level.

Figure 2-4 is a framework illustrating the concept of costing in the banking environment. It shows how direct organizational expenses build into direct cost components and then are applied for pricing, reporting, transfers, or decision analysis. It also shows the same buildup of flow for indirect expenses. The major difference is that direct expenses must be identified. This is different from being allocated as is the case with indirect expenses. The gathering of this information can either be structured (routine) or unstructured (special request).

Figure 2-4. Costing Concept

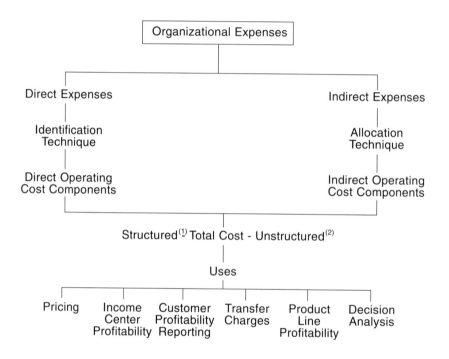

$^{(1)}$ Based on a routinized collection of relevent data.

$^{(2)}$ Special cost information for specific decisions.

Figure 2-5 pictures direct organizational studies as being conducive to either standard costing or actual costing (average item costing). Direct organizations are part of the stream of activity being costed; that is, they are contributors on a direct basis in some form. This could be an activity building toward the production or the delivery of a product.

Figure 2-5. Organization Types and Cost Methodologies

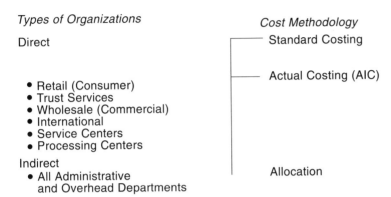

Types of Organizations

Direct

- Retail (Consumer)
- Trust Services
- Wholesale (Commercial)
- International
- Service Centers
- Processing Centers

Indirect
- All Administrative
  and Overhead Departments

Cost Methodology

Standard Costing

Actual Costing (AIC)

Allocation

Indirect organizations are away from the production or delivery of a product, perhaps in support of the process. Examples are support organizations and administrative and overhead departments.

The structure of costing is presented in figure 2-6. It shows the cost components of labor, machines, and forms as examples of directly identifiable costs. One of the uses (applications) for direct cost information is effectiveness reporting.

Compensation and other operating costs are sometimes identified in processing centers for the purpose of transferring them out to a user or client base. As a point of interest, tracking general and administrative overhead expenses provides a unique application in establishing staff support accountability. As one builds to a total cost

Figure 2-6. Costing Structure

Cost Components

Labor

Machines

Forms

Total direct cost

Compensation and other operating cost

General and adminstrative overhead

Total cost (fully absorbed)

Applications

Efficiency and effectiveness reporting

Transfer charges

Staff support accountability

Customer profitability, pricing and product management

Figure 2-7. Summary of sources and Uses of Cost Data

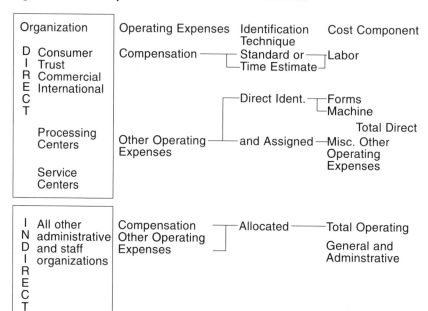

(fully absorbed) the application becomes multidimensional in terms of customer, pricing, and product evaluations.

Figure 2-7 is a summary of the sources and uses of cost data. It serves as a map guiding the analyst toward maintaining consistency in the application of costing concepts.

The costing concepts in this book are closely aligned with activity-based costing (ABC). An ABC system is defined as one that:

1. Identifies the causal relationship between the incurrence of cost and activities,

2. Determines the underlying driver of the activities,

3. Establishes cost pools related to individual drivers,

4. Develops costing rates, and

5. Applies cost to product on the basis of resources consumed (drivers).

Thus, ABC determines the activities that will serve as cost objects and then accumulates a cost pool for each activity using the appropriate activity base (cost driver).

Not only does this method assist in identifying cost drivers for cost accumulation purposes but it helps to determine economic value added and non-value added activities in an organization or process.

Work Measurement Techniques

To meet the challenges of improving productivity in financial institutions, work measurement is important. The ability to measure how long a task takes to perform against a prescriptive "how long it *should* take" is necessary. Efficiency and effectiveness go hand in hand as financial institutions seek to improve productivity.

Work measurement is important for costing and productivity measurement purposes. It helps an organization to determine how much it should cost to perform a function versus how much it is actually costing. It is useful in tracing product flows and associated work time. Work measurement is the foundation for standard costing.

This chapter explains the how to's of basic work measurement. The methods of using predetermined time standards are described but not explained in detail because the process is too highly specialized and lengthy. The reader should finish this chapter, however, with a working knowledge of self-logging or time ladders and relative value analysis techniques.

Work measurement is complementary to cost analysis. Besides measuring the frequency and duration of tasks and activities, it also provides information on staffing levels and organizational efficiency.

Aside from volume counts, the kinds of work measurement information the cost analyst is interested in obtaining is data indicating how long a particular task or activity takes to complete. The information is either prescriptive (how long it *should* take) or historical (how long it *actually* takes) to complete a task or activity.

The standard for completion of a task or activity is what the cost analyst needs from work measurement data. If the data is compiled by industrial engineers, the cost analyst may at times have to product align work measurement data. That is, the data may be arranged for staff measurement only. This is due to the staffing rather than product orientation of industrial engineers in many organizations.

Because work measurement data is not always available, cost analysts sometimes must utilize their own measurement methods in constructing relevant data. You may wish to use one of the more basic methods such as relative values or self-logging. More sophisticated approaches such as stopwatch measurement or predetermined time standards requires special training.

Before delving into the specifics of how to perform work measurement, an orientation toward terminology needs to be gained. The following terms and definitions are used in work measurement.

Actual hours   The total staff hours consumed in the completion of a task

Normal time   The amount of time it should take an experienced or trained person to complete a specific task (prior to the inclusion of time allowances)

Time allowance   A decimal factor that is multiplied and then added to the normal time to complete a job (a contingency allowance for personal needs, fatigue, and unavoidable delay)

Standard time   A measured or predetermined unit of time that it takes in order to complete a specific task; includes allowance factors and results in prescribed time

Effectiveness   The resultant net output of an organization given its utilization of resources

Efficiency   A measure of actual performance against prescribed performance

Self-logging   A work analysis technique that relies on the employee to indicate the time devoted to each task of accountability during a specified time span

Figure 3-1 depicts the relative complexity and accuracy of the various work measurement techniques. In the chart methods, time measurement (MTM) and predetermined time standards are rated as highly complex and accurate. From there the accuracy and complexity descend to stopwatch, work sampling, relative values, self-logging or time ladders, and historical averaging.

Figure 3-1. Types of Work Measurement

All of these methods have their merits. Which method or methods should be used depends on how much time, staff, and money management is willing to commit to work measurement as well as its management philosophy.

HISTORICAL AVERAGING

Historical averaging is used when the cost analyst wishes to avoid disturbing the workers at their stations or has a need only for information based on historical relationships. Historical data should only be used on an interim basis. This is because of its inherent limitations: The time value derived could be obsolete or inaccurate, and the performance of the workers cannot be rated is in other methods of work measurement.

Historical averaging involves comparing relationships of previously recorded data in order to draw inferences on the measurement of tasks. Let's take a simple example to see how this works.

Assume there is a documentation review function for consumer loan processing in the loan department and you are called upon to estimate the average time it takes for each review without contacting the department's processing staff. The information provided is for the previous year. It is as follows: 1,500 net staff hours worked (net of vacations, holidays, absences, and training) 1,200 loans processed. Historical averaging would involve dividing the net staff hours worked by the number of loans processed. Hence, 1,500 ÷ 1,200 = 1.25 hours. The derivation is only an estimate, since the analyst cannot ascertain idle time and other such factors that would tend to distort the per item average.

SELF-LOGGING OR TIME LADDERS

Self-logging, which is also called time ladders, is a method that relies on the workers to account for their individual time. The analyst usually designs a form that segments the workday into time blocks, say of 15 minutes each. Major tasks are listed as column headings. For every time block the worker must specify how many minutes were spent on each category of task. Table 3-1 is a sample form.

The advantage of using the self-logging method is that it enables the analyst to obtain data without being present. This obviously has its economic advantages. It is easily understood and simple to administer.

The disadvantages are the sole reliance on the worker's attentiveness to filling out the form in a timely and accurate manner. A participant needs to be made aware of the benefits of such a study prior to being asked to fill it out.

If the worker will be performing multiple tasks within a 15 minute segment, then a weight factor method could be included to allow for proper distribution of the work during each segment. For example, assume that from 8:00 a.m. to 8:15 a.m. the worker does some filing, opens some mail, and mostly answers the phone. The use of weight factors will allow this person to properly distribute the record of his or her work during this time segment. Based on what was done during that segment, the worker may assign weights as follows: opening mail, 20 percent; filing, 20 percent; and answering phones, 60 percent. This totals 100 percent, which could be set to account for the entire 15-minute segment. This is the *percentage of time distribution method*. Another way of accounting for this could be just deciding to set the factors to equal the total minutes within each segment. With this approach, the factors in the same example would be as follows: opening mail, 3 minutes; filing, 3 minutes; and answering phones, 9 minutes. This is the actual time distribution method. The weight factors should be designed according to their intended use and the computing process to be utilized.

RELATIVE VALUES

Under the relative value method, task or activity values are assigned by relative weight of one to another. Usually the lowest time is assigned a weight of 1.0. Everything else is then relative to it.

The use of relative values as a costing tool can be a time saver. It also can provide a base of information regarding the distribution of work according to time consumption.

The process of using relative values therefore may be explained as the assignment of weights to tasks or activities in order to determine time consumption relationships.

TABLE 3-1 Self-logging Form

Position _____Clerk_____   Date _____7/17_____

Name _____Tiggs_____

Time	Tasks					Personal Needs	Total Time/Weight Factors
	Opening Envelopes	Filing	Phones	Typing	Other		
8:00 to 8:15 am	3	3	9	–	–	–	15
8:15 to 8:30	4	3	8				15
8:30 to 8:45	6	5	4				15
8:45 to 9:00	10	1	4				15
9:00 to 9:15	13	0	2				15
9:15 to 9:30	14	0	0			1	15
9:30 to 9:45	0	10	5				15
9:45 to 10:00	0	12	3				15
10:00 to 10:15	0	14	1				15
10:15 to 10:30	0	15	0				15
10:30 to 10:45	0	14				1	15
10:45 to 11:00	0	15	0				15
11:00 to 11:15	0	15	0				15
11:15 to 11:30	0	0	1	14			15
11:30 to 11:45	0	0	0	15			15
11:45 to 12:00 pm	0	0	15				15
12:00 to 12:15	0	0	15				15
12:15 to 12:30	0	0	14			1	15
12:30 to 12:45	0	0	0			15	15
12:45 to 1:00	0	0	0			15	15
1:00 to 1:15	2	1	12				15
1:15 to 1:30	14	0	1				15
1:30 to 1:45	0	10	2	3			15
1:45 to 2:00	0	0	0	15			15
2:00 to 2:15	0	0	1	14			15
2:15 to 2:30	0	0	2	13			15
2:30 to 2:45	0	3	1	10		1	15
2:45 to 3:00	0	0	0	15			15
3:00 to 3:15	0	0	0	15			15
3:15 to 3:30	0	0	0	15			15
3:30 to 3:45	0	0	0	15			15
3:45 to 4:00	3	5	2	5			15
4:00 to 4:15	0	0	1	13		1	15
4:15 to 4:30	0	0	2	13			15
4:30 to 4:45	0	0	0	15			15
4:45 to 5:00	0	0	5	10			15
Totals	69	126	110	200		35	540

The advantages of using relative values over other methods are many. The method is easy to learn. It is not as time consuming as using a stopwatch or predetermined time standards. Because it does involve interaction with production center personnel, it is mostly based on their estimates.

There are some disadvantages of using relative values, however. They are not as accurate as accurate as a stopwatch. Moreover, they depend upon the accuracy of data supplied by production center personnel. The following is an example of how this process works.

Take a simplified production area that has three products. Assume there is no work measurement data available. However, the center's manager provides the following data.

Product	Designator	Annual Volume*
Sweep of customer balances	Product A	20,000 units
Receive and execute phone requests	Product B	11,500 units
Balance information reports	Product C	10, 000 units

Through a discussion with the analyst, the production center's manager then provides the following relative values: The total of all product A's activities takes twice as long to process as all of product B's activities. Product B's activities take 1.5 times as long as product C's to process. This particular example is a macro approach.

The manager further states there are no special costs associated with any of the products. The expenses of the center are $125,000 for staff compensation, $75,000 for other operating expenses, and $40,000 for transfers in.

The data is arranged as follows:

Product A	2 × Product B's total value
Product B	1.5 × Product C's total value
Product C	A factor of 1.0 for the total value

(By the process of elimination product C emerges as the one with the lowest value, therefore the 1.0 factor.) Rearrange for computation.

---

*The volume count is not considered in determining the weights for this example. That is, the production center's manager simply estimated the relative value of his or her center's activities based on a three-way split.

Product A = 2.0 × 1.5.
Product B = 1.5 × 1.0.
Product C = 1.0 × 1.0.

Thus, the relative value weights are

Product A = 3.0.
Product B = 1.5.
Product C = 1.0.

The expenses as given are

Compensation	$125,000
Other operating expenses	75,000
Transfers in	40,000
	$240,000

The solution to unit costs becomes algebraic at this juncture. Because in this example we are using a macro approach at the highest level we are not factoring volume counts. If the example involved the assignment of volume weights then we would apply them to the volume counts. However, this is not the case in this example. Table 3-2 shows the average item costs derived by this method.

$$3x + 1.5x + x = \$240{,}000.$$
$$5.5x = \$240{,}000.$$
$$x = \$ \ 43{,}636.36.$$

Product A = 3.0 × $43,636.36 = $130,909.08
Product B = 1.5 × $43,636.36 = $ 65,454.54
Product C = 1.0 × $43,636.36 = $ 43,636.36

Total recovery $239,999.98

The example just presented was the simplest approach to relative values. It did not include the explicit weighted value of the volume counts. Rather, it relied on a three-way split on a summary level. In the next example we will use a weighted volume approach to relative value costing.

In using the relative value method with a weighted volume approach, the product groupings must be aligned to activities and costs and a relative base factor of 1.0 must be developed. Product groupings must be appropriately aligned to the activities and tasks for product costing purposes. That is, the flow of tasks and activities to products needs to be aligned for volume counts and cost application. Frequency analysis allows for a distribution of a specific task to multiple activities and specific activity to multiple products.

TABLE 3-2 Average Item Costs

	Cost	÷	Volume	=	Average Item Cost
Product A	$130,909.08		20,000		$6.5455
Product B	65,454.54		11,500		5.6917
Product C	43,636.36		10,000		4.3636
	$239,999.98		—		—

Recovery

20,000 × $6.5455 = $130,910.00
11,500 × $5.6917 = $ 65,454.55
10,000 × $4.3636 = $ 43,636.00

$240,000.55

To develop a relative base factor of 1.0, find the product time with the lowest value (lowest processing time) and assign a factor of 1.0 to it. All other products are estimated as a ratio to that base.

As an example of using weighted volumes, assume you have two products, G and H. Product H (reviewing a credit card application) takes the least time to process; therefore you assign a value of 1.0 to it. Product G (reviewing a real estate loan application) is then estimated as a value relative to product H. For example, after researching you may decide that product G takes three times the resources to process than H. Therefore, product G's factor becomes 3.0.

The factors are then expressed as: product G, 3.0; H, 1.0. Assume product G's volume is 1,000 and product H's volume is 4,000.

From a bottom-up standpoint one can arrive at these factors by unit (time estimates). This is a microcosmic approach. If this is used then the time is estimated in minutes or hours on a per unit basis. For example, assume your time estimate for product G was 9.0 minutes and for product H it was 3.0 minutes. You can derive the relative value factors by finding the denominator that will result in a 1.0 factor for product H. In this example it is 3.0, since 3.0 minutes divided by a 1.0 factor = 3.0.

TABLE 3-3 Computing a Table of Factors

		Clean Time (Minutes)		Common Denominator		Relative Value Factors
Relative base factor	Product G	9.0	÷	3.0	=	3.0
	Product H	3.0	÷	3.0	=	1.0

The table of factors is calculated as shown in table 3-3. the time estimates (minutes) are referred to as *clean times.* It is advisable to use the factors to fully recover the available time. This is done to avoid having remaining (residual) time. Therefore, a full absorption of the available processing center needs to be accounted for. Then do the following.

1. Calculate the total activity points.

	Factor		Volume		Activity Points
Product G	3.0	×	1,000	=	3,000
Product H	1.0	×	4,000	=	4,000
	Total points				7,000

2. Determine the available processing hours. Assume the following as given.

Gross hours available	=		352
(less) Holidays	=	16	
Vacations	=	16	
Absences	=	32	
Breaks	=	14	
Training	=	8	
Total deductions		86	
Net available processing hours:			266

3. Calculate the fully absorbed unit time points by using the following formula.

Net available processing hours ÷ Total activity points = Unit points.

266 hours ÷ 7,000 = .038 Unit points.

These unit point values are then applied to a derived hourly rate.

Assume the center's expenses are $19,000 for the period being measured and only apply to products G and H. It is important that the available processing hours measurement, the volume data, and the expense data all be accumulated for the same time frame. The hourly rate is derived by dividing the $19,000 by the net available processing hours. The formula is thus:

Expenses ÷ Net available processing hours = Hourly processing rate.

Therefore, the following can be calculated:

$$\$19,000 \div 266 \text{ hours} = \$71.43 \text{ per hour.}$$

The dollar value of each unit point can now be ascertained. The formula is:

Unit point value $\times$ Hourly processing rate = Unit point dollar value.

Thus, the following:

$$.038 \times \$71.43 = \$2.7143 \text{ Unit point dollar value.}$$

Let us now apply the unit point dollar value to products G and H as a means of spreading the costs.

	Activity Points	×	Unit Point Dollar Value	=	Product Aligned Costs
Product G	3,000		$2.7143	=	$ 8,142.90
Product H	4,000		2.7143	=	10,857.20
	7,000				$19,000.10

There is an overallocation of $0.10. This is insignificant and therefore will be ignored.

At this juncture we can now calculate unit costs using the average item costing approach.

	Total Product Aligned Costs	÷	Product Volume	=	Per Unit Costs
Product G	$ 8.142.90		1,000		$8.1429
Product H	10,857.20		4,000		2.7143
	$19,000.10		—		—

Another way to apply the unit point dollar value is as follows:

	Unit Point Dollar Value	×	Relative Value Factor	=	Per Unit Costs
Product G	$2.7143		3.0		$8.1429
Product H	2.7143		1.0		2.7143

As you can see, there are variations to arriving at the same answer. It is a matter of using the same relevant factors in a different sequence. For example, for product G one could multiply the unit point value by the relative value factor to arrive at the processing time as expressed in a decimal fraction of an hour. This could then be multiplied times the hourly rate to find the per unit cost. The calculation would thus be

$$.038 \times 3.0 = .114 \text{ processing time.}$$

$$.114 \times \$71.43 = \$8.143 \text{ per unit.}$$

At this point it might occur to you that a shortcut can be achieved by ignoring the hourly rate calculation, the unit point value calculation, and the unit point dollar value calculation. It depends upon the intended use for the data and the overall context of the study. If these factors are indeed to be ignored, then the following calculations are in order.

	Activity Points	Percentage of Total
Product G	3,000	42.857
Product H	4,000	57.143
Total	7,000	100.00

Next the expenses are distributed to the products by using the percentage of total distribution.

	Total Processing Expenses	×	Percentage of Total	=	Product Aligned Costs
Product G	$19,000		42.857		$ 8,142.83
Product H			57.143		10,857.17
					$19,000.00

These costs can now be used in arriving at per unit cost. The calculation is as follows:

	Total Product Aligned Costs	+	Product Volume	=	Per Unit Costs
Product G	$ 8.142.83		1,000		$8.1428
Product H	10,857.17		4,000		2.7143

The $0.10 previous difference shows up in product G's unit cost of $8.1428 versus $8.1429.

WORK SAMPLING

Work sampling is the process of surveying the distribution of work through a form of sampling, such as randomly spaced visits. There are several ways to sample work to arrive at task and activity times; they range from estimating the sample to statistically determining the sample.

Work sampling is most helpful in sorting out multiple task times in a work unit. Take an example of a work unit that has three tasks. They are opening mail, filing, and answering the phone. The goal is to determine the time spent on each task. The easiest approach is to randomly observe and record what task the person is performing at each observation point throughout the day.

Using an example of 25 random visits to a specific work station, assume the analyst observes the following:

Task	Distribution of Work Based on Observations	Percentage of Total
Opening mail	8	32
Filing	11	44
Answering the phone	6	24
Total	25	100

The assumed work distribution is on 25 sample observations. Based on these 25 visits the observer noted the worker opening mail 8 times. The 8 observations are derived as a percentage of the total observations, $(8/25 = 32$ percent). Based on this sample, it is assumed the worker spends 32 percent of his or her time opening mail.

This is a simple approach to work sampling though it has its drawbacks in terms of representative accuracy. That is, the distribution of work based on 25 sample observations may not necessarily be representative of what the worker does within a day. More observations may be necessary to attain accuracy. Moreover, the sample day may not be representative of what usually occurs on a day-to-day basis. There may have been more filing on the sample day than what usually occurs. One can easily see there is no allowance for personal time. It was omitted in this example so that the work distribution would be fully absorbed. One could easily include an additional task and label it as "personal time away." This would allow for the capturing of randomly observed personal time away.

Assuming an 8-hour workday for this example, the following applies.

Task	Parameter of Observation (Hours)		Percentage of Total		Number of Hours Applied to Each Task
Opening mail	8	×	32%	=	2.56
Filing	8	×	44	=	3.52
Answering the phone	8	×	24	=	1.92
Totals	—		100%		8.0 hours
	(Concurrent 8-hour day)				

From the 25 observations the cost analyst now has an estimate of the person's work distribution for the day. The worker's 8-hour day is assumed to be distributed as follows:

2.56 hours for opening mail

3.52 hours for filing

1.92 hours for answering the phone

This work sampling technique is useful when volume counts are not particularly available or relevant. The method is economical and easy to work with. It also permits one to cover several work stations during the course of sample observations. The accuracy of this method is somewhat limited. As with all observation methods there is potential for worker bias in terms of work technique alteration. You may wish to resort to statistics in order to determine the number of observations necessary to achieve a stated confidence level.

STOPWATCH

Standard times may be developed with the use of a stopwatch. Sample observations are made and tasks are timed.

The sequence of steps is first carefully noted. Then a sampling is conducted. It could be random or predetermined in terms of when to conduct sample time measurement of the work being performed. The time measurement of each sample observation should be recorded. After an appropriate number of observations have been made, the data is then averaged. It is appropriate to level the time based ont he observer's estimate of the worker's efficiency. If the worker is judged below average in efficiency, then a discount factor is applied. If the worker is estimated to be average in skill then no leveling factor is necessary. Should one estimate the worker to be highly skilled and above average in efficiency, the time should be raised.

TABLE 3-5 Stopwatch Measurement

Task	Measured Time Per Observation (minutes)	Worker	Date/Time	Estimate of Worker's Efficiency
Sort an item	.012	Potter	11/7, 8: a.m.	
			−9:30 a.m.	98
	.012			
	.013			
	.015			
	.013			
	.012			
	.012			
	.016			
	.012			
	.012			
	.011			
	.013			
	.013			
Total of	.013			
15 sample	.012			
observations	.191			

In measuring a task it is suggested the observer uses a log. The column headings include the task being measured, the time measurement for each observation, the name of the worker being measured, the date and inclusive time span of observation, and your estimation of the worker's efficiency. Table 3-5 shows the results of a stopwatch measurement. There were 15 sample observations with the use of a stopwatch. The time measurement for the task of sorting an item ranged from 0.012 minutes to 0.016 minutes. The observations are totaled and then divided by 15 in order to arrive at their mean (arithmetic average). The formula is as follows:

Total time measurement ÷ The number = Average
of observations   of observations   time.

The calculation is thus

.191 ÷ 15 = .0127 Average time.

The average time of 0.0127 minute to sort an item can now be adjusted for the estimated efficiency of the worker. In this example the worker, Potter, was evaluated as being 98 percent efficient. That is, Potter's efficiency is slightly less than average. Potter's average time was 0.0127; therefore, it is assumed the work can and should be done faster by an average worker (one who is at 100 percent efficiency). The average time is thus discounted by the 98 percent factor. The formula is

$$\text{Average time} \times \text{Leveling factor} = \text{Average adjusted time}$$
$$\text{(normal time)}.$$

The calculation is

$$.0127 \times .98 = .0124 \quad \text{Average time with leveling adjustment.}$$

The next adjustment would be for personal needs, fatigue, and unavoidable delay. As an example assume a 15 percent allowance to cover these things. This allowance is added to the adjusted time. The calculation is as follows:

$$
\begin{aligned}
100\% &= .01240 \text{ minutes} \\
+ 15\% &= \underline{.00186 \text{ minutes}} \\
\end{aligned}
$$

Total processing time
for "sort" task $\underline{.01426 \text{ minutes}}$

The 0.01426 minute processing time represents the normal time, as expressed in minutes, it should take an average experienced or trained worker to sort an item. The 15 percent allowance is included in this time estimate as a means of accounting for personal needs, fatigue, and unavoidable delay.

To apply this standard to an hourly expense rate, the minutes would have to be converted to hours. Given this the following calculation is in order.

$$.01426 \qquad \div\ 60 \qquad = .0002376.$$

Normal time with allowances expressed in minutes	Minutes per hour	Normal time with allowances expressed in hours

If, for example, the hourly rate for this department is $50 then the cost of sorting an item is $0.01188 ($50 × .0002376 = $0.01188).

The hourly rate could just as well be reduced to a per minute rate. It would yield a per minute cost of $0.8333 ($50 ÷ 60 = $0.8333). The $0.8333 multiplied times 0.01426 yields the same cost of $0.01188.

PREDETERMINED TIME STANDARDS

Predetermined time standards are defined as the arrangement and classification of movements with the assignment of associated time values. Let us go next to a cursory review of predetermined time standards. The next section is written only as summary introduction to predetermined time standards. A working knowledge of methods time measurement (MTM), a specialized method, requires further training in theory and application.

MTM

Methods time measurement (MTM), is one of the best known predetermined time standard techniques. Time values are expressed in units of time called time measurement units (TMUs). One TMU has a value of 0.00001 hours.

In using predetermined standards the steps to be taken are as follows:

1. Closely observe the work activity and record by sequence a list of motions.
2. Classify the motions.
3. Assign the appropriate time values.
4. Apply frequency factors.
5. Level the values where necessary.
6. Apply personal, rest/fatigue, and delay factors.

MTM tables provide TMU factors for the following major categories:

- Reach (R)
- Move (M)
- Turn and apply pressure (T&AP)
- Grasp (G)
- Position (P)
- Release (R)
- Disengage (D)
- Eye travel time and eye focus (ET&EF)
- Body, leg, and foot motions
- Simultaneous motions
- Apply pressure (AP)

In summary, predetermined time standards have the advantages of providing accurate information, being quick and simple to apply by an experienced and trained analyst, and being relatively easy to maintain and change. The following disadvantages may apply: predetermined standards techniques are time consuming to learn; there is an initial investment in purchasing the system and training the analytical staff; and the application of predetermined standards is only reliable and practical for short-cycle and repetitive activities.

4

Average Item Costing Methodology (Nonstandard Costing) (Actual Costing)

An *average item* cost (AIC) represents the true or actual cost of an item at a specified volume. An example of an AIC study in a processing area takes up much of this chapter. Also addressed are such topics as the use of estimated actual data and the use of planned data. Estimating practical levels and time is discussed. Analyzing cost/volume relations is conceptually dealt with.

Two additional examples are presented to illustrate the AIC concepts further. One is an AIC for an administrative function; the other is an AIC for a complete product. Alternate approaches using AIC techniques are also discussed.

THE CONCEPT OF AIC

The concept of average item costing is based upon full absorption of all relevant costs. Full absorption captures all relevant costs and volumes in the same time frame. The formula is

Total relevant costs ÷ Volume = Average item costs.

Average item costing takes the total actual costs, both fixed and variable, and puts them on a per item basis.

This method is sometimes referred to as the allocation of expenses, the actual costing technique, the percentage of time method, or the nonstandard approach. These are descriptive titles for variations of average item costing.

The Sequences and Steps in Costing

A cost study that employs average item costing starts with analysis and documentation of a processing center's activities and proceeds to development of a matrix allocation of organizational (departmental) expenses to functions and products.

Analyzing and documenting a processing center's activities can be done in three steps.

1. Obtain a copy of the organizational chart. Names, with associated positions and grades would be helpful. Obtaining information on exact salaries may be difficult as well as too sensitive. Therefore, grade levels, or average salaries for members in a work pool, should suffice. It is usually best to obtain this information from the processing center manager.

2. Conduct interviews with the center manager, key processing staff, and supervisors. If the study concerns a product, interview product managers or marketing managers.

3. Review any available information that would have bearing on the project. The information being sought should include volume data, production reports, position descriptions, work documentation, revenue, and expenses. Often the analyst discovers and overabundance of information. The task of sorting out the relevant information becomes important.

Developing a matrix of organizational revenue and expenses to functions and/or products involves gathering and processing all relevant revenue and expense information. You must decide whether to use historical or planned expense information. Bases then must be developed for allocating expenses. These bases are sometimes called *concepts* to connote the conceptual reasoning behind each basis. The allocation bases could be a function of staff count, compensation, direct operating expenses, floor space, revenue, balances, machine time, or any other concept that seems appropriate and equitable.

The next step is to determine the product flow. This involves research and discussion within the processing area. Next, where appropriate, obtain estimates of percentage of time spent on various tasks. It is prudent to be flexible in allowing for changes during discussion on the logic of the time estimates. Time estimates are only as good as the logic that underlies them.

Example of an AIC in a Processing Area

In order to examine the main concepts of average item costing, let us consider the following hypothetical cost study.

The assumptions for this hypothetical project are that: (1) there are three activities being processed within the center being studied; (2) no other center is directly involved in processing these three activities; and (3) there are, however, some indirect allocations from other centers to the activities.

In the research phase the following information has been gathered: (1) there are eight distinct tasks in this center (setup, route, check, update, record, obtain phone authorization, reference check, and review), and (2) historical volume information for the past two years is indicative of the volume that is occurring year-to-date.

In this study it is found that activity A (process a request) is supported by tasks 1 (setup), 2 (route), and 3 (check). Task 2 (route) is also shared with activity B (process an inquiry), which is supported by tasks 2 (route) and 5 (record). Activity C (update customer records) is supported by tasks 4 (update), 6 (phone authorization), 7 (reference check), and 8 (review).

In studying the tasks, the dominant volumes are determined for each activity. In this study it is determined that activity A (process a request) has a dominant monthly volume of 2,500; activity B (process an inquiry), 10,000; and activity C (update customer records), 5,000. These dominant volumes are determined by finding which task measurement is most indicative of the activity volume.

Three additional tasks support the activities; tasks 9 (new customer) and 10 (photocopying) support all three activities. Task 11 (liaison) supports only activity C (update customer records). The schedule in table 4-1 summarizes the research on the tasks as they pertain to the three activities.

TABLE 4-1 Z Processing Center Tasks

Task Number	Task Description	Monthly Average Volume	Activity Volume Identifier
1	Set up	2,500	A
2	Route	12,500	A,B
3	Check	1,500	A
4	Update	5,000	C
5	Record	10,000	B
6	Phone authorization	50	C
7	Reference check	5,000	C
8	Review	5,000	C
	Support Tasks		
9	New customer	150	A,B,C
10	Photocopying	2,500	A,B,C
11	Liaison	570	C
	Dominant Volumes (Monthly Average)		
Activity A	Process a request		2,500
Activity B	Process an inquiry		10,000
Activity C	Update customer records		5,000

Assumptions

In this study it has been determined that 12 months of budget information is to be used in lieu of historical actuals. Some of the expenses have been directly linked to specific tasks. Overtime is used only for the "record" task. Depreciation is apportioned only to the "check" and "update" tasks. The schedule in table 4-2 shows the total expenses for the Z processing center. The total expenses less the direct expenses equals the amount to be ultimately apportioned or allocated to each activity in the center being costed.

This entire list of expense information in table 4-2 is transferred to column 1 of spread sheet I (table 4-3). Spread sheet I is the direct application and apportionment of the Z organization's expenses to tasks. This is only somewhat different from taking the expenses of an entire financial institution and spreading them to the various departments. The difference is the Z processing center is a microcosm. That is, the Z processing center is a department and is therefore at a lower level.

You will notice on spread sheet I there is a direct application of overtime and depreciation. This is a straightforward assignment of identified direct expenses.

TABLE 4-2 Z Processing Center 12-Month Budget[1]

Expense Categories	Plan Amount
Regular salaries ($715,000 operational staff, $150,000 supervision)	$ 865,000
Overtime (attributable 100% to record task)	15,000
Benefits (as determined by a separate study)	173,000
Entertainment	5,000
Travel	22,000
Depreciation (50% to check task; 50% to update task)	98,000
Premises	125,000
Other (including transfers in)	131,000
Total expenses	$1,434,000 [3]
Less direct expenses[2]	(113,000)
Remaining expenses to be allocated	$1,321,000

*Note: Benefits are usually frequencied with salary on a ratio (percentage basis). For purposes of simplicity assume the $173,000 was derived from another study. A 20% rate can be derived from the numbers as presented: $173,000 ÷ $865,000 = 20%.

[1]As an alternative this study could also be based on historical actuals.
[2]To be directly applied to specific tasks:
    Overtime $15,000 + Depreciation $98,000 = Total $ 113,000.
[3]To col. 1 of spread sheet I.

TABLE 4-3 Z Processing Center Spread Sheet I

Support Sched. / Org. Exps.	Col. 1 Total	Tasks								Support Tasks				Allocat. Bases
		Setup	Rte.	Check	Update	Record	Auth.	Ref.	Review	New Cust.	Photo copy	Lia-ison	Resid.	
FTE staff	39.7	4.0	5.0	2.2	6.0	6.2	.1	5.0	6.7	1.0	2.0	1.5	—	Staff reports, org. charts
A Supervision FTE	6.0	1.0	1.0	.2	.4	.4	.1	.9	1.0	.3	.4	.3		Interviews, org. charts
A Total staff	45.7	5.0	6.0	2.4	6.4	6.6	.2	5.9	7.7	1.3	2.4	1.8	—	
						($000's)								
B Compensation														
B1 Reg. salaries														
B2 Opnl. staff	$ 715.0	72.0	90.0	39.6	108.0	111.6	1.8	90.0	120.6	18.0	36.0	27.0	.4	Grade midpoints
B3 Suprvsn.	150.0	25.0	25.0	5.0	10.0	10.0	2.5	22.5	25.0	7.5	10.0	7.5	—	Grade midpoints
Total salaries	$ 865.0	97.0	115.0	44.6	118.0	121.6	4.3	112.5	145.6	25.5	46.0	34.5	.4	
Benefits	173.0	19.4	23.0	8.9	23.6	24.3	0.9	22.5	29.1	5.1	9.2	6.9	.1	@ 20% of salaries
Overtime	15.0	—	—	—	—	15.0	—	—	—	—	—	—	—	100 % to rec. per staff log
Residual									0.5				(.5)	Alloc to Rte. per mgr.
Total Comp.	$1,053.0	116.4	138.0	53.5	141.6	160.9	5.2	135.0	175.2	30.6	55.2	41.4	—	
Depreciation	98.0	—	—	49.0	49.0	—	—	—	—	—	—	—	—	Fixed asset list
Other operating expenses	283.0	31.3	37.1	14.4	38.1	43.2	1.4	36.3	47.1	8.2	14.8	11.1	—	Based on compensation
Total expenses	$1,434.0	147.7	175.1	116.9	228.7	204.1	6.6	171.3	222.3	38.8	70.0	52.5	▓	To spread sheet II

Note: Information based on interviews, statistical reports, volume data, self-logging data, and budget information. Tasks are setup, check, update, record, obtain phone authorization, reference check, and review.

Spread sheet I is set up to provide a sufficient audit trail for the cost analyst. A reference column is provided to list supporting schedules that explain the allocation bases. The tasks are labeled and divided between direct tasks and support tasks.

The full-time-equivalent (FTE) staff is listed for each task. A total is listed in order to provide a means of checking for accuracy.

A legend explaining how the information was obtained is provided. In this example it mentions the information is based on interviews, statistical reports, volume data, self-logging, and budget information.

Prior to looking at spread sheet II, it might be helpful to look at the supporting schedules A, B, and C, which the analyst appends to spread sheet I. They show the details and the basis concept or logic for the apportionment of allocations.

Schedule A (figure 4-1) is the Z processing center's organization chart. It is based on the major tasks of that organization.

An allocation of supervisorial time is spread to each task. Also the listing of FTE staff is documented.

Tables 4-4 to 4-6 are schedules B-1, B-2, and B-3, which show the details of the compensation expense calculations. Because of the proprietary nature of salaries it is advisable to not obtain them for each worker, but to use grade levels and averages instead. Turnover may negate exact salary figures anyway.

Compensation in this example includes supervisorial staff salaries, overtime, and fringe benefits. The compensation for each task was determined by a sequence of steps. For example, in task 1 (setup) there are 4.0 staff members and 1.0 supervisor. The average salary for each staff member is $18,000 per year. Therefore, 4.0 is multiplied by $18,000. The calculation is as follows: $4.0 \times \$18,000 = \$72,000$. The supervisorial salary is calculated by multiplying $1.0 \times \$25,000$. This represents one supervisor with a $25,000 annual salary. The calculation is thus $1.0 \times \$25,000 = \$25,000$. The two salary subtotals are added: $\$72,000 + \$25,000 = \$97,000$.

The fringe benefits amount is to be added next. Fringe benefits are usually expressed as a percentage of regular salaries. Therefore, the percentage is derived. In this example it was derived as 20 percent. Fringe benefit items such as medical, retirement, and other benefits were added together. They totaled $173,000.

The fringe benefits were divided by the regular salaries in order to derive the fringe rate. The calculation is thus

$$\$173,000 \div \$865,000 = 20\%.$$

In the example the fringe rate of 20 percent was added to regular salaries only. It was not added to overtime. This is because only the base of regular salaries was used as a relationship to the fringe benefits amount in determining the fringe benefits rate. Therefore, the overtime of $15,000 for the record task (task 5) was excluded from any fringe benefits calculation.

Figure 4-1. Schedule A: Z Processing Center Organization Chart

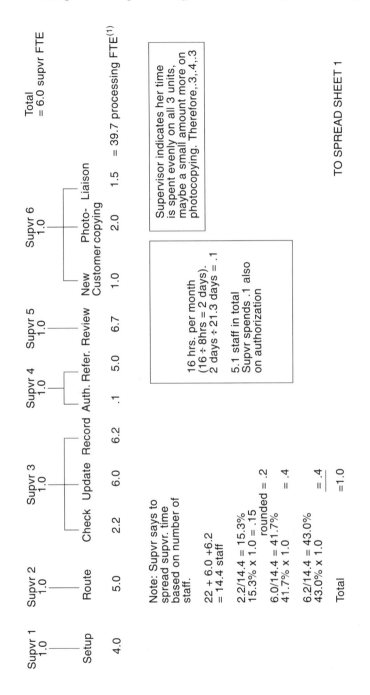

Supvr 1   Supvr 2   Supvr 3   Supvr 4   Supvr 5   Supvr 6   Total
1.0   1.0   1.0   1.0   1.0   1.0   = 6.0 supvr FTE

Setup Route Check Update Record Auth. Refer. Review New   Photo- Liaison
                                                            Customer copying

4.0   5.0   2.2   6.0   6.2   .1   5.0   6.7   1.0   2.0   1.5   = 39.7 processing FTE[1]

Note: Supvr says to
spread supvr. time
based on number of
staff.

22 + 6.0 + 6.2
= 14.4 staff

2.2/14.4 = 15.3%
15.3% × 1.0 = .15
         rounded = .2

6.0/14.4 = 41.7%
41.7% × 1.0   = .4

6.2/14.4 = 43.0%
43.0% × 1.0   = .4
                      ___
Total   =1.0

16 hrs. per month
(16 ÷ 8hrs = 2 days).
2 days ÷ 21.3 days = .1

5.1 staff in total
Supvr spends .1 also
on authorization

Supervisor indicates her time
is spent evenly on all 3 units,
maybe a small amount more on
photocopying. Therefore, .3, .4, .3

TO SPREAD SHEET 1

TABLE 4-4 Z Processing Center
Schedule B-1: Compensation

The center manager says most of the staff
members are grade 18's and the supervisors are
grade 22's. Therefore, we will use midpoint
salaries.

Grade 18 annual salary at midpoint = $ 18,000.

(39.7 × $18,000 = $714,600.)

Grade 22 annual salary at midpoint = $ 25,000.

(6.0 × 25,000 = 150,000.)

		Recovery
	Operational staff	$714,600
	Supervision	150,000
	Total salaries at midpoint	$864,600
less:	Budgeted salaries [1]	865,000
	Under recovery	$ (400)

[1]Could also be based on last year's historical or
this year's actual (year-to-date). However, this
example is basing the AIC on budgeted expenses.

To continue with task 1 (setup) as the example, the salary total of $97,000 is multiplied by the derived fringe rate of 20 percent. This amounts to $19,400. The total compensation for task 1 then is $116,400 ($97,000 + $19,400).

In schedules C (tables 4-7 and 4-8) the detailed calculations of allocating other operating expenses to each task are shown. The allocations are based on each task's percent of compensation to the total compensation of the center.

The calculation for task 1 (setup) on Schedule C-1 (Table 4-7) is a derivation of its percentage of total compensation. The resultant figure is 11.0541 percent. Therefore, task 1 will absorb 11.0541 percent of the total operating expenses to be apportioned or allocated. The amount to be apportioned was previously determined to be $283,000. The $283,000 is then multiplied by 11.0541 percent to find the amount of other operating expenses to be allocated to the setup task. The calculation, therefore, is $283,000 × 0.110541 = $31,283. This is done for each task. The $283,000 is now apportioned to all 11 tasks based on each task's percentage of total compensation. These calculations are detailed in schedule C-2 (Table 4-8).

TABLE 4-5 Z Processing Center Schedule B-2:
Regular Salary Operational Staff Apportionment

Task No.	Task	(From Schedule A) No. of FTE Staff	×	Annual Salary Factor	=	Total Regular Salaries
1	Set up	4.0		$18,000		$ 72,000
2	Route	5.0		18,000		90,000
3	Check	2.2		18,000		39,600
4	Update	6.0		18,000		108,000
5	Record	6.2		18,000		111,600
6	Authorization	0.1		18,000		1,800
7	Reference	5.0		18,000		90,000
8	Review	6.7		18,000		120,600
9	New customer	1.0		18,000		18,000
10	Photocopy	2.0		18,000		36,000
11	Liaison	1.5		18,000		27,000
	Residual					400
	Total budgeted operational salaries					$715,000

TABLE 4-6 Z Processing Center Schedule B-3:
Regular Salary Supervisory Staff Apportionment

Task No.	Task	(From Schedule A) No. of FTE Staff	×	Annual Salary Factor	=	Total Regular Salaries
1	Set up	1.0		$25,000		$ 25,000
2	Route	1.0		25,000		25,000
3	Check	0.2		25,000		5,000
4	Update	0.4		25,000		10,000
5	Record	0.4		25,000		10,000
6	Authorization	0.1		25,000		2,500
7	Reference	0.9		25,000		22,500
8	Review	1.0		25,000		25,000
9	New customer	0.3		25,000		7,500
10	Photocopy	0.4		25,000		10,000
11	Liaison	0.3		25,000		7,500
	Residual					—
	Total budgeted supervisorial salaries					$150,000

TABLE 4-7 Z Processing Center Schedule C-1:
Other Operating Expense Allocation ($000's)

		Task	Compensation[1]	Derived Percentage of Total Comp.
Entertainment	$ 5.0	1 setup	$ 116.4 [2]	11.0541 [3]
Travel	22.0	2 route	138.0	13.1054
Premises	125.0	3 check	53.5	5.0807
Transfers in	131.0	4 update	141.6	13.4473
Total to		5 record	160.9	15.2802
be allocated	$283.0	6 authorization	5.2	0.4938
		7 reference	135.0	12.8205
		8 review	175.2	16.6382
		9 new customers	30.6	2.9060
		10 photocopy	55.2	5.2422
		11 liaison	41.4	3.9316
			$1,053.0	100.0000 %

[1]Includes processing staff and supervision salaries, overtime and fringe benefits, from spread sheet I (in $000s).

[2]Task 1 setup

(a) $4.0 \times \$18.0 = \$72.0$ processing staff

(b) $1.0 \times \$25.0 = \$25.0$ supervision

(c) $\$72.0 + \$25.0 = \$97.0$ Processing + supervison salaries

(d) $\$173.0 \div \$865.0$ =   20%

    Fringe   Regular   Fringe

    benefits   salaries   benefits rate

(e) $\$97.0 \times .2 = \$19.4$ Fringe benefits calculation

(f) $\$97.0 + 19.4 = \$116.4$ Task 1 (setup) compensation (Regular salaries + Fringe benefits)

[3]$\$116.4 \div \$1,053.0 = 11.0541\%$ Task 1 (setup) compensation Percentage of total derivation

$11.0541 \times \$283,000$ total indirect expenses to be allocated = $31,283 to spread sheet I

**TABLE 4-8 Z Processing Center Schedule C-2:
Other Operating Expense Allocation**

Task No.	Task	Percentage of Derived Total Compensation	×	Total to Be Allocated	=	Resultant Allocation
1	Set up	11.0541%		$283,000		$ 31,283
2	Route	13.1054		283,000		37,088
3	Check	5.0807		283,000		14,378
4	Update	13.4473		283,000		38,056
5	Record	15.2802		283,000		43,243
6	Authorization	0.4938		283,000		1,397
7	Reference	12.8205		283,000		36,282
8	Review	16.6382		283,000		47,086
9	New customer	2.9060		283,000		8,224
10	Photocopy	5.2422		283,000		14,836
11	Liaison	3.9316		283,000		11,127
	Total allocated expenses					$283,000

To spread sheet I

The total expenses for each activity are next moved from spread sheet I to spread sheet II. Spread sheet II is used for aligning task expenses to activities.

The task identifier number, literal description, and amount are listed. Activity identifiers are associated with each task. This column shows which activities are associated with each task listed. There are three activities in this example. They are labeled activity A (process a request); activity B (process an inquiry); and activity C (update customer records). Task 1 (setup), only supports activity A. However, task 2 (route), supports activities A and B.

There is a column for each activity. The task expenses are apportioned to each activity according to volume. No relative value weights have been applied. Therefore, it is assumed all volumes within each task are equal in effort and expense applied.

For task 1 (setup), the annual volume to be applied is 30,000 (2,500 × 12 = 30,000) units. Since all of its is attributable to activity A (process a request), there is no separate distribution of the expenses.

The volume count is of the same time frame as for the expenses: 12 months. The dominant annual volumes for each activity are given as follows:

Activity A   2,500 × 12 = 30,000
(process a request)

Activity B   10,000 × 12 = 120,000
(process an inquiry)

Activity C   5,000 × 12 = 60,000
(update customer records)

As mentioned before, task 2 (route), flows to activities A and B. The distribution of task 2's expenses is based on its representative activity volume to total volume. The activity volumes are added together to form an allocation basis. Thus 30,000 + 120,000 = 150,000 total volume representation for the task. The expense distribution for it is based on volume. The total expense of $175,100 for task 2 is apportioned as follows:

Activity A $\qquad \dfrac{30,000}{150,000} \times \$175,100 = \$35,020$

Activities A and B $\qquad\qquad\qquad\qquad\qquad$ Allocation
$\qquad\qquad\qquad\qquad\qquad\qquad\qquad\qquad\qquad$ to activity A

Activity B $\qquad \dfrac{120,000}{150,000} \times \$175,100 = \$140,080$

Activities A, B $\qquad\qquad\qquad\qquad\qquad\qquad$ Allocation
$\qquad\qquad\qquad\qquad\qquad\qquad\qquad\qquad\qquad$ to activity B

$35,020 + $140,080 = $175,100 total allocation of
task 2 (route) to activities A (process a request) and
B (process an inquiry.)

Assume the decision has been made to round the extensions to the nearest $100 at this point. Therefore, $35,020 becomes $35,000 and $140,080 becomes $140,100.

The activity support tasks are apportioned to each activity based on volume. The base is determined by adding all of the activity volumes; that is, A (process a request) = 30,000; B (process an inquiry) = 120,000; and C (update customer records) = 60,000. The aggregate is thus 30,000 + 120,000 + 60,000 = 210,000.

When all of the center's task aligned expenses have been allocated to the activities they are totaled by activity. There is a column for each activity.

From spread sheet II (table 4-9) the totals for each of the activities are as follows:

Activity A (process a request)	$ 315.1
Activity B (process an inquiry)	406.4
Activity C (update customer records)	712.5
Total	$1,434.0

**TABLE 4-9 Z Processing Center Activity Alignment of Expenses:
Spread Sheet II ($000's)**

Tasks		Amount	Activity Identifier	Activity A Proc Rqst	Activity B Proc Inq	Activity C Update Rcrds
1	Setup	$ 147.7	A	$147.7	$ —	$ —
2	Route	175.1	A,B	35.0[1]	140.1[2]	—
3	Check	116.9	A	116.9	—	—
4	Update	228.7	C	—	—	228.7
5	Record	204.1	B	—	204.1	—
6	Authorization	6.6	C	—	—	6.6
7	Reference	171.3	C	—	—	171.3
8	Review	222.3	C	—	—	222.3
	Product Support Activities					
9	New customer	38.8	A,B,C	5.5[3]	22.2[4]	11.1[5]
10	Photocopying	70.0	A,B,C	10.0[6]	40.0[7]	20.0[8]
11	Liaison	52.5	C			52.5
	Total	$1,434.0[9]		$315.1	$406.4	$712.5

Activity Volumes
  A — Process a request   30,000
  B — Process an inquiry   120,000
  C — Update customer records   60,000

Notes:
Frequency Analysis
[1]Task 2   activity volume   (30,000/150,000) × $175.1 = $35.0 (30,000 + 120,000 = 150,000).
[2]Task 2   activity volume (120,000/150,000) × $175.1 = $140.1.
[3]Task 9   activity volume   (30,000/210,000) × $38.8 = $5.5 (30,000 + 120,000 + 60,000 = 210,000).
[4]Task 9   activity volume (120,000/210,000) × $38.8 = $22.2.
[5]Task 9   activity volume   (60,000/210,000) × $38.8 = $11.1.
[6]Task 10 activity volume   (30,000/210,000) × $70.0 = $10.0.
[7]Task 10 activity volume (120,000/210,000) × $70.0 = $40.0.
[8]Task 10 activity volume   (60,000/210,000) × $70.0 = $20.0.
[9]From spread sheet I.

This is a checkpoint for making sure the total for the activity-aligned expenses equals the total task expenses. The activity-aligned expenses of $1,434,000 indeed equal the task aligned expenses of $1,434,000.

Now that the expenses are activity aligned, they are called *costs* and we are ready to calculate the average item costs. To be used next is the following formula:

Total costs + Total volume = Average item cost (AIC).

Total cost here represents the total cost attributed to each activity within the processing center only. It does not include the institution's general and administrative overhead (G&A). In doing those cost projects that cross organizational lines the term. *Total cost* may have a broader meaning.

Table 4-10 shows the average item cost for each activity.

The item costs are multiplied by the annual volume as a verification of recovery. The only differences that will show up in this kind of costing example are those that occur as a result of rounding each unit cost to five decimal places. Therefore, the error is minimal. Table 4-11 summarizes the recovery of the calculations for the Z processing center.

The processing center's costing is now completed. However, the next order of costing has to do with overhead and allocations or transfers from other processing centers.

In this example there are three processing centers under an administrative department that has an annual budget of $65,000. The other two centers are designated × and Y. The total budget for these two other centers is $1,566,000. Therefore, the total budgeted amount for all three centers is $3,000,000 ($1,566,000 + 1,434,000 = $3,000,000). Since the administration expense of $65,000 is in close organizational proximity to the processing centers it will be referred to as "local overhead."

The formula for calculating the local overhead burden rate is as follows:

$$\frac{\text{Local overhead organizational expenses}}{\text{Processing centers' budgeted expenses}} = \text{Burden rate.}$$

TABLE 4-10 Average Item Cost Calculations

Formula:	Total cost	÷	Total volume	=	AIC
Activity	*Total Annual Cost*	÷	*Total Annual Volume*	=	*Average Item Cost*
A (process a request)	$315,100	÷	30,000	=	$10.50333
B (process an inquiry)	$406,400	÷	120,000	=	$ 3.38667
C (update customer records)	$712,500	÷	60,000	=	$11.87500

Note: The next step is to verify the recovery of the center's expenses given the item (unit) costs. The data in columns 1 and 2 are from spread sheet II.

TABLE 4-11 Z Processing Center Projected Recovery Calculation

Cost to be recovered = $1,434,000
(from spread sheet II)

Activities	Average Item Cost	× Annual Volume	= Total Recovery[1]
A (process a request)	$10.50333	30,000	$ 315,100
B (process an inquiry)	3,38667	120,000	406,400
C (update customer records)	11,87500	60,000	712,500
Recovery			$1,434,000
center costs			1,434,000
Total over/underrecovery			$ 0

[1]Rounded to nearest whole dollar

In applying the formula to the example, the following occurs:

$$\frac{\$65,000}{\$1,566,000 + \$1,434,000} = 2.1667\%.$$

Therefore, the local overhead burden rate for all three centers is 2.1667 percent.

The next step is to apply the burden rate to the average item costs. The local overhead burden can be unitized. In this example the local overhead burden cost for activity A, (process a request) is $0.22758 ($10.50333 × 2.1667% = $0.22758).

TABLE 4-12 Z Processing Center Calculation of Administrative Burden Costs (Local Overhead)

Activity	col. 1 Average Item Cost	×	Local Overhead Burden Rate	=	col. 3 Local Overhead Burden Cost	(col.1 + col. 3) Local Average Item Cost
A (process a request)	$10.50333		2.1667%		$0.22758	$10.73091
B (process and inquiry)	3.38667		2.1667		0.07338	3.46005
C (update customers records)	11.87500		2.1667		0.25730	12.13230

When it is added to the average item cost, we now have a unit cost of $10.73091 ($10.50333 + $0.22758 = $10.73091). The $10.73091 unit cost is called the "local average item costs." It is designated as such in order to acknowledge the inclusion of local overhead. The addition of local overhead is illustrated in table 4-12.

The last item to be added to the item costs is the general and administrative overhead (G&A) expenses of the financial institution.

In this example we must assume two givens: the G&A expenses of the financial institution have been determined as $2,622,466, and the total operating (noninterest) expenses of the bank as $18,000,000. In order to spread the G&A expenses properly, it is necessary to express the amount as a function of the total expenses of the financial institution.

The formula and calculation are as follows:

$$\frac{\text{G\&A overhead expense}}{\substack{\text{Total financial institutionwide operating expenses} \\ \text{including activities A, B, C and} \\ \text{their respective local overhead}}} = \text{G\&A overhead recovery rate.}$$

$$\frac{\$\ 2,622,466\ \text{(given)}}{\$18,000,000\ \text{(given)}} = 14.57\%$$

(*Note:* The source is not reflected in this example. Therefore, the $2,622,466 and the $18,000,000 figures are to be accepted as given.)

With the derived rate of 14.57 percent we are now prepared to finalize the buildup of each activity's unit cost. The G&A may be expressed on a per unit basis. Thus the activity A's local average cost of $10.73091 is multiplied by 14.57 percent. This equals a G&A cost of $1.56349 per unit for the activity. The total per item cost is then $12.2944 ($10.73091 + $1.56349 = $12.2944). Table 4-13 illustrates the calculation for each activity.

TABLE 4-13 Z Processing Center Products Total Cost Calculation

Activity	col. 1 Local Average Item Cost	×	G&A Overhead Rate	=	col. 3 G&A Overhead	(col.1 + col. 3) Total Per Item Cost
A (process a request)	$10.73091		14.57%		$1.56349	$12.2944
B (process an inquiry)	3.46005		14.57		0.50413	3.96418
C (update customer records)	12.13230		14.57		1.76768	13.89998

TABLE 4-14 Reconciliation to Total
Financial Institution Expenses

Average Item Cost $\times$ *Volume*		*Total Local Overhead*		*Total General Overhead*		*Total Financial Institutionwide Expenses*
Direct expenses + Allocated expenses	+		+		=	

We now have fully absorbed item costs for each of the three activities in this study. It should be mentioned here that there are other approaches to allocating general financial institution overhead to activities and products. They are all based on some form of arbitrary assignment. (A detailed discussion of allocation bases is presented in chapter 8.)

If the financial institution decides to charge customers for activities A, B, and C and there are no other direct or indirect costs related to these activities elsewhere in the financial institution then they can simply be reclassified as products.

In doing a cost study it is important to maintain the integrity of the costing methodology and framework as established within the financial institution. Table 4-14 schematizes the integrity one must strive for in doing a cost study. If this is diligently followed, then errors of double counting and omission will be minimized.

Cost Study Completion Checklist

A checklist can serve as a guide and reminder to the analyst during the course of a study. The checklist should include at least the following entries.

Revenue data (if applicable)

Expense data

Volume data

Balances (if applicable)

Time standards (if available)

Addition/subtraction of exceptional items

Organizational chart

Organizational alignment of: revenue; staff; compensation; and other operating expenses.

Functional (activity) alignment of: revenue; staff; compensation; and other operating expenses.

Product alignment of: revenue; staff; compensation; other operating expense; and volume data.

Relative value analysis (if applicable)

Average item cost calculation

Center expense recovery analysis

Local overhead burden development

Local average item cost calculation

Development of general and administrative (G&A) burden

Total average item cost calculation

DATA TYPES

Historical Data

In using historical data for a AIC study it is imperative the data be representative of a normal operation. This means that exceptional items must be sorted out and dealt with on an individual basis. The data may need to be smoothed out. Through the interviewing exceptional items on revenue, expense, and volume data can be brought to the surface. The analyst must exercise good judgment in determining what is exceptional. Overall, the data being used should be indicative of the normal status of the organization being studied.

In the case of a new organization there is little or no history to resort to. This may pose some difficulty until a steady state (normal operation) is achieved. However, the analyst may find it necessary to construct a forecast based on limited historical data. The impact of the exceptional items should be diminished.

Estimated Actual Data

Estimated actual connotes taking some historical data and using it as a basis for estimating the remainder of the year. This is also referred to as annualizing the data.

Again, the exceptional items need to be dealt with in order to smooth out the estimate. Exceptional or one-time-only occurrences may be difficult to find or isolate. Interviews are most helpful in this regard.

To annualize data, divide the data by the number of actual months, then multiply by 12. For example, assume a small financial institution has seven months of actual data. Its gross expenses are $785,000. The exceptional items to be subtracted amount to $57,000. Assume there is $13,000 to be added as an exceptional omission. (Exceptional omissions are those things that did not show up as expenses but should have during the course of normal operations.) The expense adjustments are as follows:

Gross expenses	$785,000
Less: exceptional items	−57,000
Plus: exceptional omissions	13,000
Net to be annualized	$741,000

$$\frac{\$741,000}{7 \text{ months}} = \$105,857.14 \qquad \text{Average expenses per month.}$$

$$\$105,857.14 \times 12 \text{ months} = \qquad \$1,270,285.60$$
Estimated actual
for year.

This amounts to seven months of actual data that has been annualized to 12 months. The adjustments for exceptional items serve to refine the data further.

Planned or Budgeted Data

The cost study presented earlier in this chapter was based on planned data. In some processing centers, such as data processing, planned data is used extensively for cost analysis purposes. This is the DP center's way of making a commitment to deliver services at a price agreed to in advance. Policy may state that the DP center would absorb any underrecoveries.

Planned or budgeted data must, however, be used with caution. The analyst is advised to test the data for reality and appropriateness. If the data is inaccurate, the cost study will provide useless data. Sometimes a cost study based on plan data will reveal inconsistencies between what is planned and what is actually occurring.

Estimating Practical Levels and Time

In defining what a normal level of processing is, the analyst may find there are differences of opinion as to what is normal. The goal is to determine what the normal operational state is for a center, free of any abnormalities. Historical data may be helpful. The extremes to be avoided are underutilization on one end and capacity filling levels on the other. A practical level is somewhat prescriptive in that it says what the normal level should be.

It is important to determine the capacity parameters and find what is considered practical and hence normal. Discussions with processing center personnel will help reveal what they consider practical levels. Use approximate ranges to find an agreeable level.

Processing center personnel are usually knowledgeable enough to help the analyst estimate comparative ranges for handling either tasks or activities. An extension of the estimates against volumes should bring any distortions to the surface. It may take two or more passes at refining the data before it is acceptable.

Determining practical levels and building time estimates requires good judgment on the part of the analyst. It also requires working closely with the processing center personnel to attain accuracy.

AVERAGE ITEM COSTING IN AN ADMINISTRATIVE FUNCTION

The following example is based on an administrative function. Assume a cost study is to be done in the marketing department. Assume a direct mail solicitation was made for one product-charge card, with a total of 200,000 solicitations mailed to a multiple region base. The study is to determine how much it costs to bring in each new customer.

Assume that you find that on the average, for every 100 solicitations there are two responses. Only half of the responses become customers. Therefore, the ratio is one new customer for every 100 solicitations: $(2 \times 0.5 = 1)$.

Assume that you have obtained the following information. The advertising manager estimated 45 hours of her time was spent on the project. Her annual salary is $55,000. Fringe benefits raise it another 20 percent ($11,000). Her total compensation therefore is $66,000 ($55,000 + $11,000). The total regular work hours for a year are 2,080 (52×40). However, holidays, vacations, absences, and conferences account for 18 percent of this person's total time. Therefore $0.18 \times 2,080 = 374$ hours of time away from work. This person is available for 1,706 hours of on-site work per year. The compensation is now calculated to yield an hourly figure of $38.69 ($66,000 $\div$ 1,706 = $38.69). It therefore costs $38.69 per available hour of this person's time. Assume the other administrative expenses (other operating expenses), as determined by a separate study, for this manager are 10 percent of her compensation. The cost for 45 hours of her time is then calculated as follows:

$38.69	Hourly compensation
× .10	Administrative cost factor
3.869	Hourly administrative expenses
$38.69	Hourly compensation
+ 3.869	Hourly administrative expenses
$42.559	Total compensation and administrative expenses per hour for the advertising manager

$$\$42.559 \times 45 \text{ hours} = \$1,915.16.$$

Total managerial expenses for the mailing campaign

Next the invoices for artwork, layout, printing, and mailing need to be considered. In this example they total $180,000.

An outside agency handled the responses and did the follow-up. The invoice from them totaled $19,500.

Assume the financial institutionwide G&A rate is 12 percent after the direct cost of marketing has been factored out to prevent double counting. (This issue will be taken up in more detail in chapter 7, on allocations.)

However, debatable questions need to be addressed at this point. Should the G&A rate be applied to only the internally generated expenses such as compensation, or should it be applied to invoices received from outside such as the agency bill of $19,500? The answer depends upon how the G&A base was built to begin with. If it includes outside expenses, then it should be applied. However, an argument for the other side of the issue (not applying G&A) would be relevant if a product's processing is done 95 percent outside the financial institution. This is especially true if an invoice is sent monthly, it is paid, and little else is done in conjunction with the expenses as invoiced.

Another question is whether the G&A should be applied to one-time-only projects. This depends on the philosophy of management. A belief in full absorption of costs for all projects would necessitate the inclusion of G&A expense. On the other hand an incremental approach may exclude G&A from the study.

In this example assume the G&A base was constructed to include outside vendors. Therefore G&A will be applied to all expenses. There are obviously a variety of other expenses to consider for inclusion in this study. However, for purposes of brevity they were not included.

The expense buildup is as follows:

Administration	
($42.559 × 45 hours)	$ 1,915.16
Artwork, printing, and mailing	180,000.00
Response screening	19,500.00
Total expenses	$201,415.16
before G&A	
G&A @ 12%	24,169.82
(0.12 × $201,415.16)	
Total expenses	$225,584.98

With 200,000 solicitations mailed and the expected response ratio 2 to 100, this indicates a response of 4,000 potential customers (200,000 × 2/100 = 4,000). However, experience has shown that only half of these become new customers. Therefore, the marketing effort in 2,000 new customers (200,000 × 2/100 = 4.000); (4,000 × 0.5 = 2,000). The average cost of attracting each new customer then is $112.79. ($225,584.98 ÷ 2,000 = $112.79). Carrying the study further, the cost per solicitation is $1.1279 ($225,584.98 ÷ 200,000 = $1.1279).

AVERAGE ITEM COSTING FOR A COMPLETE PRODUCT

For the next example, assume there is a product R (for reconcilement), that flows through several organizations before it is consummated as a delivered, completed product. All numbers are to be accepted as givens. (See table 4-15.) Each unit cost summarized in table 4-15 would have been the result of a cost study on the function being represented.

It is important to take a comprehensive approach in costing a product on a financial institutionwide basis. This means

- Using the same time frame for all data

- Subtracting double counted amounts

- Including all applicable and relevant costs

TABLE 4-15 Costing Product R, Reconcilement

Direct Costs	Activity Cost Per Unit	
Processing center A	$0.4239	Local unit cost
Processing center D	$0.0860	Local unit cost
Processing center F	$0.0351	Local unit cost
Subtotal	$0.5450	(Product cost)
Indirect (support) costs		
Advertising	$0.0244	
Product sales	$0.0318	
Product administration	$0.0139	
Subtotal	$0.0701	
Total before G&A	$0.6151	
G&A @ 15%	$0.0923	($0.6151 × .15 = $0.0923)
(without advertising, sales, and product administration included as part of the overhead percentage)		
Total product cost per unit	$0.7074	

- Using appropriate volume data
- Making allowances for other products that share the same processing center(s)

This goal may be difficult to achieve but is worth striving for.

COST/VOLUME RELATIONS

In an average item cost (AIC) setting, volume plays a big role in determining the unit costs. Generally the costs are higher during low volumes and lower during high volumes. That is, an inverse relation exists between costs and volume in AIC. This is especially true if there is a great amount of fixed costs. This relation is graphed in figure 4-2.

Using the example of a processing center, assume the following: The annual fixed costs have been defined and listed. Fixed costs are defined as those being stationary, regardless of any volume changes, and regardless of whether utilization is zero or at peak capacity. That is, fixed costs here are those expenses that are not subject to volume swings. Another definition of fixed costs is costs that would continued even if the operations were to cease; this strict definition is used when considering discontinuance of an operation but is not generally used in product costing.

The fixed costs for this study are as follows:

Managerial compensation	$ 75,000
Supervision	174,000
Premises costs	247,000
(those that will continue even if the premises are unoccupied)	
Equipment and fixtures, including depreciation and leasing	
(costs that will remain and those that are contractual obligations	
of greater than one year)	153,000
Total fixed costs	$649,000

The variable costs have been defined as those that change with volume. At 2,000,000 units the following annual expenses were realized:

Operations staff compensation	$482,000
Travel	9,000
Entertainment	400
Equipment maintenance	12,350
Telecommunications	28,100
Subscriptions	200
Utilities	15,700
Stationery and supplies	26,900
Total	$574,650

Figure 4-2. Trend of Unit Cost/Volume Relations within an AIC Technique

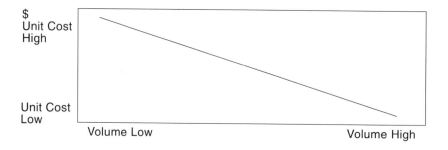

After interviewing the center management, it is decided that for purposes of the study, the following items and amounts that are part of annual expenses just listed, are more fixed than they are variable. The decision is made to include them with the fixed base.

Travel	$ 3,275
Telecommunications	200
Subscriptions	1,820
Utilities	4,129
Stationery and supplies	5,850
Total	$15,274

The fixed costs now total $664,274 ($649,000 + $15,274 = $664,274). The variable costs now total $559,376 ($574,650 − 15,274 = $559,376).

At 2,000,000 units the center costs are as follows:

	Per Unit
Fixed	$0.332137
($664,274 ÷ 2,000,000 = $0.3321)	
Variable	$0.279688
($559,376 ÷ 2,000,000 = $0.2797)	
at 2,000,000 volume	$0.611825

One assumption is generally made regarding variable costs. The assumption is that the per unit value remains constant regardless of the volume. That is, the total variable costs move with volume but each unit cost remains the same. This is not always true, since some variable costs reach plateaus and the unit value changes after a certain range.

Under the fixed costs as defined, the per unit value changes with volume. The value in this example is $0.3321 per unit for 2,000,000 units. It will drop as the volume increases above that level. Conversely the per unit value will increase when the volume drops below the 2,000,000 volume. However, under any volume the total fixed cost of $664,274 remains the same. The total cost for 2,000,000 units is $1,223,650 ($664,274 + $559,376 = $1,223,650).

It is interesting to graph the cost per volume relations and observe the resultant total cost and unit value changes, as done in figure 4-3.

Taking the same data we could calculate the total per unit cost at any given level. At 2,000,000 volume the per unit cost was $0.611825. For a moment assume the hypothetical extreme at either end. With a volume of only one, the cost for that one unit is 664,274.279688 ($664,274. + $0.279688).* With a volume of 5,000,000 the per unit cost is $0.4125428.** As you can see, the total per unit cost in this example decreases

Figure 4-3. Cost per Volume Relations

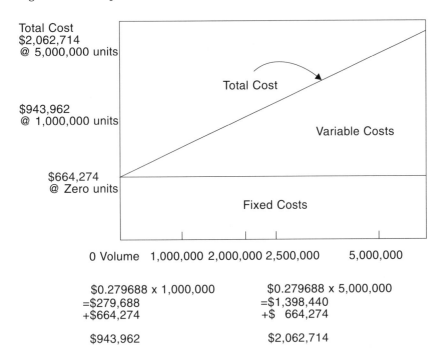

Total Cost
$2,062,714
@ 5,000,000 units

$943,962
@ 1,000,000 units

Total Cost

Variable Costs

$664,274
@ Zero units

Fixed Costs

0 Volume   1,000,000 2,000,000 2,500,000   5,000,000

$0.279688 x 1,000,000 $0.279688 x 5,000,000
=$279,688   =$1,398,440
+$664,274   +$ 664,274

$943,962 $2,062,714

*Some would appropriately argue the impossibility of this occurrence. The variable cost would also probably be higher because of imperfections of categorizing variable costs.
**[$664,274 + (5,000,000 × $0.279688)] ÷ (5,000,000) = $0.4125428.

with volume. Product management or marketing may become particularly concerned
when the analyst uses the AIC method at the lower end of the volume range. Their
concerns may be appropriate, particularly if the product is new and not fully developed—
hence a low volume. Figure 4-4 shows the per unit costs at given levels beginning with
250,000 units. You will notice the per unit cost decreases less dramatically at the
higher end of the volume scale. For purposes of brevity the variable unit cost values
have been rounded to four decimal places and the resultant total unit cost values to
two decimal places.

Figure 4-4. Per Unit Costs at Different Levels

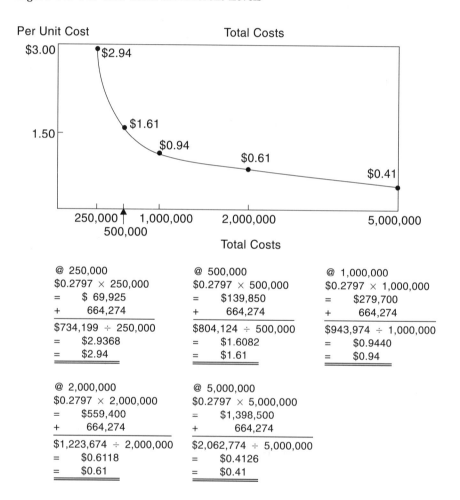

Figure 4-5. Sample Timesheet

PRODUCT TIME SURVEY

Staff Member's Name __Clemmons_____

Phone Number __x 864_____

Branch Name __Willows_____

Branch Number __10_____

Date __12/10/XX_____

Indicate the percentage of your time spent on the Product Groups as listed. This data will be used for the development of average unit times. The percentages should reflect your best estimate of the time you spend on each group listed in a typical workday.

	Product Group	Product Line	Products
Product Group A	80%		
(Deposit services)			
Product line A1		60%	
Demand deposits)			
Product A1a			40%
(Business checking)			
Product A1b			20%
(Consumer checking)			
Product line A2		20%	
Product A2a			5%
Product A2b			10%
Product A2c			5%
Product Group B	20%		
Product line B1		5%	
Product B1A			2%
Product B1b			1%
Product B1c			2%
Product line B2		5%	
Product B2a			5%
Product line B3		10%	
Product B3a			1%
Product B3b			3%
Product B3c			5%
Product B3d			1%
	100%	100%	100%
	Total product groups	Total product lines	Total products

ALTERNATIVE APPROACHES USING AIC (NONSTANDARD) TECHNIQUES

Many creative cost analysts are inventing new methods and techniques in the non-standard costing environment. Some of these techniques compensate for inadequate management information systems. Others are devices permitting the analyst to develop good cost data in the absence of industrial engineering time standards.

Time Estimates for Products at the Customer Contact Level (Branch Office)

Industrial engineering standards are not always available for time estimates at the point of product delivery, such as customer contact in a branch. Forms that allow each staff member to show how his or her time is allocated to the various in a typical workday product are quite useful. Such timesheets must be designed to account for all of the staff member's time and to list the product information being sought. Questions should be simple and direct. Figure 4-5 illustrates such a form. It stratifies the information according to the three levels: product groups, product lines, and products.

In addition to supplying data for product average unit times, this form can be used as a basis for allocating expenses to product groups, products lines and products. The data is collected and aggregated by product for each branch. The data is then extended against the hours available for work for the staff members in a typical workday.

| Percentage of time for product Ala (business checking) | × | Number of hours available for work for one day for each reporting staff member in the branch who entered data for this product | = | Average amount of time spent on product Ala in a typical work day |

This data is then divided by volumes in order to develop average unit times for a specific branch.

Consider the following example. There are five staff members in a branch. They indicated on the questionnaire they spend some of their time on product Ala, which is business checking. Their percentages and available time for work are as shown in table 4-16.

No allowances will be made for holidays, vacations, and absences in the unit time factor. This is due to the net available staff hours already being calculated and used in determining the hourly rates. For this example assume a total average daily volume count of 125 units at this branch for product Ala, business checking. For simplicity assume the unit count represents deposits only.

TABLE 4-16 Time Survey

col. 1	col. 2	col. 3	col. 4
			Average
	Percentage of		Individual
	Time on		Time Spent on
	on Product Ala	Average Available	Product Ala
Staff Members	(Business Checking)	Work time	(hours)
Hernandez	40%	7.0	2.80
Lee	10	7.5	0.75
Nelson	05	6.0	0.30
Peterson	73	7.0	5.11
Sullivan	22	7.0	1.54
Other staff	0	150.0	0
Total	—	184.5	10.5

Derived average 5.69%   (10.5 ÷ 184.5 = 5.69%)

Note: Column 3 includes allowances (subtractions) for personal time such as breaks and lunches.

The base average unit time is calculated by the following formula:

Total average time spent on a given product at the branch ÷ Total average volume for that product at the branch = Average unit time.

Thus we compute 10.5 hours ÷ 125 units = 0.084 average unit time for the business checking product. This is 5.04 minutes (0.084 × 60 = 5.04). However, minutes will not be used in this study.

Once the average unit time for each product is developed, a recovery calculation is made. To check against time recovery multiply each product's average unit time against its annual volume. This provides for an accounting of the annual time for each product. These annual times are then totaled. The total is then checked and verified against the total available staff time for work at the branch. Major differences should be researched. A reconciliation of any distortions should also be made.

Now that the time factors have been dealt with in this methodology, let us focus on the expense side of the methodology. If time factors have been developed on an hourly basis for each product unit, then it is appropriate to develop expenses on an hourly basis. Assume for purposes of example that the annual expenses for the branch are $1,020,000. Also assume the cost analysis research is summarized as follows:

Compensation	$ 780,000
Other operating expenses	227,000
Transfers-in	13,000
Total	$1,020,000

In each of the three categories there were direct expenses to be subtracted and applied to specific products. The adjustment is summarized in table 4-17.

In practice one would prepare a detailed schedule of direct expense applications. It would list the specific category and amount being directly applied to a specific product. Assume the following. The direct expenses for product A1a, business checking, are overtime, $8,000; other marketing, $3,400; and data processing, $2,085. The remainder of the direct expenses went to other products.

TABLE 4-17 Applying Direct Expenses to Specific Products

Category	Total before Adjustments	Portion to Apply Directly to Specific Products	Net Available for Hourly Rate Development
Compensation	$ 780,000	$24,000[1]	$756,000
Other operating expenses	227,000	10,000[2]	216,000
Transfers-in	13,000	7,100[3]	5,900
Total	$1,020,000	$41,600	$978,400

Notes:
[1] Overtime
[2] Marketing
[3] Data processing.

The staff count in this branch is 30 persons. The annual net available hours for work after personal time and holidays, vacations, and absences is 46,500 hours. This averages out to 1,550 available hours for work for each staff member per year.

The hourly rate for the branch could be calculated by using the following formula: Total net expenses ÷ Total net available hours for work = Net hourly expense rate.

In the example the computation is as follows: $978,400 net expenses ÷ 46,500 net hours = $21.04 per hour.

There are 31,500 units (125 units × 252 days = 31,500) of volume for product A1a on an annual basis. The adjusted average unit time was previously developed as 0.084 hours.

Therefore, the following calculation occurs for determining the total annual hours for product A1a, business checking:

$$\text{Total annual units} \times \text{Average unit time} = \text{Total annual hours.}$$

The computation is as follows: 31,500 × 0.084 average unit time = 2,646 annual total hours for product A1a. This calculation is necessary for two reasons. The first is to provide an hourly base for spreading the direct expenses, and the second is to verify expense recovery.

The direct expenses for the product totaled $13,485 ($8,000 + $3,400 + $2,085 = $13,485). This is spread on an hourly basis by dividing the total direct expenses by the total hours for the product. The computation is thus, Product A1a $13,485 direct expenses ÷ 2,646 total hours = $5.0964 per hour direct expenses.

The cost buildup for product A1a then appears as follows: $21.0400 branch hourly expense rate + $5.0964 direct expense hourly rate = $26.1364 total hourly rate.

The per unit time is multiplied by the hourly rate to arrive at the per unit cost: $26.1364 total hourly expense rate × 0.084 average unit time = $2.1955 per unit cost.

This is to be done for each product. A check of expense recovery is to be made by multiplying the total volume (units) for each product by their respective per unit costs. These extensions are then totaled and checked against the total branch expenses. In this example business checking accounted for $69,158.25 (31,500 units × $2.1955 per unit cost = $69,158.25) of the branch's expense. This can be verified by using the original derived percentage, 5.69 percent, and multiplying it by the $978,400 net expenses. The result is $55,670.96 (0.0569 × $978,400 = $55,670.96). We then add the $13,485 in direct expenses to this. The result is $69, 155.96 ($55,670.96 + $13,485 = $69,155.96). The difference between the two, $2.29 ($69,158.25 − $69,155.96 = $2.29), is attributable to rounding errors. Holidays, vacations, and absences were accounted for by using the net available hours for the branch. Net available hours were used in the hourly rate development. Therefore, development of a special HVA factor was not necessary.

This method is most useful when the analyst needs to develop unit times for products and there are no time standards available. Questionnaire forms are used to develop unit times by applying the data against available hours. The expense data is then developed on an hourly rate.

Pros and Cons of AIC

Among the many advantages of the AIC approach are the following.

- True or actual item costs are visible at a given moment. This may be important to the bank's decision makers.

- The cost information is more easily obtained and compiled than with other methods. This method is relatively simple to use and is easily learned.

- There are no standards to maintain. This can save expenses as the development and maintenance of standards can be costly and time consuming.

The AIC method has several disadvantages as well, such as the following ones.

- Average item costs are volume sensitive. That is, they are subject to fluctuations in cost and volume.

- Inefficiencies of a processing area are often invisible to management. They are undiscernible and difficult to isolate given average item costs.

- The fixed and variable aspect of the costs becomes more pronounced during the extremes of volume. Therefore, the optimal deployment of resources may be difficult to achieve.

- Excess capacity may be difficult to ascertain. In the absence of a standard measurement there is little visibility on the prescriptive capacity of a processing area.

- Spending variances are more difficult to isolate than with a standard methodology. There is generally no residual expense pool to analyze as exists in the standard methodology.

5

Standard Costing
Methodology

Standard costing is a prescriptive methodology for cost development. The essence of standard costing is to prescribe what the costs *should be* given certain parameters and techniques.

In this chapter standard costing for a processing center is covered from start to finish, with examples of how to do it. The beginner should have no difficulty grasping the essentials of this methodology, but there is sufficient depth to challenge the intermediate and senior analyst to refine techniques within this approach. The manager who reads the chapter will come away with an awareness of the need for flexibility and change within a standard costing framework.

THE CONCEPT OF STANDARD COSTING

To perform a cost study using the standard costing approach, a standard cost system must already be in place or standards must be available for costing. In using standards there are three basic functions to be performed: (1) analyze and document the processing center's activities, (2) develop activity- or product-aligned standard times, and (3) perform frequency analyses.

Analyze and Document the Processing Center's Activities

In this phase of the assignment the analyst researches and documents the major activities of the processing center being costed. A brief listing should be completed that shows the sequence of tasks leading to the completion of an activity.

Interviews with appropriate center personnel such as the center's manager, supervisors, and key staff members may be most helpful. If there is an industrial engineer familiar with the center's operation and the time standards, a review with that person should be a priority. In many financial institutions, however, the cost analyst is the one who sets the standards. This is especially true in the smaller institutions.

Next product management or marketing personnel should be interviewed to obtain their input on cost categories. They may have special requirements in regard to the alignment of costs by activity or product. It is not necessary to interview everyone involved in the process, however. The emphasis should be on good research in an effort to gain knowledge and understanding of the processes being costed.

If the work measurement standards have been previously established they need to be reviewed for possible revisions. Review for possible update

The source(s) of volume counts

The applicability of volume counts

The applicability and appropriateness of the time standards

Changes in equipment and or procedures

Develop Activity-Aligned Standard Times

Developing activity-aligned standard times entails the use of one or more work measurement techniques. The analyst decides what techniques to use on the basis of experience, the amount of time available for the study, the standard cost system in place (if any), and the general availability of data for development of standards.

In this phase there also may be the task of converting standard times from minutes to hours. This depends on the methodology that is employed in measuring the work.

Perform Frequency Analyses

Some activities have a lower or higher volume than that of the product they support. Such activities must be "frequencied." In performing a frequency analysis a ratio of activity to product volume is developed.

An example would be an activity volume of 250 that flows to a product volume of 8,000. The ratio is 250 to 8,000, or 0.03125 to 1.0; that is, for every product unit there is 0.03125 unit of this particular activity. The importance of this result becomes manifest when a unit cost is developed for the activity; then the cost is frequencied at $0.03125 \times$ activity unit cost for each unit of the product it flows to.

Assume for a moment the unit cost of a particular activity is $0.19. On a frequency basis it costs $0.0059375 for this activity for each product unit (0.19×0.03125 = $0.0059375). In other words for every unit of the product there is an associated cost of $0.0059375 for this activity.

Now let's take an example of an activity volume that is greater than the product volume. Assume the activity volume is 11,500 and the product volume is 10,800. The ratio to be developed will use the following formula:

$$\text{Activity volume} \div \text{Product volume} = \text{Frequency ratio.}$$

Thus the calculation is as follows:

$$11,500 \div 10,800 = 1.0648 \text{ to } 1.0.$$

This is expressed as 1.0648 activity units to 1.0 product units.

Assume the activity cost is given as $0.32 per unit. The cost for this activity as it is frequencied to the product would then be

$$\$0.3407$$
$$(\$0.32 \times 1.0648 = \$0.3407).$$

Another way of looking at this is how to see what the overall cost is.

$$\$3,680$$
$$(\$0.32 \times 11,500 = \$3,680).$$

For this activity the total cost of $3,680 is to be frequencied. It can be spread to the 10,800 product units. This can be accomplished by dividing the $3,680 by the 10,800 unit product volume. The result is

$$\$0.3407 \text{ unit cost}$$
$$(\$3,680 \div 10,800 = \$0.3407).$$

In summary, frequency analyses are used to spread the unit costs of activities with volume variations from that of a specific product to that specific product.

Elements of Standard Cost System

Given that standard costing is the use of prescribed data, there are certain elements to maintain. Standard costing systems should contain the following at a minimum: labor and time standards, time allowances, labor rates, and other operating cost rates.

The development of *labor and time standards* is the core of standard costing. Based on the developed standards the cost data is aligned to those standards. Hence, standards facilitate the development of unit costs.

As mentioned in chapter 4 there are several methods to use in developing labor standards. If possible there should be consistency throughout the institution since comparability of data is important. Not all financial institutions are geared toward maintenance of a detailed standards systems. Sometimes a significant commitment of staff is required in order to maintain labor standards. Standards can be developed using a simple format such as self-logging, though the accuracy is somewhat less than with the other methods.

A refinement of labor standards would include the use of *time allowances* to cover personal time, fatigue, and delay. These components may change in value over time. Reorganizations, changes in physical layout, personnel policy, and other such factors could alter the value of each one.

Labor rates are the result of salaries, overtime, temporary work, bonuses, and benefits being aligned to the available hours of a center being measured. Labor rates are the result of calculating compensation on an hourly basis. Because each of the components is subject to change, it is wise to revise labor rates at least annually.

In developing the labor rates the analyst should be diligent in striving for a full recovery of compensation. The rates could be based on available hours for the processing center. One exception to this may be bonuses. Since they are relatively volatile, one may find it prudent to handle them separately, perhaps as an overhead expense.

The *other operating costs* of a center are everything incurred as expense except compensation. It essentially includes all operating expenses other than compensation. It may be adjusted to include amortization for such things as research and development (R&D), which are not listed on the expense reports. It also may include provisions for extraordinary items.

Other items to consider are the treatment of transfers-in from other centers. Because their cost impact may be difficult to predict, some cost systems are developed with a framework that excludes transfers-in from the other operating cost rates. In such systems transfers-in are unitized on an actual cost to actual volume basis.

This other operating cost rate is usually developed based on available staff hours for the center being costed. In the nonstandard costing method it is usually based on volume count.

Periodically the other operating cost rates of a processing center should be updated.

STANDARD COSTING OF A PROCESSING AREA WITH MULTIPLE ACTIVITIES

One of the first things to be calculated for a processing center with multiple activities is the total accountable hours—that is, the total paid hours for the staff in the center. The usual aggregate hours to be considered and sorted out are supervision and production staff; holidays, vacations, and absences; and training. The objective is to arrive at the net hours available for supervision and processing. This is done by subtracting from the total hours any "down time"—any holidays, vacations, absences (paid and unpaid), and any other nonprocessing occurrences that diminish the availability of staff for production.

In some centers there is a management level to be considered. Allocation techniques such as those used for supervision would be appropriate. The management hours will probably have to be spread over a larger base than the supervision hours, however.

In this cost study the standards developed are initially expressed in minutes. We start at the lowest level: a task.

TABLE 5-1 Z Processing Center Conversion of Minutes to Hours

Standard Number	Task	Standard Minutes	÷ 60 =	Standard Hours
1	Setup	15.9		0.26500
2	Route	3.7		0.06167
3	Check	12.2		0.20333
4	Update	9.6		0.16000
5	Record	5.4		0.09000
6	Phone authorization	5.5		0.09167
7	Reference check	9.2		0.15333
8	Review	12.0		0.20000
	Activity Support Tasks			
9	New customer	69.6		1.16000
10	Photocopying	7.5		0.12500
11	Liaison	25.2		0.42000

Assumptions: There are three activities processed within this center. No other center is directly involved in the processing of these three activities. There are some indirect overhead allocations from elsewhere in the institution to these activities, however. Accept as given the following: the standard times; the monthly average volumes; and activity identifiers. The three activities are designated as: activity A (process a request); activity B (process an inquiry); and activity C (update customer records).

The hierarchy builds from tasks, to activities, to products, to product lines, up to product groups. In this book the lowest level for a unit time is at the task level; the lowest level for a unit cost is at the activity level; and the lowest unit level for revenue reporting is at the product level.

This example will carry the study in detail through the activity level. However, should the institution decide to charge customers for activities A, B, and C then they can simply be reclassified as products. Products, product lines, and product groups will be covered in chapter 9.

Since the standard time per unit is expressed in minutes it is divided by 60. This is done to convert the standard unit times into an expression of standard decimal hours. The formula (applied in table 5-1) is as follows:

Standard
minutes   ÷ 60 minutes = Standard decimal hours per unit.
per unit

For example: 15.9 minutes per unit task ÷ 60 minutes = 0.26500 hours per unit task.

TABLE 5-2 Z Processing Center Volume Identification

Task Standard Number	Task	Standard Hours per Unit	Monthly Average Volume	Activity Volume Identifier
1	Setup	0.26500	2,500	A
2	Route	0.06167	12,500	A,B
3	Check	0.20333	1,500	A
4	Update	0.16000	5,000	C
5	Record	0.09000	10,000	B
6	Phone authorization	0.09167	50	C
7	Reference check	0.15333	5,000	C
8	Review	0.20000	5,000	C
	Support Tasks			
9	New customer	1.16000	150	A,B,C
10	Photocopying	0.12500	2,500	A,B,C
11	Liaison	0.42000	570	C

Dominant volumes (monthly average)
Activity A   2,500
(process a request)

Activity B   10,000
(process an inquiry)

Activity C   5,000
(update customer records)

TABLE 5-3 Z Processing Center Total Standard Hours

Task Standard Number	Tasks	Standard Hours Per Unit	×	Monthly Average Volume	=	Monthly Total Task Hours
1	Setup	0.26500	×	2,500	=	662.5
2	Route	0.06167	×	12,500	=	770.9
3	Check	0.20333	×	1,500	=	305.0
4	Update	0.16000	×	5,000	=	800.0
5	Record	0.09000	×	10,000	=	900.0
6	Phone authorization	0.09167	×	50	=	4.6
7	Cross reference	0.15333	×	5,000	=	766.7
8	Review	0.20000	×	5,000	=	1,000.0
	Total task hours					5,209.7
	Support Tasks					
9	New customer	1.16000	×	150	=	174.0
10	Photocopying	0.12500	×	2,500	=	312.5
11	Liaison	0.42000	×	570	=	239.4[1]

[1]Assume that through research it has been determined task 11 (liaison) goes directly to activity C (update customer records).

The next thing to accomplish is to identify volume. Three things must be done by the analyst: (1) identify the volume count for each task; (2) decide what the dominant activity volumes are; and (3) identify which activities the tasks flow into. In this example three tasks flow into activity A (process a request). They are setup, route, and check. The routing task also supports activity B (process an inquiry).

As you can see from table 5-2, some tasks will have to be frequencied into their respective activities. For example, task number 3 (check), which has a volume of 1,500, will have to be frequencied into activity A (process a request), whose volume is 2,500. The dominant volumes are selected as most representative of a specific activity.

For each of the tasks and support tasks, the analyst needs to do an extension of standard hours times task volume. That is, all the total standard hours (monthly total task hours) need to be calculated for each task. Table 5-3 shows these calculations.

The analyst is now ready to compute what can be referred to as an *activity burden rate*. This rate is developed as a means of frequencying support tasks to tasks as they are to be applied to the activities. The formula is as follows:

$$\text{Activity burden rate} = \frac{\text{Support tasks}}{\text{Direct tasks}}$$

As mentioned before, task 11 (liaison) will be directly applied to activity C (update customer records). Therefore it will be excluded from the support tasks in this calculation.

The support tasks common to all three activities are:

Task 9	New customer	174.0
Task 10	Photocopying	312.5
	Total support hours	486.5

The formula applied is thus

$$\frac{486.5 \text{ support hours}}{5{,}209.7 \text{ task hours}} = .09338 \text{ Activity burden rate}$$

This is a form of frequency analysis. It is a method of using a frequency ratio to account for the support tasks. For each task hour there is 0.09338 hours of support tasks being performed.

The next step is to increase each standard time by the support burden rate. This allows for full recovery of all standard task hours, including the support tasks within the center. The aim is to have an accounting of all the hours at standard.

TABLE 5-4 Z Processing Center Burden Standards

Standard Number	Tasks	Standard Hours	×	Burden Rate	=	Burdened Standard Hours[1]
1	Setup	0.26500		1.09338		0.28975
2	Route	0.06167		1.09338		0.06743
3	Check	0.20333		1.09338		0.22232
4	Update	0.16000		1.09338		0.17494
5	Record	0.09000		1.09338		0.09840
6	Phone authorization	0.09167		1.09338		0.10023
7	Reference check	0.15333		1.09338		0.16765
8	Review	0.20000		1.09338		0.21868

Note: The *burden standard hours* include support tasks except for task 11 (liaison), which will be allocated directly to activity C (update customer records).
[1]1.0 factor + 0.09338 = 1.09338.

TABLE 5-5 Z Processing Center Activity Alignment of Tasks: Activity A (Process a Request)

Standard Number	Tasks	Burdened Standard Hours[1]	Frequency Analysis		Adjusted Standard Unit Time	Monthly Activity Volume		Standard Processing Hours Recovery
1	Setup	0.28975	× 1	=	0.28975 ×	2,500	=	724.4
2	Route	0.06743	× 1	=	0.06743 ×	2,500	=	168.6
3	Check	0.22232	× 0.6[2]	=	0.13339 ×	2,500	=	333.5
	Total activity SUT[3]				0.49057 ×	2,500	=	1,226.5

The dominant monthly average volume for activity A is 2,500.

[1]From table 5-4.

[2]1,500 ÷ 2,500 = 0.6.

[3]SUT = Standard unit time.

Note: Adjusted standard unit times are additive, whereas burdened standard hours are not.

The next step is to align the appropriate tasks to specific activities. The burdened standard hours are carried over from the previous schedule, which reflects their buildup. The burdened standards are then frequencied to arrive at the adjusted standard unit times.

Task standard 1 (setup) need not be frequencied as it has the same volume as activity A (process a request), which it folds into. However, task standard 3 (check) needs to be frequencied. It has a volume of 1,500, which is different from activity A's volume of 2,500. It folds into activity A. When applied as a function of the dominant activity volume it becomes a ratio. This frequency analysis as illustrated by task 3 is applied against activity A's volume of 2,500. The relation is thus established as a ratio. Hence 1,500 ÷ 2,500 is a ratio of 0.6, or 60 percent. For every unit of activity A, processing a request, a 0.6 unit of task 3, checking, occurs. Performing a frequency alignment makes the individual task standards additive; that is, they can be aggregated to equal an activity standard. Before this was accomplished they were not additive.

The burdened standard hours are referred to as adjusted standard unit times after they are frequencied. When they are totaled they become an activity's *standard unit time* (SUT). In table 5-5 the buildup of activity A's SUT is illustrated.

This same process is repeated for all activities. The computation for activity B (process an inquiry) is shown in table 5-6. Again an activity SUT is developed by aggregating the adjusted standard unit times for the activity-aligned tasks.

TABLE 5-6 Z Processing Center Activity Alignment of Tasks: Activity B (Process an Inquiry)

Standard Number	Tasks	Burdened Standard Hours[1]		Frequency Analysis		Adjusted Standard Unit Time		Monthly Activity Volume		Standard Processing Hours Recovery
2	Route	0.06743	×	1	=	0.06743	×	10,000	=	674.3
5	Record	0.9840	×	1	=	0.09840	×	10,000	=	984.0
Total activity SUT[2]						0.16583	×	10,000	=	1,658.3

The dominant monthly average volume for activity B is 10,000.

[1]From table 5-4.
[2]SUT = Standard unit time.

The last alignment of tasks to activities is for activity C (update customer records). There are five tasks supporting this activity. Three of them require no frequency alignment; two others, tasks 6 (phone authorization) and 11 (liaison) do require frequency alignments. See table 5-7 for the computation.

TABLE 5-7 Z Processing Center Activity Alignment of Tasks: Activity C (Update Customer Records)

Standard Number	Tasks	Burdened Standard Hours[1]		Frequency Analysis		Adjusted Standard Unit Time		Monthly Activity Volume		Standard Processing Hours Recovery
4	Update	0.17494	×	1	=	0.17494	×	5,000	=	874.7
6	Author	0.10023	×	0.01[2]	=	0.00100	×	5,000	=	5.0
7	Reference	0.16765	×	1	=	0.16765	×	5,000	=	838.3
8	Review	0.21868	×	1	=	0.21868	×	5,000	=	1,093.4
11	Liaison	0.42000	×	0.114[2]	=	0.04788	×	5,000	=	239.4
Total activity SUT[3]						0.61015	×	5,000	=	3,050.8

Total dominant monthly average volume for activity C is 5,000.

[1]From table 5-4, except for task 11, which comes from table 5-3.
[2] 50 ÷ 5,000 = 0.01.
   570 ÷ 5,000 = 0.114.
[3]SUT = Standard unit time.

The frequency alignment for task 6 is

$$0.10023 \times \frac{50}{5,000} = 0.00100.$$

The frequency alignment for task 11 is

$$0.42000 \times \frac{570}{5,000} = .04788.$$

This is the one support task that was to be directly applied to activity C only. It was not part of the support task burden rate.

In this study assume the standard costs are being developed with budgeted expenses. Table 5-8 shows the details of the budgeted expenses for this center.

Also assume in the research phase it was determined that overtime is 100 percent attributable to activity B so it is directly applied to that activity. Depreciation is to be divided evenly between activity A and activity C. All of these direct expenses total $113,000.

They will be separated from the expense allocation process and be directly routed to the appropriate activities. The net expense after transfers-in and direct expense reduction then is $1,321,000. This amount will be used in developing an hourly rate for the processing center.

Holding the expenses off to the side temporarily, let's take a look at the staffing hours at the Z processing center. There are 45.7 budgeted full-time-equivalent (FTE) staff members in the center. If you multiply the 45.7 FTE by 2,080 hours, the result is 95,056 gross staff hours for the year. From this, all nonprocessing hours are to be subtracted. This includes management, supervision, holidays, vacations, absences, and training. After this is subtracted we have what is called the *net anticipated hours* available, "net hours" for short.

TABLE 5-8 Z Processing Center 12-Month Budget[1]

Expense Categories	Plan Amount
Regular salaries	$ 865,000
Overtime (attributable 100% to activity B)	15,000
Fringe benefits	173,000
Entertainment	5,000
Travel	22,000
Depreciation (50% to activity A, 50% to Activity C)	98,000
Premises	125,000
Other (including transfers-in)	131,000
Total expenses	$1,434,000
Less: Direct expenses[2]	(113,000)
Net processing (remaining) expenses	$1,321,000

[1]This could also be based on historical actuals.
[2]To be directly allocated or charged to the specific activities of: overtime $15,000; depreciation, $98,000. They total $113,000.

TABLE 5-9 Z Processing Center Staff Analysis

	Staffing			*Anticipated Hours*
Budgeted FTE Staff[1]	×	Annual Hours Per FTE Staff[2]		
Gross available hours				
45.7	×	2,080		= 95,056
Less: Nonprocessing hours				
6.0	×	2,080	Supervision	(12,480)
39.7	×	80	Holidays	(3,176)
39.7	×	80	Vacations	(3,176)
39.7	×	60	Absences	(2,382)
39.7	×	50	Training	(1,985)
Net processing hours available				71,857

[1]Or could be historical average
[2]52 weeks × 40 hours = 2,080 hours.

In this example the net hours are 71,857. Dividing by 2,080 we arrive at 36.6 FTE processing staff availability. (See table 5-9.)

We are now ready to develop an hourly expense rate for Z processing center. The formula is as follows:

Z's Net budgeted expenses, annual (12 months) ÷
Z's Annual net anticipated hours available = Z's Hourly rate.

$1,321,000 ÷ 71,857 = $18,38373.

It is appropriate to point out here that a combination of fixed and variable costs is built into the standard hourly rate. Therefore, the cost is likely to be affected by changes in volume.

We have derived all of the necessary data for computing the standard unit costs. Multiply the adjusted standard unit time (SUT) by the hourly rate to arrive at the standard unit cost. Then add any direct costs to arrive at the adjusted standard unit cost.

As an example of how this is done, we will use activity B (process an inquiry). The adjusted standard unit time of 0.16583 is multiplied by the hourly rate of $18.38373 to arrive at the standard unit cost of $3.04857. The direct unit cost of $0.12500 is added to this: $15,000 overtime + 120,000 annual units + $0.12500. The resultant adjusted standard unit cost is $3.17357. (See table 5-10.)

**TABLE 5-10 Z Processing Center Computation of Standard Unit Costs
for All Activities in the Center**

Activity	Adjusted SUT	Hourly Rate	Standard Unit Cost	Per Unit Direct Cost	Adjusted Standard Unit Cost
A	0.49057	$18.38373	$ 9.01851	$1.63333[1]	$10.65184
(Process a request)					
B	0.16583	18.38373	3.04857	0.12500[2]	3.17357
(Process an inquiry)					
C	0.61015	18.38373	11.21683	0.81667[3]	12.03350
(Update customer records)					

[1]Depreciation: $98,000 × .5 = $49,000.
  2,500 monthly volume × 12 = 30,000 annual units.
  $49,000 ÷ 30,000 = $1.63333.

[2]Overtime = $15,000.
  10,000 monthly volume × 12 = 120,000 annual units.
  $15,000 ÷ 120,000 = $0.12500.

[3]Depreciation $98,000 × .5 = $49,000.
  5,000 monthly volume × 12 = 60,000 annual units.
  $49,000 ÷ 60,000 = $0.81667.

The potential recovery of the adjusted standard unit costs should be checked. When each activity's unit cost is multiplied by the annual volume a potential recovery is indicated by the result. In this cost study the potential recovery for the three activities totals $1,422,393. This is calculated as follows:

Activity A $10.65184 × 30,000 = $319,555;

Activity B $3.17357 × 120,000 = $380,828;

Activity C $12.03350 × 60,000 = $722,010.

Therefore $319,555 + $380,828 + $722,010 = 1,422,393. This compares to the total budgeted expenses of $1,434,000. There is a $11,607 shortfall in recovery, which is explained by analyzing the available hours in conjunction with the hours at standard.

TABLE 5-11 Z Processing Center Projected Recovery Calculation

Activity	Standard Unit Costs	+	Direct Costs	=	Adjusted Standard Unit Costs	Annual Volume[1]	Total Recovery (Underrecovery) at Standard
A (process a request)	$ 9.01851		$1.63333		$10.65184	30,000	$ 319,555
B (process an inquiry)	3.04857		0.12500		3.17357	120,000	380,828
C (update customer records)	11.21683		0.81667		12.03350	60,000	722,010
Total recovery							$1,422,393
Total to be recovered							1,434,000
Underrecovery							$ (11,607)

The available hours were 71,857. However, the hours at standard for the three activities is 71,228. The calculation for this appears on the projected recovery calculation schedule shown in table 5-11. The difference between the two most likely is attributable to excess capacity. In this case it is excess staff. It equates to 629 hours (71,857 − 71,228 = 629). This excess capacity can be translated into numerical staff equivalencies. Assume the gross annual hour per staff person is 2,080. From this we subtract such things as holidays, vacations, absences, and training. In this example they are accounted for as follows:

Gross staff hours	2,080
Less	
Holidays	80
Vacations	80
Absence	60
Training	50
Net available hours per operating staff Member	1,810

Dividing the excess hours of 629 by 1,810, equals the availability of 0.3 FTE staff (629 ÷ 1,810 = 0.3). This is not a large number but it essentially represents a surplus (idle) equivalency of 0.3 FTE. If this number were larger, obviously management would be motivated to curtail it, particularly as it became visible through the under-recovery of the center. This kind of data is an example of the benefits of using a standard cost analysis system.

TABLE 5-12 Accounting for Net Processing Hours

Hours	FTE Staff
71,857 available hours	39.7
629 hours of assumed idle capacity	.3
71,228 hours accounted for at standard	39.4

$$629 \div 1,810 \text{ hours} = .3$$
$$71,228 \div 1,810 \text{ hours} = \underline{39.4}$$
$$39.7$$

It should be mentioned here that there is a significant variability of work flow within a financial institution by hour of the day, day of the week, week of the month, and so forth. It is rarely possible to completely balance the available staff with the available work at any given time. Some amount of staffing for peaks is inherent to financial institutions and depends in part on the level of service that management wishes to maintain.

Tables 5-12 and 5-13 illustrate the accounting for the net processing hours available and for monthly hours at standard, respectively.

Our next task is to calculate the projected recovery for the center (as in table 5-11) with the thought of explaining any differences that may exist. First, the recovery is calculated for the center on an activity by activity basis. Comparing the recovery of $1,422,393 against the amount to be recovered of $1,434,000, we find an underrecovery of $11,607.

Next, we calculate the total annual hours at standard for all activities, which gives a total of 71,227.2 annual standard hours. Subtracting this from the total annual processing hours available for the center of 71,857.0, we have a remainder of 629.8 (71,857.0 − 71,227.2 = 629.8) excess hours.

Multiplying the excess hours by the hourly expense rate for the center of $18.38373, the result is $11,578. This figure essentially represents expenses that are attributable to excess capacity. If we subtract the underrecovery of $11,607 from this amount, we are left with a difference of $29, which is due to rounding errors.

The next step is the development of local standard unit cost. This is the result of adding the adjusted standard unit costs to the unitized local overhead burden costs.

At this point it must be emphasized there are many stages in the development of standard unit costs. One can also see that unit costing possibilities exist at all levels.

TABLE 5-13 Z Processing Center Monthly Hours Calculation (Rounded)

Activity	Volume	×	Unit time	=	Monthly Processing Hours at Standard
A	2,500	×	0.49057	=	1,226.5
(Process a request)					
B	10,000	×	0.16583	=	1,658.3
(Process an inquiry)					
C	5,000	×	0.61015	=	3,050.8
(Update customer records)					
Total monthly hours					5,935.6
				×	12
Total annual hours at standard					71,227.2
Net processing hours at available					71,857.0
Less: Annual hours at standard					71,227.2
Excess hours					629.8

Expenses due to excess capacity:
  (629.8 excess hours × $18.38373 hourly expense rate = $11,578)

Expenses due to rounding errors:
  $ 11,578 Excess capacity expenses
  + $(11,607) Underrecovery
  $ (29) Attribute to rounding errors

At what level costs are determined and with how much detail is a function of management philosophy.

With this in mind the next issue to deal with is the development of a burden rate for local overhead expenses. These would be in lieu of direct transfers-in. In the example we are working with here, there is an administration department that manages three centers, X, Y, and Z. The annual budget for this department is $65,000. This expense must be allocated to the three centers in an equitable manner. The decision is made that each center's percentage of total expense will serve as a basis for allocation.

The formula for developing this burden rate is

$$\frac{\text{Local administration expenses}}{\text{Operating centers' expenses}} = \text{Burden rate.}$$

Therefore, the calculation is

$$\frac{\$65,000}{\$1,566,000 + \$1,434.000} = 2.1667\%.$$

Figure 5-1. Calculating Local Overhead Burden Rate

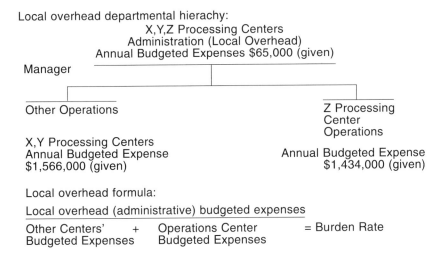

Local overhead departmental hierachy:

X,Y,Z Processing Centers
Administration (Local Overhead)
Annual Budgeted Expenses $65,000 (given)

Manager

Other Operations

X,Y Processing Centers
Annual Budgeted Expense
$1,566,000 (given)

Z Processing
Center
Operations

Annual Budgeted Expense
$1,434,000 (given)

Local overhead formula:

$$\frac{\text{Local overhead (administrative) budgeted expenses}}{\text{Other Centers' Budgeted Expenses} + \text{Operations Center Budgeted Expenses}} = \text{Burden Rate}$$

Figure 5-1 presents the conceptual framework used in developing local overhead.

We take this overhead burden rate and multiply it against the adjusted standard unit cost for each activity, as shown in table 5-14. The result is an overhead burden cost for each activity. The burden cost for each activity is then added to each respective activity's adjusted standard unit cost. The result is a local standard unit cost for each activity.

At this juncture the activities could be identified as products if management decides to charge customers for these activities. If this is the case, we will continue with this example, adding the institution's overhead.

TABLES 5-14 Z Processing Center: Calculation of Administration Burden Costs (Local Overhead)

Activity	col. 1 Adjusted Standard Unit Cost	×	Local Overhead Burden Rate	=	col. 3 Overhead Burden Cost	(col. 1 + col.3) Local Standard Unit Cost
A	$10.65184		2.1667		$0.23079	$10.88263
B	3.17357		2.1667		0.06876	3.24233
C	12.03350		2.1667		0.26073	12.29423

TABLE 5-15 Activity Costs for Activities A, B, and C

Standard Unit Costs	Z Processing Totals	Center Recovery
A ($ 9.01851 × 30,000)	$ 270,555	
B ($ 3.04857 × 120,000)	365,828	
C ($11.21683 × 60,000)	673,010	
Total	$1,309,393	$1,309,393
Direct Costs		
A (1.63333 × 30,000)	$ 49,000	
B (0.12500 × 120,000)	15,000	
C (0.81667 × 60,000)	49,000	
Total	$ 113,000	$ 113,000
		$1,422,393
Local overhead		
A ($270,555 × 2.1667%)	$ 5,862	
B ($365,828 × 2.1667%)	7,926	
C ($673,010 × 2.1667%)	14,582	
Total	$ 28,370	N/A
Institutionwide G&A overhead (derived)		
A ($319,555 × 14.57%)	$ 46,559	
B ($380,828 × 14.57%)	55,487	
C ($722,010 × 14.57%)	105,197	
Total	$ 207,243	NA
Residual recovery ($ 11,607 ÷ 1,309,393 = .88644%)		
A ($270,555 ×.88644%)	$ 2,398	
B ($365,828 ×.88644%)	3,243	
C ($673,010 ×.88644%)	5,966	
Total	$ 11,607	$ 11,607
		$1,434,000

NA = Not Applicable

The next step is thus to develop an institutionwide general and administrative (G&A) expense rate. The formula for this is as follows:

$$\frac{\text{Total institution general and administrative overhead expense}}{\text{Total activity costs at standard}} = \text{General Overhead recovery rate}$$

For this study there are some givens. Assume the general overhead expense anu the total activity costs of the institution at standard are given amounts. That is, their source is not reflected in this analysis. Therefore, the figures of $2,622,466 for general overhead and $18,000,000 of activity costs at standard for the institution are to be accepted as given.

The calculation is thus

$$\frac{\$\ 2,622,466}{\$18,000,000} = 14.57\%.$$

This rate is to be applied to each unit cost as its absorption of the institution's general and administrative expenses. (For more details, see chapter 7.) Much caution must be exercised to ensure there is no double counting or omissions in this process. Several approaches can be taken in allocating general institution overhead, but all methods are arbitrary and subjective.

The schedule in table 5-15 accounts for the standard costs of the Z Processing Center. Again these costs are at the activity level. The cost accumulation for the standard unit costs plus the direct costs and a residual recovery are listed. The residual recovery occurs as a closeout routine. It is allocated to the various products as an add-on. This allows for closing out all the center's expenses. It also allows for the visibility of residuals to those who would be interested in knowing what they are. It indicates the magnitude of the potential underrecovery.

We can rearrange the data to show the buildup of unit costs for each activity using the five components of cost indicated.

Activity A (Process a Request)

Standard unit cost		$ 9.01851
Direct cost		1.63333
Local overhead	($ 5,862 ÷ 30,000) =	0.19540
Institution G&A	($46,559 ÷ 30,000) =	1.55200
Residual	($ 2,398 ÷ 30,000) =	0.07993
Total cost		$12.47917

Activity B (Process an Inquiry)

Standard unit cost		$ 3.04857
Direct cost		0.12500
Local overhead	($ 7,926 ÷ 120,000) =	0.06605
Institution G&A	($55,487 ÷ 120,000) =	0.46239
Residual	($ 3,243 ÷ 120,000) =	0.02703
Total cost		$ 3.72904

Activity C (Update Customer Records)

Standard unit cost		$11.21683
Direct cost		0.81667
Local overhead	($ 14,582 ÷ 60,000) =	0.24303
Institution G&A	($105,197 ÷ 60,000) =	1.75328
Residual	($ 5,966 ÷ 60,000) =	0.09943
Total cost		$14.12924

To recap:

Activity		
A (Process a request)	$12.47917 × 30,000 =	$ 374,375.10
B (Process an inquiry)	3.72904 × 120,000 =	447,484.80
C (Update customer record)	14.12924 × 60,000 =	847,754.40
Total		$1,669,614.30
Less rounding error		1.30
Total product recovery		$1,669,613.00

Total product recovery:
   ($1,434,000 + $28,370 + $207,243 = $1,669,613)

In standard costing it is essential to be able to reconcile calculated costs to the total costs of the institution. In this example there could have been other activities in the upward succession of flow to products, product lines, and product groups. They were omitted for simplicity of presentation in order to focus on the procedural aspects of standard costing.

To summarize this example, the following must be completed at a minimum in order to maintain data integrity in a standard costing system.

Calculate:

• Total costs at standard

• Total direct costs

• Total local overhead costs

• Total general overhead costs

• Total residuals

Figure 5-2 Reconciliation of Activity Level Costs to Total Institution Expenses

The sum of these is to equal or be reconcilable to the total expenses of the institution. This is illustrated by figure 5-2, which is a flowchart of reconciliation of activity level costs to the total costs of the institution. This diagram reflects the aggregation of all costs assuming an institution is totally on a standard costing system. The total is reconcilable to the total institutionwide expenses. Should an institution be partially on a standard cost system then any nonstandard costs that exist would have to be added to the total in order to reconcile to the total institutionwide expenses.

ACTUAL VERSUS ESTIMATED DATA

Using Current or Historical Data

The use of historical cost as a basis entails using actual expense data rather than budgeted expense data. The costing example that was just completed could have been based on historical data instead of budgeted data. To do so is a matter of management philosophy. Some institutions may have the sophistication in their system to do both. If this is the case then you can use "plan to actual" comparisons and analyses and thus expand the usefulness of the standard costing approach. Using actual expense data provides a means of continuously monitoring what is occurring to expenses in each center.

Using Estimated Actual Data

Estimated actual data is a combination of what has occurred and what is forecasted based on the actuals. For example, the estimated actual data for a center could be based on nine months of actual data plus three months of forecasted data. The three months of forecasted data could be based on what has actually occurred for the first nine months of the year.

If the cost system is highly sophisticated and flexible enough for sensitivity (what if) kinds of analyses, then estimated actual scenarios can be produced. These are based on current year-to-date information plus revised projections for the remainder of the year. The impact of changes on unit costs can be readily known in such analyses. They can point to potential difficulties or areas requiring immediate attention.

Using Planned or Budgeted Data

Planned or budgeted expenses are essentially a forecast of future expenses. Costing based on planned expenses is only as reliable as the planned data itself. If the plan has been realistically constructed, then the data will be meaningful and useful for costing purposes.

The example used in this chapter was based on planned (budgeted) data. This is useful in establishing cost objectives. It allows both the user and the provider the opportunity to review and approve costs prior to the beginning of a new year, quarter, or month.

Some institutions used planned data for the whole year. They account for the difference between planned and actual in a management residual pool at year's end.

VARIANCE ANALYSIS

No matter what the method or the system there are going to be variances from standard in comparison to actual occurrences. The more complex the system the more difficult it is to sort out and explain any variances.

There are basically three types of variances: efficiency, spending, and volume. The monetary impact of these will be reflected in the residual pool.

Efficiency variances are those attributable to work flow and processing. Time is emphasized here. Some people are faster than the time standard and hence more efficient. If the work force is taking more time than prescribed to do something, then the extra time will surface as an inefficiency variance (assuming the cost system has a mechanism built in specifically to sort out this kind of variance).

Some processing center managers may not wish to sort out variances to this degree. They may also be reluctant to use the term "efficiency." Variance analysis may also distract from the standard costing system's objective of providing data on the cost of doing business. One can avoid controversy and only provide the quantitative dollar impact for "assumed efficiency variances," deferring further discussion to the jurisdiction of others.

Spending variances can occur at any time. The purchase of supplies, compensation, and other such controllable expenditures vary from month to month. Management needs to know the difference between variances attributable to activity and those attributable to changes in spending levels. The details of defining such variances can be difficult to work out sometimes and the result not worth the effort.

The ability to sort out changes in costs due to changes in volume is an important feature to have in a standard cost system. If the system is based on planned data, then the standard unit costs will not change. Instead the residual pool will reflect these changes.

Variances due to differences in efficiency spending, and volume should be part of the residual pool of expenses. The overages and underrecoveries would then be explained based on all three.

To see how the process works, let us consider another example. Assume a one-activity processing department with a budget as follows:

- 0.125 hours per unit, as determined by work measurement

- 1,000 units, the planned volume for the processing department

- 125 hours (0.125 hours × 1,000 units = 125 hours), the total budgeted processing hours for the center

- $1,000 expenses, the expense budget for the processing department

- $8 per hour processing expense ($1,000 ÷ 125 hours), a derived hourly rate for the processing department. (This particular rate includes all expenses such as compensation and other operating expense.)

Assume the actuals occurred as follows:

- 0.1317307 hours per unit, derived from a reported total of 137 actual hours (total hours consumed 137 ÷ 1,040 units = 0.1317307 hours derived).

- 1,040 units, the actual volume reported

- $1,200 expenses, the actual expenses incurred

We are now ready to calculate the variances.

Efficiency/(inefficiency) variance

$$
\begin{array}{ll}
0.125 & \text{standard unit hours} \\
-\ 0.1317307 & \text{actual unit hours} \\
=\ 0.0067307 & \text{hours inefficiency variance.}
\end{array}
$$

Multiply the variance times the actual volume:

$$
\begin{array}{llll}
0.0067307 \times & 1,040 & = & 6.999928 \\
\text{Per unit} & \text{actual} & & \text{total inefficiency hours} \\
\text{inefficiency} & \text{units} & &
\end{array}
$$

Therefore, the inefficiencies for this department as compared against standard totaled 6.999928 hours for the time period being reported.

TABLE 5-17 Favorable/Unfavorable Variances

Efficiency
6.999928 hours × $8 per hour budget rate =   ($56) inefficiency

Volume
40 units over budget × $1.00 per unit budget =   ($40.)

($1,000 planned expenses ÷ 1,000 planned units = $1.00 per unit.)

Spending [derived]
$1,200 actual expenses – $1,000 budgeted expenses – $56 insufficiency – $40 volume = ($104)

    Total variances   ($200)

Summary recapitulation

Budget	$1,000
– Actual	1,200
Total explained	$ (200)

Spending variance. This amount is derived as a residual after the efficiency/(inefficiency) and volume variances are accounted for.

Volume. To find the volume variance we subtract the actual volume count from the budgeted volume.

> 1,000 budgeted units – 1,040 actual units =
> 40 units over budget.

The dollar amount of each category is quantified in table 5-16.

SMOOTHING OUT VOLUME LEVELS

As in any system or methodology there are exceptions to contend with. Volume counts can be a difficulty if an activity is new and therefore has not reached a steady state. *Steady state* is defined as a stable volume level, stable in the sense of having a similar level from one period to the next. It is therefore somewhat predictable.

In cases where the operations have not reached steady state, the analyst must depend on projections with little or no verifiable history. In such cases it is prudent occasionally to check on the volume count and compare it to what was used in setting the standard.

ALTERNATIVE APPROACHES USING STANDARD COSTING TECHNIQUES

Hourly Rate Calculation

There are those who advocate the development of two hourly rates—fixed and variable. This requires a more complex calculating and reporting system. The interpretation of what is fixed and what is variable is often cause for debate.

Moreover, the need for such data is often dubious. Users may ask for it but have no real purpose or application for the data in mind.

The merits of this kind of breakout need to be weighed against the cost of alignment and calculation of the data as defined. Even if the information is not maintained on an ongoing basis, one should have the ability to strip out the fixed cost component. Management frequently asks questions such as "What will it cost us to take on this high volume customer?" or "How much would we save if we eliminated this service?"

Some institutions go to a finer level of detail by categorizing staff and expense within a center according to work units. They also develop a separate hourly expense rate for each unit according to its staffing availability, compensation, and other operating expenses. While this method has its merits, there must be a specific use for the data since it entails extra work.

The Advantages of Standard Costing

There are many advantages to using the standard costing methodology. This technique is used when senior management has mandated establishing prescriptive bases for determining what the costs should be.

The first advantage is that any inefficiencies of an operating area can be measured. The time standards are useful when applied to volume data in sorting out inefficiencies especially for determining staffing levels. It can also help the processing center managers decide where to concentrate their efforts toward productivity improvement. Cost analysis usually quantifies any inefficiencies and labels them as residuals.

The cost impact of volume variances can readily be separated from that of spending variances. This is an important differentiation to make in some processing areas. In using the average item costing (AIC) method it is not usually possible to sort out the two variances. By distinguishing them, however, the manager of the center can better control work scheduling and have a better grasp of the spending variances. The recipients of charges from a center usually respond favorably to the use of standard costs for this reason. Obviously unfavorable variances have to be absorbed by someone. The cost impact of unfavorable variances may be absorbed by the center management and be labeled as a "management pool."

The excess capacity of a center may become more visible. For the activities and products to be set at standard, a definition of "normal" capacity must be established. This is based on the volume at an average level. Obviously, idle equipment and staff is a sign of excess capacity. This will show up as a volume variance. However, when processing is sustained a plateau above normal for a time the efficiency factor of the center may exceed 100 percent. Management then becomes aware of the possible upper capacity limits of the center. Standard costs are not affected by volume variances. By definition, standard costs remain stable; they don't change with volume as do AIC costs. The recipients of standard cost generated transfer charges generally appreciate their stability and predictability. Standard costs allow for more stable planning of costs by the recipients of such transfer charges.

The Disadvantages of Standard Costing

The disadvantages of standard costing must be weighed against the advantages and the overall bank management philosophy before a decision is made about adopting such a methodology. Like any costing methodology, standard costing has its disadvantages. They are as follows.

The true item costs may not be represented. Standard costs are prescriptive. They tell what the costs *should* be. In order to find out what the true costs are it is necessary to allocate the residual costs of a center back to the item costs. The differences between actual costs and standard cost can be significant at times.

It is sometimes difficult to adapt a standard costing system to change. Many of the standard systems that are installed are inflexible to change in organizations, products, and customer bases. Some are "hard wired" to the extent that makeshift modules must be added in order to accommodate change.

Often a residual management pool of expenses must be reallocated. This is done in order to clear out the expenses of a processing center that uses the standard costing approach. The residual is the difference between standard costs and actual costs. The movement of residual expenses sometimes causes misunderstandings between a provider organization and its user organizations.

At times standards can be too burdensome and costly to maintain. The larger the organization the more complex the standard system is likely to be. Having a standard cost system requires a commitment to maintain it by keeping it current in all respects. This can be a heavy commitment for some organizations. It is easier to control a standard cost system and maintain it in smaller banks. A standard cost system requires having a cadre of analysts, industrial engineers, and programmers on staff in order to maintain it. This can be expensive.

There is a possibility of confusion on usage of the data. The concept of standard costing may be difficult for some to understand. There is more possibility of it being misunderstood than if it were an actual costing system. The abundance of data that comes out of some of these systems may be overwhelming to some people. Most recipients of data prefer it be presented in a self-explanatory format. Herein lies the difficulty. To some people standard cost systems provide data that is more elaborate than their data requirements. They may require interpretation of what some of the reports contain.

Data Processing Costing*

In today's world of high technology and computers, we see an unprecedented expansion of automation and productivity gains. The innovations seem endless.

Computer technology is literally changing daily. Rapid obsolescence is a problem to managers who must decide on acquisition of equipment and design of data processing facilities.

In the area of workflow automation, financial institutions have realized significant gains in productivity, from both a processing standpoint and from the standpoint of delivery to users. Computers have made the workday more productive for many.

In terms of technology the one area that is tentative and subject to change at all times is data processing. There the pace of technological advance is very rapid.

We all must keep abreast of these changes in order to maintain a consistent and accurate approach to costing. The variations are numerous on how to arrange, analyze, and present data.

DATA PROCESSING IN FINANCIAL INSTITUTIONS

Data processing (DP) facilities exist today in financial institutions as a result of technological advances and as a result of the need for a systematic and well-defined sequence of operations to be performed on data as it flows in and out of the financial institution. DP as a function handles, sorts, merges, computes, arranges, reports, and delivers information.

*For a thorough in-depth coverage of DP costing, the reader is encouraged to consult *EDP Cost Accounting* by Terence A. Quinlan.

The DP budget can consume a gargantuan share of an institution's expense budget. This is especially true if the DP management's philosophy is geared to technological synchronization with the needs of a growing and changing organization.

Knowledge of computer networking is essential. In smaller institutions there may be little or no difficulty in this regard. However, in the medium size and larger institutions the linkages may be mercurial. In such networks a primary system feeds data to another system. The other system may have several feeds into it. The more the feeds, the more the complexity. Cost analysts need to know how these flows work and what measurement information is available.

The volume measurement capability of each system is knowledge one must have in order to carry on a cost study. These kinds of needs must be made known to the systems personnel prior to implementation of a new system.

The development of cost data provides a valuable service to the institution's DP organization. The cost data often clarifies how much the DP services are costing the organization and what DP capacity remains uptapped.

The cost data provides answers to the following questions management may raise.

- What is the capacity utilization for the mainframe computer and printers?

- What are the peak times and days?

- What has been the volume trend for the last two years?

Those performing cost studies may be called upon to provide information on the cost of initiating or continuing certain projects and on the price of alternatives.

DP PLANNING

At the start of the planning cycle the planned demand for DP services is determined. There are several ways to gather the information needed. Sending out questionnaires and following up with phone calls will yield some response. The users need to be prompted and informed, starting with meetings with the key users. A good tool is a user profile to be filled out by each client user. The profile should include the user's volume data and seasonal trend usage. A basis from which to plan is essential in gathering accurate and usable data. The planning process assumes an ongoing installation is the object of planning. In startup situations planning becomes a matter of estimating ranges. Capacity planning is another major responsibility of data processing management. It usually needs to be done over a longer time span than the annual planning cycle. This is because of the long lead time required to complete systems projects, obtain equipment, and deal with interface issues. A financial institution's DP plan needs to be an integral part of its strategic plan.

Those performing cost studies need information on projects, ongoing operations, and product innovations. This translates into human and machine resource requirements. The cost study process assists in their quantification. The main elements to cost in a DP center are

- Central processing unit (CPU)

- Direct access storage device(DASD)

- Magnetic ink character recognition processing (MICR) device

- Printing devices

Many questions regarding the demand for DP services need to be answered in the planning process. The specific demands for each function need to be known. The translation of the demand resources needs to be quantified. The nature of the demand such as volume trends, seasonality, and anticipated hourly peaks should be known. The longevity of each major project needs to be quantified. The expected benefits should also be noticed. With this information the analyst performs a capacity utilization analysis on each major DP function.

The tasks that a person doing a DP cost study must perform are as follows:

- Gathering and formatting planned volume data

- Translating planned volumes to the utilization of human and machine resources

- Analyzing capacity

- Analyzing project cost/benefit, impact, and priorities

- Developing transfer rates

Much interaction with the DP providers and the DP users is entailed throughout this process. The objective for the cost analyst is to balance the needs for quantification of DP resources and determination of their economic impact between the providers and the users.

In planning for new and continuing projects there must be established accountability measures. Such things as "managed to" benefits, payback period, earnings per share impact, and internal rate of return are essential accountability benchmarks. "Managed to" benefits are potential savings that are committed to by management. For example, if an automation project is justified on staff savings then a commitment would require that management hold to those savings by keeping the staff levels at the savings level. This is called "managing to" the savings.

In data processing the bulk of the resources to quantify are in two basic categories: (1) human and (2) machine or plant. Human resources are closely tied to the utilization of machines. These two are the raw materials of a DP center.

One should try to identify soft dollars during the planning process. These are areas where costs should or could be reduced without interruption of essential services (more on this in chapter 13).

In planning for existing services there is usually sufficient ongoing volume and expense data for deriving rates and assessing the impact of the plan on DP resources. However, where the service is new and there is no data, substitute data must be employed. One should then look for a similar service and use analogies in constructing a probable activity and expense scenario for the new service. Hence, the data of one service is used as a substitute for another service. This is the essence of projecting the history of one service to the elements of another. Flexibility for accommodating changes and performing sensitivity analyses is necessary in any planning system. The planning process for a DP cost study is diagrammed in a flowchart shown in figure 6-1.

Figure 6-1 Planning the DP Cost Study

Send out questionnaires to survey planned usage for next year. Include current and historical usage data.

↓

Make contact with major users and interview them to obtain further information.

↓

Prompt all recipients to respond.

↓

Obtain volume and other pertinent plan data.

↓

Quantify impact on human and machine resources.

↓

Develop planned capacity utilization pro formas.

↓

Develop rates.

DP COSTING CONCEPTS

Costing a DP organization focuses on the triad of provider, services, and users. DP costing is unique in that not only does the analyst cost the services but he or she may also recommend transfer pricing. This is different from the product costing environment, where product management or marketing is usually accountable for recommending pricing. Moreover, DP costing has a large impact on what will occur within the internal transfer charge mechanism of the institution. In this regard DP costing is potentially more visible as the self-interests of some organizations may cause a focus on certain costs. Hence the analyst must be aware of the overall cost recovery concept and its provisions for underrecoveries.

Determining the costs of a DP center entails studying the processing center, identifying its tasks and activities, measuring what they are costing, recommending transfer pricing, and then implementing transfers upon approval. This multistage process requires a working knowledge of the interplay of several factors. The relationship of one center to another must be known, as well as the interface of one system to another. Figure 6-2 summarizes this process.

The ultimate flow of activities to products must be considered in determining an overall costing framework. The idea here is to ensure the costs are appropriately structured so they are additive in determining a product cost. This often requires diligent research and calculation. The benefits are enormous when one considers the resultant ability to add activities from different centers together to form a product.

Frequency analysis is the technique that allows for the additive alignment of one product to another. It is not always possible to align a single activity's cost to fit all subsequent products. A host of products may have different volumes from one another—hence the need for individual frequency analysis.

The challenge is to bring together the reporting of various processing centers into a cost and transfer system that is logical, equitable, and understandable. A comprehensive approach is the goal.

In performing cost analyses one looks for natural value units for volume measurement for each task or activity. These units of measurement serve as a basis for unitized costs, transfer pricing, and recovery analysis. They are the elements of transaction that take place in building tasks into activities and subsequently products.

Processing Pools

In arranging data for costing purposes processing pools are to be configured. These configurations are made in order to bring about the costing of common processing elements. They are needed so that an orderly arrangement of cost data can be produced. A configuration, therefore, is a grouping of equipment, processing volumes, and expenses according to an activity or process that is common to these elements.

Figure 6-2. Interrelation of DP Costing Concepts

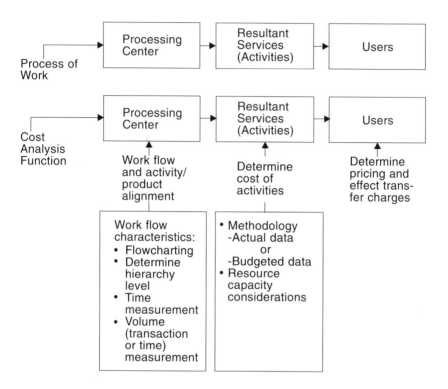

Once the alignment of equipment, processing volumes, and expenses is made, the configurations are called expense pools.

The pools are arranged according to functions. The arrangement of the pools is usually dependent upon the organizational structure of the DP facility.

The processing pool for computer services may be configured so as to include the following:

- Processing center administration

- Computer operations

- Data entry

  Batch

  Key

- Printer operations
  Impact
  Laser
- Tape and disk operations
  Dynamic
  Storage
- Technical support
- Time share operations

The matching of equipment and expense to their respective functions is the first step in the costing process. It is the beginning of expense pooling.

For each operation there should be an equipment pool configuration. This facilitates the aggregation of all applicable equipment expenses for each function or operation.

Usually a fixed asset listing will aid the analyst in tracking down and sorting out equipment according to the functional or operative areas. An equipment pool may be configured as shown in table 6-1.

TABLE 6-1 Computer Services Equipment Pool: Printer Operations

	Direct Maintenance Repairs (If Known)	Depreciation Amortization (If Applicable)	Equipment Rent/Lease (If Applicable)	Total
Impact				
10 D-500 printers	$1,200	$1,000	0	$ 2,200
2 X-29 printers	240	0	0	240
5 modems	120	0	0	120
5 M-500 printers	1,500	0	0	1,500
5 feeder/sorters	1,800	0	900	2,700
Subtotal	$4,860	$1,000	$900	$ 6,760
Laser				
4 high-speed Z-10	2,700	1,200	0	3,900
3 processors	500	800	0	1,300
Subtotal	$3,200	$2,000	0	$ 5,200
Total	$8,060	$3,000	$900	$11,960

Note: Carry each total to the cost pool schedule.

TABLE 6-2 Computer Services Cost Pool

							Cost Categories							Total Before Admin. Allocat.	Admin. Allocat.	Total After Admin. Allocat.
Function	Salaries	Overtime	Benefits	Temp. Staff	Travel	Phone	Contract/ Consult	Main./ Repairs	Premises	Equip. Rent	Deprec./ Amort.	Stat./ Supplies	Misc.			
Center Admin.[1]	$ 75,000	$ 0	$15,000	$ 0	$3,000	$ 2,000	$5,000	$ 0	$ 3,000	$ 0	$ 0	$ 500	$ 100	$103,600	(103,600)	$ 0
Computer operations																
(CPU)	50,000	5,000	10,000	1,000	0	3,000	2,000	8,000	10,000	4,000	1,000	3,000	1,000	98,000	23,175[2]	121,175
Data entry																
Batch	30,000	1,000	6,000	1,500	0	2,000	0	3,500	8,000	5,500	1,500	2,500	1,500	63,000	14,901	77,901
Key	40,000	800	8,000	2,500	0	3,000	0	1,000	6,500	4,000	1,200	2,000	500	69,500	16,444	85,944
Printer operations																
Impact	20,000	0	4,000	0	0	500	0	4,860	3,000	900	1,000	3,000	0	37,260	8,813	46,073
Laser	25,000	0	5,000	0	0	500	0	3,200	3,000	0	2,000	3,000	0	41,700	9,863	51,563
Tape and disk operations																
Dynamic	10,000	0	2,000	0	0	500	0	1,000	2,000	1,000	500	1,000	0	18,000	4,257	22,257
Storage	10,000	0	2,000	0	0	500	0	1,000	4,000	500	1,000	2,000	0	21,000	4,967	25,967
Technical support	40,000	0	8,000	0	0	2,000	1,500	0	2,000	500	250	200	100	54,550	12,902	67,452
Time share operations	25,000	0	5,000	0	0	1,500	0	900	1,500	500	250	250	100	35,000	8,278	43,278
TOTAL	$325,000	$6,800	$65,000	$5,000	$3,000	$15,500	$8,500	$23,460	$43,000	$16,900	$8,700	$17,450	$3,300	$541,610	0	$541,610

[1]Close out to computer operations, data entry, printer operations, tape and disk, technical support and time share operations based on their percentage of total expenses.

[2]Example of administrative allocation $98,000 / ($541,610 − $103,600) × ($103,600).
$98,000 ÷ $438,010 = 22.37%. $103,600 × 22.37% = $23,175 Admin Allocation.

**TABLE 6-3 Computer Operations (CPU)
Rate/Recovery Schedule**

Elements	Expenses [1]	÷	Volume	=	Derived Rate (Rounded)
Processor time	$106,175		232,108		$0.45744
			CPU cycle seconds		
I/O time	$ 15,000		53,191		$0.28200
(input/output)	_____		I/O time		
Total expenses	$121,175				

[1] From the cost pool schedule.

Each cost category may have its own supporting schedule. It will depend upon the level and complexity of the costing effort and the center's information availability. Maintenance, repairs, equipment rental or lease costs, and depreciation and amortization should be compiled for each function or operation in their respective pool schedules.

The schedule in table 6-2 provides an example of how the costs for a computer services organization are spread to various functions, such as computer operations, data entry, printer operations, tape and disk operations, technical support, and time share operations. It is important to note that although the center administration receives an allocation of certain expenses, these expenses are to be reallocated to the functions. They can be reallocated on a percentage basis, which could be translated into an overhead decimal factor.

The total for each function or operation is carried to a rate development and recovery schedule. For example, the computer operations schedule may appear as shown in table 6-3. Within that schedule the expenses may be broken down into elements based on some measurement algorithm.

Rate Development Bases

In developing rates there may be several possible units of measure for a particular element. For use in transfer rate development, there must be some causal relation between the unit of measure and cost. In some areas this may be difficult to discern. The availability of unit measurement is usually the determining factor in structuring rates.

The issue of time measurement versus transaction measurement will be taken up later in this chapter. However, the following are possible units of measurement for each function as indicated so far in this chapter. Some are alternatives. Some are mutually exclusive; that is, if you use one you cannot use another. Others are additional elements to consider for charge to users.

Mainframe(CPU)and time share
  Kilobyte hours or seconds
  Core per second
  Execute command program
  CPU time
  Number of I/O's (Input/Output)
  I/O time
  Program controlled interruption (PCI)

Data entry
  Hours
  Minutes
  Number of cards
  Number of keystrokes

Printer operations
  Hours
  Minutes
  Seconds
  Per unit (printer/terminal)charge (monthly)
  Number of lines
  Number of pages

Tape/disk operations
  Number of tracks (per day/month)
  Number of tapes (per day/month)
  Number of cylinders (per day/month)
  Number of disk packs (per day/month)
  Number of mounts

Technical support
  Hours/minutes
  Monthly charge per unit
  Number of calls

Other DP-related areas include:

MICR processing (magnetic identification code recognition)
Microfilming operations—Computer output microfiche (COM)
Scanning operations

Costs can be developed on a per unit, or transaction, basis for each of these.

Associated with each of the bases just listed are algorithms or formulas for computation. The results of computation may vary, depending on the basis selected and the transfer rate system being used. It should be noted there that it is difficult to develop reliable standard costs in a DP center. The variations can be enormous at times. Hence the average item cost (AIC) approach is usually the basis for DP costing. Having covered the basic elements of rate development for DP, we should look at what constitutes a data processing center as a whole.

FUNCTIONAL ORGANIZATION OF A DATA PROCESSING CENTER

There are many ways to functionally organize a DP center. The choice depends upon the size of the institution, the physical proximity of the center, and the management philosophy of the institution. Figure 6-3 shows the organization of an integrated data processing center.

Figure 6-3. Functional Organization of a DP Center

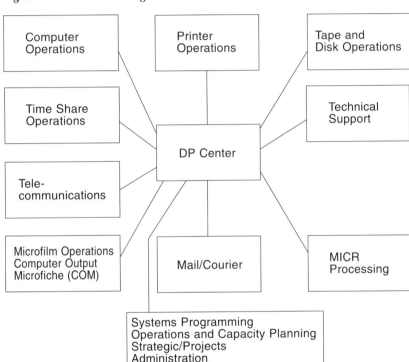

LIFE CYCLE OF A DP CENTER

Each of the functions of a DP center is subject to change as the institution changes. Change is inevitable in data processing. It comes from three basic sources: technological advances, changes in institution functions, and changes in processes. New technology, new business, organizational growth, and management changes may necessitate additional DP activities and changes in others. These changes may best be explained in terms of a life cycle, as shown in table 6-4. When a DP center is formed it is in the startup stage. As time goes on there are new systems and designs to be implemented. This occurs as the benefits of DP automation are sought as goals for the institution. Steady state is reached when there is little change occurring and the expense budget is not significantly changing.

TABLE 6-4 DP Center Life Cycle

Phase	Activities	Change
Startup	Staffing; facilities and equipment acquisition and planning	Shift of work from outside vendors to in-house utilization of equipment and personnel. A significant budget commitment.
Systems design and interface	Integral design of major systems with the goal of having each system compatible and communicative with the others	Characteristically high growth in expenses due to staffing increases and additional equipment
Steady state	The systems and processes are functioning as planned. Volume and activities have leveled out.	Little change is occurring. The budget reflects nominal increases.
Enhancements needed	Increased demands due to volume increases. Technological advancements are implemented. Continued growth places a strain on the operations.	Upgrading of equipment is needed. Additional staffing makes moderate increase in budgets necessary.
Major systems redesigns needed	The enhancements can no longer accommodate the growth. A retooling of major systems is necessary. Many projects are established.	Redesigns of systems and the expansion of equipment cause a major increase in the budget. Staffing increases.
Steady state	Steady state is achieved. The conversion to new systems is complete.	A contraction of resources. Staff levels are reduced. Consolidations through reorganization causes a slight decrease in the budget.

Enhancements are eventually needed on the original systems. They are followed by major system redesigns. Then steady state is reached once again. The cycle repeats itself over the years.

Steady state should be management's goal in systems design. This is the point when all the processing is done in an efficient manner and an effective cost. It is the optimal point of matching resources to needs at the lowest possible cost.

When determining rates, the stages of the DP life cycle must be kept in mind. Since change in data processing can greatly alter the cost bases of a product within an organization, the analyst must be prepared to accommodate change while establishing DP costs.

PRODUCT POOLS

In constructing a product pool one tries to find the best fit of the organization's unique processes and systems to that of a transfer charge mechanism. There are many variations to the method that is being presented here for product pool construction. Whichever variation is chosen, it is important to be consistent, practical, and logical.

Figure 6-4 shows how the costs from cost centers flow into product pools. It also shows how additional costs such as local overhead, G&A, and costs from other departments are allocated. The result is a total institutionwide capturing of costs for each product.

Figure 6-4. The Flow of Costs to Product Pools

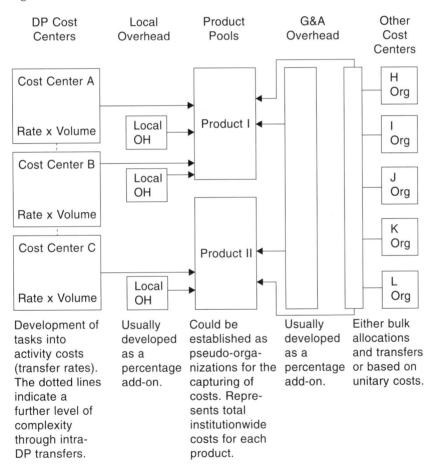

DP Cost Centers	Local Overhead	Product Pools	G&A Overhead	Other Cost Centers
Cost Center A				H Org
Rate x Volume	Local OH	Product I		I Org
Cost Center B	Local OH			J Org
Rate x Volume				K Org
Cost Center C		Product II		L Org
Rate x Volume	Local OH			
Development of tasks into activity costs (transfer rates). The dotted lines indicate a further level of complexity through intra-DP transfers.	Usually developed as a percentage add-on.	Could be established as pseudo-organizations for the capturing of costs. Represents total institutionwide costs for each product.	Usually developed as a percentage add-on.	Either bulk allocations and transfers or based on unitary costs.

TABLE 6-5 Product Cost Pool

Providing Organization	*Algorithm (Basis for Determination)*		*$ Extensions*
Center A	Rate × volume	=	Transfer cost
Local overhead	@ % transfer cost (center A)	=	Overhead transfer
Center B	Rate × volume	=	Transfer cost
Local overhead	@ % transfer cost (center B)	=	Overhead transfer
Support organization (H,I,J,K,L)	Rate × volume or some allocation technique	=	Transfer cost
Subtotal			Transfers/ allocations
G&A	@ % subtotal		Allocations (G&A)
Total costs			$ X X X

There are several ways product pools can appear in terms of capturing costs. The details may be based on organizational or functional transfers. Table 6-5 is an example of how this may appear.

A broader perspective of cost systems is presented in chapter 15. Our purpose here is to understand ways of accounting for DP costs such that they become integral to product pools that may be accounted for outside of a DP organization.

COST DEVELOPMENT TECHNIQUES

In the DP environment the cost analyst finds an abundance of information to work with. It must be sorted out so that only relevant data is processed and used in the costing process. The essential elements for development of DP costs are

- Volumes

- Equipment pools and expenses

- Processing pools and expenses

- Capacity utilization

- Transfer mechanism

Volume data must be accumulated at a level high enough to be usable in the transfer mechanism. The lower the level at which volume is tracked in the processing stream, the more complex will be the costs. Reruns, abnormally ended runs (abends), and other nonroutine occurrences need to be accounted for as well.

The alignment of equipment to the various processing pools is a function of the expense-recording mechanisms that are in place. Processing pools include staff, equipment, and other operating expenses. The pools are usually developed so as to accommodate the existing transfer mechanisms.

A capacity level of utilization for costing purposes needs to be established. Later in this chapter the issue of capacity determination is covered. At this point it is sufficient to indicate that certain DP costs are developed based on a percentage of full capacity.

The transfer mechanism determines what the format should be for transfer cost development. Costs must be developed to conform to the transfer mechanism that is in place. Obviously as things change over time the mechanism may need to be modified.

The following is a simple example of a DP costing. Assume there are four activities to be costed. The equipment pools have equipment expenses allocated as follows:

$755,000 for activity 1 (mainframe)

$158,000 for activity 2 (spool)

$ 12,500 for activity 3 (tape operations)

$ 79,000 for activity 4 (disk operations)

TABLE 6-6 DP Schedule I

Measurement Component	Annual Volume	Cost Pool Distribution Equipment	and Processing[1]	=	Total Expenses
Activity 1 (Mainframe)					
Job steps executed	25,025	$ 12,000	$ 53,000		$ 65,000
CPU seconds	1,803,675	697,500	235,000		932,500
Execute command programs	51,860,465	45,500	66,000		111,500
Total		$755,000	$354,000		$1,109,000
Activity 2 (Spool)					
Print lines	35,000,200	$ 77,000	$ 52,200		$129,200
Key strokes	23,577,981	50,800	103,400		154,200
Pages(1 part)	6,848,000	30,200	55,400		85,600
Total		$158,000	$211,000		$369,000
Activity 3 (Tape Operations)					
Tape mounts	54,888	$ 1,500	$122,000		$123,500
Tape storage per day	459,016	11,000	45,000		56,000
Total		$12,500	$167,000		$179,500
Activity 4 (Disk Operations)					
Track days	1,397,462	$79,000	$30,000		$109,000

[1]The cost breakdown represents a more detailed study of each activity's components. Accept the data as given at this point.

The processing pools (exclusive of equipment pool expenses) have the following expenses:

$354,000 for activity 1 (mainframe)

$211,000 for activity 2 (spool)

$167,000 for activity 3 (tape operations)

$ 30,000 for activity 4 (disk operations)

TABLE 6-7 DP Schedule II

Activity	Measurement Component	Total Cost[1]	÷ Volume	Unit = Cost	70% of × Capacity[2]	Net Unit = Cost
Mainframe						
1A	Job steps executed	$ 65,000	25,025	$2.59740	.7	$1.81818
1B	CPU seconds	932,500	1,803,675	0.51700	.7	0.36190
1C	Execute command programs	111,500	51,860,465	0.00215	.7	0.00151
	Total mainframe cost	$1,109,000				
Spool						
2A	Print lines	$ 129,200	35,000,200	0.00369	.7	0.00258
2B	Key Strokes	154,200	23,577,981	0.00654	.7	0.00458
2C	Pages (1 part)	$ 85,600	6,848,000	0.01250	.7	0.00875
	Total spool cost	$ 369,000				
Tape operations						
3A	Tape mounts	$ 123,500	54,888	2.25004	.7	1.57503
3B	Tape storage days	56,000	459,016	0.12200	.7	0.08540
	Total tape cost	$ 179,500				
Disk operations						
4	Disk track days	$ 109,000	1,397,462	0.07800	.7	0.05460
Total disk track cost		$ 109,000				

[1]The represents an aggregate of equipment and processing costs. For example, $12,000 + $53,000 = $65,000 for activity 1A.

[2]This represents an estimate of used capacity. The idea here is to not charge the users for the cost of excess capacity. This is a transfer pricing decision however. With the 70% factor there will be a 30% residual cost remaining in the center. Some centers transfer this residual to a "management pool," where it is redistributed to the user base.

TABLE 6-8 DP Recovery Schedule

Activity	Measurement Component	Net Unit Cost	× Volume	(col. 3 × col. 4) = Recovery	Total Cost	(col. 5 − col. 6) Over/(Under-recovery)	(col. 7 ÷ col. 6) % Over/(Underrecovery)
1A	Job steps executed	$1.81818	25,025	$ 45,500	$ 65,000	$ (19,500)	(30.0%)
1B	CPU seconds	0.36190	1,803,675	652,750	932,500	(279,750)	(30.0%)
1C	Execute command programs	0.00151	51,860,465	78,309	111,500	(33,191)	(29.8%)
2A	Print lines	0.00258	35,000,200	90,301	129,200	(38,899)	(30.1%)
2B	Key Strokes	0.00458	23,577,981	107,987	154,200	(46,213)	(30.0%)
2C	Pages (1 part)	0.00875	6,848,000	59,920	85,600	(25,680)	(30.0%)
3A	Tape mounts	1.57503	54,888	86,450	123,500	(37,050)	(30.0%)
3B	Tape storage days	0.08540	459,016	39,200	56,000	(16,800)	(30.0%)
4	Disk track days	0.05460	1,397,462	76,301	109,000	(32,699)	(30.0%)
	Totals			$1,236,718	$1,766,500	($529,782)	(30.0%)

Assume the costs are to be based on 70 percent of capacity for this center. The transfer rates may be set up as follows:

The first task to develop costs for is activity 1 (mainframe operation). Each category, or measurement component, is listed in a schedule with its annual volume and cost pool data, for both equipment and processing. The intent of DP schedule I (table 6-6) is to list the total expenses for each activity by category. Schedule II (table 6-7) shows the development of unit costs. The total cost for each category from schedule I is listed. It is divided by its associated volume. The derived unit cost is then multiplied by a capacity discounting figure. This results in a net unit cost figure.

Schedule II could serve as a format for an itemized resource billing report that would be sent to users. Such a billing statement needs such entries as:

Activity description (literals)

Measurement component (e.g., CPU seconds)

Volume

Unit transfer price

Total charge

The schedules in tables 6-6 and 6-7 do not include all the elements and components to consider in costing a data processing computer operation. However, they represent the basics. In building equipment pools there are two things to consider: (1) equipment pools for charging users based on their direct equipment usage and (2) equipment pools as a subset of the DP center. An example of the former is printer terminals used by organizations other than DP. An example of the latter is the computer mainframe, which is part of the DP operations center.

Whenever rates are determined projections should also be made of the potential recoveries. In this example the rates were set to recover only 70 percent of the computer operation's costs. Therefore, 30 percent of its costs will be residuals in the center. The recovery schedule appears as table 6-8.

CAPACITY DETERMINATION

There are several capacity levels to be considered in planning acquisitions of additional DP equipment and also in developing transfer costs. The capacity hierarchy may begin with a measurement of average use and then work upward to practical capacity, reserve capacity, usable limit, and absolute limit. (See figure 6-5 for a graphic representation.) There may be times when a DP system is pressed to the limits during daily, weekly, or monthly peaks. DP management may look at the frequency of peak usage in formulating additional equipment acquisition plans. Cost analysis will look at it in terms of calculating relevant transfer rates.

Figure 6-5. Capacity Hierarchy

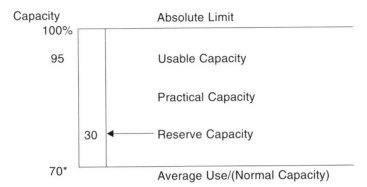

*The 70% figure is for illustration purposes only.
Average use percentages are derived after careful
study of a system's usage.

Capacity planning is a necessary function in costing DP. It involves determining the appropriate level of resources needed to meet the total processing requirements based on two assessments. One is the assessment of service level usages and commitments. The other is the determination of an optimal capacity utilization level. An optimum will be cost effective as well as processing efficient. Through this type of planning the cost analyst determines the appropriate level of usage on which to base costs. You will find utilization tracking particularly helpful in assessing the potential for cost recovery within a system.

Several of the steps of capacity planning provide useful data on a system's present utilization and prognosis for the future. Such techniques as linear projections (time series and regression techniques), simulations, and benchmarking are used in planning. Capacity planning involves at least the following steps.

1. Workload definitions—job characteristics, transaction counts, job applications identification, and scheduling.

2. Resource utilization measurements—via programs that measure and report the nature of activity in a given system.

   a. Data extraction/analysis—determination of a 24-hour work profile, identification of peak periods, and computation of peak-to-average ratios.

   b. Forecasting of future workloads—trend analysis, volume growth and modifications, and new requirements determination.

If there is an adequate capacity planning function in the DP center, then the information just listed should be readily available. The job of capacity determination for costing is much easier if such information is available.

Capacity determination for costing is a matter of policy. If the policy is one of stable transfer rates from month to month or from one year to the next, then an artificial capacity for costing purposes will be used. It is generally higher than the present average utilization level. That is, there will be little or no discounting of the rates for cost of unused capacity, which may translate into initially higher rates. This is based on the premise of not lowering rates because of excess capacity costs. It also is premised on having stable rates for a specific duration.

However, if the policy is to charge for all costs incurred based on average capacity utilization, then only the average capacity utilization for the present and near future needs to be determined. The rates are then set according to the costs at the average utilization level. This is a form of average item costing. (Divide the expected volume into the anticipated costs.) This form of costing obviously derives higher unit costs for lower volumes and lower unit costs for higher volumes. The rates become somewhat unpredictable if the costs are adjusted frequently, such as monthly.

A form of standard or prescriptive costing is to adjust the costs and hence the rates for such things as capacity utilization. This provides a benefit of more stable and predictable rates.

TRANSACTION VERSUS HOURS AS A BASE

In a DP center there are some applications that can be measured either on a per transaction basis or a per unit of time basis. In measuring on a time basis it is difficult sometimes to measure the underlying intensity of processing. That is, for two jobs one minute of time can mean a great deal of difference in the utilization of computer resources. This is something to be aware of in using time as a measurement for costing. Relative value factors may be useful in applying weights for costing purposes for such applications.

Many cost analysts prefer to develop costs based on per transaction elements whenever such a basis is logical and measurable. The bottom line is to use whatever method makes sense in preparing a costing structure. (Developing overall standard costs for a data center may be a difficult undertaking. At best, predetermined artificial rates for a stable charge are a consideration to strive for within this context. However, artificial rates will create a recovery that is different from the actual costs being incurred. A reconciliation exercise will then have to be undertaken in order to explain any differences.)

The following are computer time measurements to consider.

- Production time

- Data conversion time

- Setup time

- Testing time

- Software time

- Hardware time

- Down time

These measurements are denoted by such terms as *CPU seconds, elapsed time, days,* and *active hours.*

Some of the computer transactions to consider for volume purposes are

- Job steps executed

- Execute-command-program requests

- Print lines

- Key strokes

- Pages

- Tape mounts

- Entries

- Frames

Other charges may be fixed. However, they are usually based on some common denominator.

RESEARCH AND DEVELOPMENT: CAPITALIZING VERSUS EXPENSING

Research and development (R&D) expenditures can be substantial in an expanding and growing DP center. R&D embraces research; creation of new products, processes, systems, and equipment configurations; and major improvements of existing products processes and systems. The development phase would include costs associated with any testing, whether it be pilot or simulation.

In a service industry, for purposes of outside financial reporting, R&D is mostly charged to expense as incurred. However, for management reporting there are other possibilities. These include initial capitalization and subsequent amortization of the expenditures. The variable here would be length of time for amortization.

There are several ways of accounting for R&D in the management information reporting structure. The alternatives are as follows:

a. Treat R&D as a period expense and charge it off as incurred. Categorically account for it as expensed R&D.

b. Capitalize and amortize R&D in a manner similar to depreciation on capital expenditures such as buildings and equipment.

c. Ignore the categorization of R&D and expense as incurred.

Let's expand on these possibilities and look at the issues for each one. If you treat R&D as a period expense and charge it off as incurred, the following consequences occur. The per item costs charged with R&D tend to be higher in the years of R&D absorption than during the later part of the product life cycle. This approach is on the conservative side in terms of reflecting immediate recognition. Per item costs will tend to fluctuate yearly as a result of R&D period costs. This is especially true if R&D expenditures vary from month to month and from year to year. Associated product profitability will be adversely affected in the earlier years and eventually smooth out when product maturity is attained. If this method is used there should be an annual recosting to take into consideration any changes in item costs that have occurred as a result of R&D expenditures.

Capitalizing and amortizing R&D has the following consequences. It tends to smooth out the associated item costs, making them more stable, predictable, and comparable. Calculations for assessing the payback period become distorted under this method and need to be modified to the period cost method. The length of amortization is arbitrary; a judgment factor must be used in deciding the criteria for amortization. Because accounting for R&D can be time consuming and troublesome, a commitment of staff resources must be made in order to maintain the integrity of tracking amortization.

Should capitalizing and amortizing R&D be used, there needs to be a logical and consistent method for determining the length of amortization for each R&D activity. An accurate and well maintained tracking system must be in place and maintained. A reliable audit trail is essential.

If the cost analyst chooses to ignore categorization of R&D and expense it as it is incurred, the following disadvantages occur. Capturing of costs relevant to delivered products and hence full absorption becomes impossible. Cost accountability for R&D functions is lost. With the absence of a product or project burden of R&D, the

costs unaccounted for become G&A or unassigned. This tends to smooth ou
to the whole financial institution, making R&D costs unidentifiable. If this method is
used there should be a clearly stated policy that accountability and charging are nonas-
sociative and, therefore, R&D should be spread to multiple organizations as overhead
or reside in a management pool.

TABLE 6-9 Systems Maintenance, Enhancement, and Research and Development

Type of	Existing Systems		Future Systems
Systems	Maintenance	Enhancement	Research and Development
Computer operating systems	Maintain DASD-CPU interfaces[1]	Improve DASD-CPU interfaces	Design and develop state of the art data links
Application systems			
Product related	Maintain DDA system	Improve DDA system for faster processing	Design and develop a system for a new product line
Overhead related	Maintain organizational reporting system	Change organizational hierarchy and relationships	Design and develop a new reporting system

[1]DASD is direct access storage device; CPU is central processing unit.

Usually research and development is distinguished separately from maintenance
and enhancement activities. Table 6-9 describes the differences between maintenance,
enhancement, and R&D. Maintenance costs should be treated as period costs. That
is, they should be recognized, for management reporting purposes, in the period they
are incurred.

TRANSFER PRICING

Transfer pricing is an interesting subject to study, review, and participate in for decision making. Many factors affect transfer pricing. Decisions made regarding transfer
pricing affect internal profitability measurement on an institutionwide basis. Therefore much study and care should be undertaken in tackling this subject. One of the
ideal methods of costing for DP services is to develop cost pools, route the costs to
activities, and ultimately transfer the costs to the user base, including product pools.
Some DP centers simply transfer charges for the services they provide at actual cost.
Others transfer charges below cost. Others may transfer them at a price above cost.

The determining factor behind transfer pricing is management's philosophy and policy on this subject. DP center management generally has two major concerns: (1) effective resource utilization and allocation and (2) operating expense recovery. Given the institution's view on these two topics, a policy statement should be drafted as to pricing. The discussion that follows will explore some alternative policies and their impact on the DP center.

In data processing, as in other service activities, the objective should be to charge for services rendered as opposed to allocating costs that are not associated with a specific service provided.

Maximizing Cost Recovery

Cost recovery can be maximized by setting rates at actual cost. This is done by setting rates as a function of anticipated operating costs divided by anticipated usage. Other factors to consider are R&D costs and potential growth (historical plus trend growth). If the rates are significantly higher than rates in the marketplace, they will drive some users to the outside. However, a policy of prohibiting outside vendor use would preclude such occurrences.

Alteration of Demand Patterns

To alter DP usage patterns, encourage use of normally low utilization periods through favorable rates. For example, have discount rates for evening hours usage. Set rates such that a rate is disproportionately higher for use of one resource than another. The higher rate would be set as a disincentive from using a resource and thereby an encouragement to use an alternative resource. The rate would be set lower for the alternate resource. In other words, rates would be set to encourage use of a particular resource to the exclusion of other resources(s). This is often done when management wishes to discourage the use of an older and outdated computer and encourage the use of a lower cost and more efficient one. Setting rates at a certain percentage below market prices may or may not cause a "profit" or residual to occur in the providing organization's cost pool. Rates are sometimes based on historical costs and usage with no provision for trend growth or change.

There are two basic views regarding the operating expense base for transfer pricing. One view says to set rates based on actual or perhaps anticipated usage but to charge for the unused capacity of the resource. The other is based on charging only for those resources that are available to the users and excluding charges for unused capacity. Its usage may also be predicated on actual or planned usage. Charging for unused capacity transfers all of the costs to the users. Not charging for unused capacity leaves a residual of costs in the center. The residual resulting from the center's absorption of an underrecovery due to capacity costs remains in the center's management pool. It could be allocated out later if the transfer-out policy in the institution permits. The following is a list of the characteristics, advantages, and disadvantages of the two bases.

Actual/Anticipated with Full Capacity Charge

- Historical information is adjusted by a growth rate to arrive at an anticipated usage.

- Present actual usage may be affected by the current rates in effect. Demand patterns are influenced to a certain extent by the pricing structure.

- Growth rates in a rapidly changing environment are difficult to predict at times.

- Unused capacity costs can be high. Passing them on to the users could distort the value of the services being provided to them.

Available Capacity

- The unavailable and unused capacity is not charged to the users.

- The rates are somewhat prescriptive in nature.

- Generally some resource capacities are unknown and therefore cannot be calculated.

Allocation Pools for Transfer Rates

In developing primary rates the operating expenses are grouped into activity pools. These are categorized as direct expenses or direct allocations. There are often expenses that cannot be directly identified with a particular activity. They are to be allocated based on a logical and consistent methodology. The allocation methodology could be based on volume, time, weighted expenses, head count, or square footage occupied.

There are further allocations to consider above these primary rates. These would be indirect allocations such as supervisors' compensation and general center overhead items. All of this is important if a full recovery of expenses is a stated goal.

Pricing Issues

As in any decision regarding pricing there are several issues to consider. They may briefly be summarized as follows:

User understanding of the transfer rate schedule and the invoices

Determination of allocation bases for indirect expenses

Equipment configuration development

The treatment of fully depreciated assets

How to charge for new products

To assure user understanding, the transfer rate structure should be published and made known to all users. It should be easy to understand. Invoice billing should provide enough information so the users can easily discern and understand what their usage was and how the associated charges were arrived at. The easier the invoice billing process is to understand, the more acceptable it will be to the users.

In determination of allocation bases it is important to bring appropriate indirect expenses into the pricing structure if the intent is to fully charge out DP costs. This may provide a controversy within the user base, however, especially if the rates are inordinately high. Therefore, a policy decision must be made and reasons communicated in regard to the treatment of indirect expenses.

The configuring of equipment for pricing purposes requires the ability to track usage and invoice it. The pricing must be fair and motivate a desired use. Bringing in new equipment and pooling it with old equipment for pricing may provoke resistance from users. They may decline old equipment assignments and insist on newer equipment at the same price. Therefore, a pricing differentiation may be beneficial as a means of optimal utilization of equipment.

The treatment of fully depreciated assets is a pricing issue that needs to be resolved. The decision must be made whether to continue to charge for equipment once it becomes fully depreciated. The advantage of a continued charge is the buildup of a synthetic replacement pool. This is obviously a negative expense to the DP center and hence a "profit." It provides management with a beneficial measurement of the equipment beyond its useful life. It also alerts them to the possible need for the replacement of certain equipment. The disadvantage of charging for depreciated equipment is the potential for misunderstanding recovery effectiveness due to distortions caused by such negative expenses.

How to charge for new activities is another common pricing question in DP costing. With new activities there is no track record on which to base pricing decisions. Usually the best that can be done in this kind of situation is to develop a pricing structure and charges that are similar to an existing activity that has the same pattern and structure of occurrences.

Other Pricing Issues and Considerations

Chargeback systems (transfer charging) provides accountability. It matches the identification of resources with the user base. This accountability allows for a better allocation of DP resources. In effect there must be a willing provider and a willing user given the process of accountability measurement via a transfer charging mechanism.

Transfer charging allows for project accounting and control. The cost or price of resources used by a DP center on behalf of a certain project can be ascertained through a transfer charging mechanism.

The user base will force improvements in efficiency and effectiveness if they have to pay the price for the services provided them. The users become more practical in their demands for services when they have to pay for them. "Nice to have" requests are minimized through a chargeback system.

Any differences between the costs of providing services and the price paid for those services needs to be explained. This is part of the necessity of accountability to the users.

BUILDING A COST TRACKING SYSTEM

Much will be said in chapter 15 about cost tracking systems. The need for capturing costs in an efficient and organized manner is shown by the following schema.

Unit of measure (volume)	×	*Unit costs*	=	*Extensions*
Seconds		Relevant costs as derived on a per unit		DP cost
Transactions		basis		accountability
Lines				
Pages				

One measures the services provided to users by some unit of activity and then applies cost data. A data processing center is accountable for its costs. Combining units of activity (volume) with unit costs gives the total DP costs to be accounted for.

Measuring the cost of services provided establishes accountability in keeping the cost of providing services to an acceptable level. It also helps in keeping the use of these services to only those things that are necessary.

The following schema depicts the effects of combining unit volume measurement with unit pricing. The resultant recovery may be different from the DP cost accountability. That is, there could be an overrecovery or an underrecovery. This provides DP center management with feedback on how effective they will be in transferring their prices to the users.

Unit of measure (volume)	×	Unit prices		=	Extensions
Seconds Transactions Lines Pages		DP rates (unit pricing)			DP recovery

The DP center's transfer charge effectiveness (net recovery) is derived as follows:

Total DP costs (actuals incurred)	–	Total DP recovery (total transfer charges)	=	DP transfer charge effectiveness (net recovery)

This formula provides DP center management with feedback on how effective they are in transferring out their costs to the users.

Building a Cost Tracking System

In order to measure the impact of transfer pricing on the DP center there must be an adequate cost tracking system. The construction of such a system is a function of relying on state-of-the-art software and a well-planned and defined methodology. Given previous formulas it is easy to see why many DP centers charge out for their services at cost. They simply may not wish to consume time in explaining the differences between prices and costs.

The ideal cost tracking system in a DP center would have the following characteristics: It would be compatible with and accept information feeds from other systems. It would properly account for cost flows from activities to product pools. It would account for and/or reconcile the differences between stated costs and actual occurrences. It would specifically list any volume and spending variances. The dollar impact of each would be quantified. Overhead costs would be properly aligned and accounted for.

Identifying Startup Costs

When new projects and new systems are being considered or are in the development phase, accountability for them necessitates costing. Even before a new project is approved management may require pro forma financials. In other words management wants to know what something is going to cost before it happens. Pro forma analyses and ongoing tracking are parts of the ever increasing need for cost control in DP centers. It is a function of financial administration to account for DP activities. The costs should be broken down between hard dollar and soft dollar occurrences. From there it is a matter of identifying expenses as staff compensation and other operating expenses. In projects and startup operations there may be significant outside vendor costs to account for.

Expenditures for projects and startup operations should be accounted for as they affect profit and loss and cash flow. The cash flow basis is needed for calculating such things as a payback period and internal rate of return. (Refer to chapter 11 for specific instructions on accounting for these items.)

The Need for Multidimensional Cost Tracking

In a DP center, costs for R&D, projects, production, maintenance, improvements, and administration are incurred on behalf of organizations, products, and customers. The ideal tracking system would capture, and accurately account for, all costs with respect to all three. Many R&D and other projects are on behalf of product offerings that translate into an ultimate benefit for the customer base. Sometimes there is disagreement over who should pay for what. Some projects are beneficial to the entire institution and therefore become part of the corporate overhead structure. The assortment of functions in the DP center needs to be viewed according to use by organization, product, and customer during the expense planning cycle.

SPENDING VARIANCES AND VOLUME VARIANCES

For purposes of illustration, assume a unit cost for an activity was calculated to be $0.42 based on an anticipated monthly volume of 1,575,000 units. The anticipated cost then is $661,500 ($0.42 × 1,575,000). If the results for this activity for a given month came out as $889,500 in costs with a volume of 1,623,000 units, the two types of variances would be calculated as follows:

$$\$0.42 \times 1,575,000 \ = \ \$661,500 \quad \text{anticipated cost}$$
$$\$0.42 \times \quad\ 48,000 \ = \ \$\ 20,160 \quad \text{volume variance}$$
$$\underline{\hspace{2cm}} \quad (1,623,000 - 1,575,000)$$

Total cost
at standard $681,660

We next subtract the calculated total costs at standard from the actual costs for the month. The difference, which is $207,840, is assumed to be spending variances.

$889,550	Total cost for the month
− 681,660	Total cost at standard
$207,840	Assumed spending variance

The accounting for this is summarized as follows:

$661,500	Anticipated cost
20,160	Additional cost attributable to volume variances
207,840	Additional cost attributable to assumed spending variances
$889,500	Total actual cost for this activity for the month reported

The volume variance is an explanation of additional cost attributable to increases in volume. The spending variance is derived as a result of subtracting the anticipated cost and the volume variance cost from the total cost incurred.

There are variations to this methodology as presented. It becomes more complex as additional variable are brought into the situation. This kind of analysis is valuable in determining the reasons for overrecoveries or underrecoveries, increases or decreases in costs, and budget variances.

7

Allocation Concepts and Systems

Allocations are arbitrary, the result of someone's judgment and decision. Hence, the bases for deciding how much goes where must be developed. Good research lays the groundwork.

The allocation process that is developed must be understood by users to be accepted. The cost analyst should therefore arrange the data logically and clearly. The integrity and accuracy of the data is also very important.

Allocations are developed apart from the financial books of the institution and serve as substitutes for that data for management information purposes. As part of management information they are in the realm of internal financial accounting (reporting).

Allocations are for funding, revenue, and expenses and may be routed to organizations, products, and customers. Funding allocations are used in determining balances. This could either be funds provided or funds used by organizations, products, and customers. Either an interest credit or a charge for funds is given. Usually a main issue to be decided for funding allocations is the determination of interest rates.

Revenue allocations are generally used in order to give revenue credit to organizations and products. This type of allocation is most helpful in establishing some form of revenue sharing. Revenue sharing occurs when there are two or more organizations or products participating in the generation of the same revenue stream. Because of the often unclear and indirect nature of identification that takes place as the bases are established, this type of allocation is known as "shadow reporting."

Expense allocation are those requiring a considerable amount of time for equitable determination. They are given to a wider spectrum of allocation bases than are funding and revenue allocations. The candidates for expense allocations permeate the bank.

All allocations must be equitable, consistent, logical, and conceptually explainable. The core of any allocation system is its credibility.

These topics will be covered in more depth. The intent of this chapter is to provide ideas that will assist the reader in conceptually designing a new allocation system or improving an existing one.

FUNDING ALLOCATIONS

In most institutions there are organizations that have a surplus of funds and there are those with a need for funds. In the dynamics of operating a financial institution, the deposit takers are not always in a position to place all their funds externally. There may be a central function that pools these funds for placement. They find other organizations that have a need for funds so they can place the pooled funds either internally or externally. A credit for funds would then be given to the providing organizations. Those who receive intrainstitution funds from the providers may refer to their acquired balances as "pooled funds used." Those who provide the surplus funds may refer to their placing as "pooled funds placed." The provider certainly would like to receive an internal revenue credit (interest income) for placing the funds. In this context the providers would like their balances to be appropriately accounted for. Those who are recipients of the funds usually have no objection to paying an internal charge for the use of the funds. They may question the rate structure, however. Figure 7-1 illustrates internal fund allocation by showing how $100 in surplus funds of one organization is transferred on an internal pool basis to other organizations within a financial institution.

Organization A has $100 in surplus funds. Two other departments in the institution have shortfalls in funding. Organization B uses $25 of organization A's funds; organization C uses the remaining $75.

A credit (interest income) for funds is given to organization A. A charge (interest expense) is levied on organizations B and C for their use of internal pooled funds. A policy needs to be established on giving internal credit for funds placed and charging for funds used. One issue is whether the placing rate should be the same as the using rate. Also the criterion for establishing interest rate levels needs to be established.

The funds could be used for any length of time from overnight to several days. Most financial institutions have pooled funds available as a first echelon of use before going to the outside. Therefore, it is important to have in place a balance tracking mechanism and an appropriate charge and credit mechanism.

Figure 7-1. Internal Funds Allocation

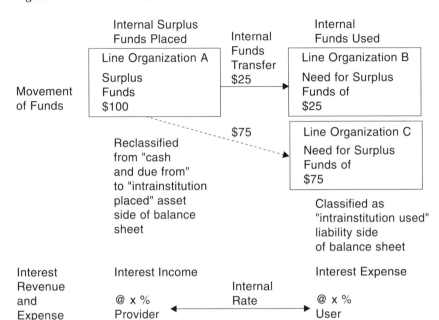

Allocation of funds and the consequent charge and credit for funds is a major issue. It is the essence of internal funds transfer pricing.

Risk is not usually an issue for funds placed internally. Some may argue it is. In the ultimate placement of funds to products and customers, the aim is to be equitable in transferring the cost of funds from one organization to another and to compensate the providing organization adequately. Funds transfer pricing is often clearer and more straightforward than is transfer pricing for noninterest costs.

A policy must be determined on the methodology for developing funds transfer pricing. The accounting for balances and the cost of funds must be simple. The real or actual cost of funds may be elusive. Some organizations circumvent this issue by using outside market rates as benchmarks.

There obviously is going to be an artificial difference between some outside market rate and the real average cost of funds to the institution. This means there will be distortions in the internal profitability reporting. The cost of funds will be somewhat arbitrary. How is the difference to be accounted for? Maybe it need only be accounted for in a management information pool. The issue is how to account for the differences between actual and market pricing. The pricing at some market rate may be an incentive for the using organizations (departments) to be more judicious in their use of funds.

This whole issue can be compounded further by having provider and user contract spreads established with asset/liability management. The issue of overall market rates and yields could be part of asset/liability management's funds management accountability. The idea is to place surplus funds optimally, to the benefit of the institution as a whole. Whatever the method, whether it be simple or complex, it must embrace this concept of looking at the institution as an integral organization.

A further complication is matched funding. This is where balance sheet sources and uses are closely matched in terms of maturity (duration), funds cost, and market or customer risk. Its complexity increases with the size of an institution. Smaller financial institutions are at a distinct advantage in their ability to administer matched funding.

Some financial institutions, especially those with branches, have a centralized funds management function. This function manages the book entry tracking of placings and takings of internal funds. It also gives appropriate credits and charges for funds as provided and used, respectively. On a branch profitability measurement basis some branches may be at a distinct advantage over other branches. Some branches may have a relatively low-cost deposit base while others may have a higher cost deposit base that is beyond their control. On the basis of profit contribution measurement this may seem inequitable. It is such issues that need to be discussed and resolved prior to the design and implementation of a system for measuring branch profitability by using credits and charges for funds as a line item.

Table 7-1 is a sample balance sheet of a funds providing organization. We see in the table an overall cost of funds of 4.3333 percent. The income yield is an overall 12.0252 percent including the internal placement of funds amounting to $100 at 11 percent. If the providing organization were to charge for its surplus funds at average cost then the $100 would be placed internally at 4.3333 percent. The managers of the providing organization may take exception to this, however, arguing they are missing out on opportunity income by not placing the funds on the outside market. This provides a good reason for pricing internal funds placements at some designated market parity rate.

One might also look at the funds sources of the providing organization. They have $240 in borrowed money and are paying 11 percent. This is outside funding. It is also the highest rate they are paying for funds. Hence an additional factor in pricing internal funds at something higher than the average cost of funds rate.

We have covered the placement of surplus funds, but the allocation of funds includes such sources as deposits and capital. It also includes the allocation of assets, such as loan balances and other funds-placing activities. These are generally organizational issues.

TABLE 7-1 Balance Sheet of a Funds-Providing Organization

Assets		Yield %	Liabilities and Capital		
Cash and due from	$50		Demand Deposits	$ 700	
loans	$1,000	15%	Interest bearing demand deposits	300	7.5%
Investments	60	10	Time deposits	150	6.0
Placements	180	9	Borrowed money	240	11.0
Other Assets	200	4	Capital & Equity	200	5.5
Intrainstitution Funds placed	100	11			
Total	$1,590		Total	$1,590	

Assets: Weighted Average Calculations

Balance	Percentage of Total		Yield (%)		Weighted Yield
$ 50	3.1447	×	0	=	0
1,000	62.8931	×	15	=	9.4340
60	3.7736	×	10	=	0.3774
180	11.3207	×	9	=	1.0189
200	12.5786	×	4	=	0.5031
100	6.2893	×	11	=	0.6918
$1,590	100.0000				12.0252

Liabilities and Capital: Weighted Average Calculations

Balance	Percentage of Total		Cost of Funds (%)	Weighted Yield of Funds (%)
$ 700	44.0252	×		
300	18.8679	×	7.5	1.4151
150	9.4340	×	6.0	0.5660
240	15.0943	×	11.0	1.6604
200	12.5786	×	5.5	0.6918
$1,590	100.0000			4.3333%

To be taken into consideration in developing a funds transfer mechanism are the capability and availability of a system for identifying and tracking surplus funds. The financial institution's management must establish a policy on funds pricing. The financial institution's overall objective for having a fund's transfer mechanism must be clearly stated and understandable.

Some situations require the allocation of shared revenue and balances between departments. Generally this occurs in the presence of shared revenue generation between organizations and products or in the presence of overlapping accountabilities and servicing.

It can be difficult at times to distinguish the exact breakout of revenue credit between multiple entities. This is true whether it be for balance sheet products or fee-based products.

REVENUE ALLOCATIONS

Revenue allocations can be the result of two or more departments sharing revenue for their part in performing a service. They also can be the result of organizational, product line, or customer-generated revenue that needs to be sorted out and allocated based on categories. An example of revenue sharing allocations would occur when one organization takes deposits and books loans on behalf of another organization in the institution. When this happens, that service-providing organization within the institution may ask for its share of the revenue. This is a typical request when bottom line organizational accountability is measured and rewards for performance are dispensed based on a management reporting system that tracks revenue. The other kind of allocation is more basic. Some financial institutions simply do not categorize their revenue by organization, product, or customer. They must resort to some form of allocation in order to approximate these breakouts.

Revenue allocations may be necessary in the absence of a subsidiary general ledger for a specific profit center (revenue-producing department) or when there is a need for revenue sharing. Considerations when establishing revenue sharing and general revenue allocations are as follows:

- What is the present availability of revenue measurement? Is it by line (revenue-producing) organization?

- If it is by line organization, can it be reconciled to the consolidated general ledger?

- If it is not, what are the present means for estimating the revenue? Is there sufficient detail by product or by customer to allow for a general allocation to each income-generating organization?

If there is no organizational reporting, you then need to work up a rudimentary method as a first cut at the data. This can be done by reviewing revenue by product and customer profiles (if available). Let's take an example of the allocation of revenues identified by product and customer.

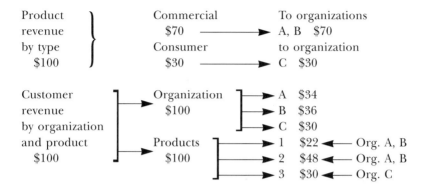

This list represents the process of taking different cuts at the same data. From the information available we see that $100 in revenue could be split between commercial and consumer bases, by organization and by the type of product being sold. At this juncture all we know is that two organizations (A and B) share $70 of commercial revenue income since they are the sum total of commercial-income-generating organizations.

TABLE 7-2 Allocation of Revenue by Product and Customer

	Organization A	*Organization B*	*Organization C*
Revenue by customer	$34	$36	$30
Revenue by business type			
Commercial	34	36	
Consumer			30
Revenue by product type			
1	$10.7	$11.3	0
2	23.3	24.7	
3	0	0	30

(1) $34 + 36 = $70
    $34 ÷ 70 = .4857
    .4857 × $22 = $10.7

    $36 ÷ $70 = .5143
    .5143 × $22 = $11.3

(2) .4857 × $48 = $23.3
    .5143 × $48 = $24.7

In this example organization C is the only consumer-revenue-generating organization. A close study of customer profiles tells us that organization A's customers generated $34 to the institution, organization B's $36, and organization C's $30.

We also see that products 1, 2, and 3 account for $22, $48, and $30 of the same revenue. Organizations A and B share the $22 and $48 revenue; organization C has $30 revenue from product 3.

This provides us with the necessary information to complete the allocation process. The allocation thus appears as shown in table 7-2.

In table 7-2 we can see a pattern of revenue approximations for products 1 and 2. The customer data and the organizational data provided a basis for these allocations. This is done by working with available data and grouping the information into common patterns.

EXPENSE ALLOCATIONS

The issue of expense allocations is probably the most frequently dealt with issue in cost analysis. Basically there are cost centers and income centers that incur expenses on behalf of organizations, products, and ultimately customers. It is the cost analyst's job to allocate these expenses equitably for the purpose of measuring profitability. Figure 7-2 illustrates how this process works in a financial institution.

The net expenses are initially captured at either the cost center level or the income center level. They are analyzed and accounted for on some allocation basis. The concept of allocations is to account for expenses that remain in centers after the transfers out and transfers in have occurred—that is, the net expenses. In many institutions there are organizations that do not transfer their expenses. Instead they allocate them out to the triad of organizations, products, and customers.

The most interesting allocations are those of organization to organization. This is especially true if the recipient organization has leverage (control) over whether to accept the allocation and services or to reject them. Financial institutions that use interorganization allocation along with much senior management dialogue have been able to isolate discretionary and unnecessary functions. Hence cost control is a beneficial byproduct of this type of allocation.

Cost allocation systems are built when there is a purpose for a further accounting of expenses. Sometimes the intent may be to account for residuals according to the triad of organizations, products, and customers. On a more comprehensive level a cost allocation system may be the central core for cost analysis. When this occurs the complexities of item costing by product, including capturing overhead, usually occur with the ultimate reporting of costs by organization.

Figure 7-2. Expense Allocation in Financial Institutions

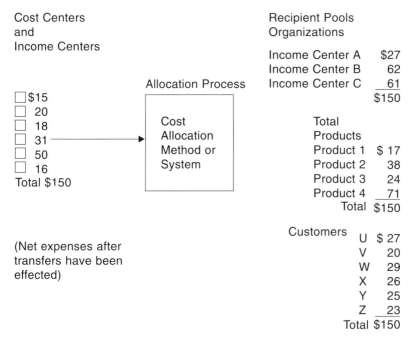

Cost Centers
and
Income Centers

Allocation Process

☐$15
☐ 20
☐ 18
☐ 31 ——————→
☐ 50
☐ 16
Total $150

Cost
Allocation
Method or
System

(Net expenses after
transfers have been
effected)

Recipient Pools
Organizations

Income Center A	$27
Income Center B	62
Income Center C	61
	$150

Total Products	
Product 1	$ 17
Product 2	38
Product 3	24
Product 4	71
Total	$150

Customers

U	$ 27
V	20
W	29
X	26
Y	25
Z	23
Total	$150

DETERMINATION OF BASES OR CONCEPTS

The basis of concept to use in allocating expenses is a function of whatever common measurement of usage makes sense. Recipients must be able to understand the allocations.

Some of the items that can be used in formulating a basis for allocation are these:

- Number of accounts
- Balances
- Number of staff
- Number of items processed
- Time logged or spent
- Income

- Direct expense

- Measured resource utilization

- Compensation

- Interest expense

- Space occupied

A specific concept or basis should be selected as one that best fits or explains the apportionment of the expenses being allocated. Ideally, it should be a function of what is being allocated. For example, fringe benefits are a function of having a paid staff. Allocating benefits using staff count is not a best fit though. A closer fit would be to use salary as a determinant for benefit allocations. It is generally closer to how benefits are incurred. One may argue, however, that medical benefits are generally a function of age. The concept could go further into the minutia of what is being allocated. Always try to use a concept or base that is representative but at the same time not costly to determine and administer.

The concepts used in allocating costs fall into the following categories:

- Percentage of time spent

- Weighted average

- Percentage of total

- Unit/volume

- Direct identification

Building an Equitable, Consistent, and Acceptable System

There are essentially two methods for allocation of expenses: sequential and simultaneous closeout.

Under the sequential method the expenses are closed out from one center to another, or from one echelon to another. No other reallocation within the structure occurs at the time of closeout. The process appears as shown in figure 7-3.

Once a cost center allocates its expenses there is no reallocation back to it. For example, once cost center A has allocated its expenses, it is closed out. There can be no allocations to cost center A after this has occurred. After it allocates its expenses it is closed out from further participation in the process.

The simultaneous process on the other hand involves multiple allocations between centers concurrently. Under this method it is possible for a center to receive an allocation from a center that is also a recipient of its allocation. Therefore we have

Figure 7-3. Sequential Method of Closeout

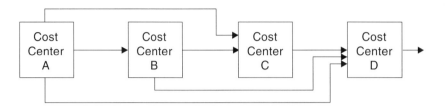

different allocations occurring at the same time. For example, cost center A could be allocating to cost center B while cost center B is allocating to cost center A. This method can be complex both in formula development and in execution. There are algebraic equations that can accommodate this process. It is known as the simultaneous method of close out. Figure 7-4 is a diagram of how this method operates. For an example of how this method works, refer to the appendix at the end of this chapter.

In building an allocation system it is important to have a reconciling feature. The numbers need to tie or reconcile to the general ledger.

It is also important to have control reports. They should be on a "to-from" and a "from-to" basis. It is essential that the allocator and the recipient have access to the same data. An example of this is table 7-3. Table 7-4 shows what each of the three organizations receives as a statement.

Figure 7-4. Simultaneous Method of Closeout

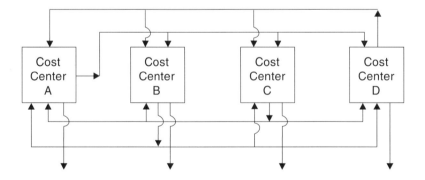

TABLE 7-3 Report 1: Cost
Center A, Total Expenses,
$325,000

Allocations to	Percentage	Amount
Organization X	26	$ 84,500
Organization Y	34	110,500
Organization Z	40	130,000
Total	100	$325,000

Obviously report 2 is discreet and simple. The example makes the point that allocations should be made known to the recipient in such a manner as to answer the basic questions of where did the allocation come from.

One may find at least one additional report to be helpful. It is a summary total report showing the total matrix of allocations. It would appear as shown in table 7-5.

TABLE 7-4 Sample Statements of
Allocations (Report 2)

Report 2
Organization X
Total $84,500

Allocations from (Org.)	Percentage of Expenses	Amount
Cost center A	26%	$ 84,500

Report 2
Organization Y
Total $110,500

Allocations from (Org.)	Percentage of Expenses	Amount
Cost center A	34%	$110,500

Report 2
Organization Z
Total $130,000

Allocations from (Org.)	Percentage of Expenses	Amount
Cost center A	40%	$130,000

**TABLE 7-5 Report 3: Allocations to
                Recipient Organizations**

Allocations Received (from Org.)	To Org.A	...	To Org.Z	Grand Total
Org.A	$		$	
.				
.				
.				
Org.Z				
Total				

In this kind of arrangement the question of an organization's allocations to itself needs to be answered. If it is a support or overhead organization there probably should be no self-allocations. If it is an income center, however, then it will probably allocate a substantial portion of its expense back to itself.

In setting up an allocation system a basic question must be answered: What is the purpose of the allocations? That is to say, What is the system's intended use? The answer is important because these systems can become complex. There also is a variety of dimensions on how they can be configured. Examples are as follows:

- Cost centers to income centers only

- Cost centers to cost and income centers

- Cost centers to cost centers and then to income centers

- Cost and income centers to income centers

The list could go on. Again it is the intended purpose that should determine who is to allocate to whom.

Allocations can be of a direct or an indirect nature. Direct allocations are those of a known support base. The allocator is in direct support to its recipient organizations. Indirect allocations may be based on a more broadly defined base of support. That is, some linkages exist between the allocator and the recipient organization, but they are not clearly defined.

For allocation purposes organizations may be defined as being in one of the following categories:

- Staff organization (direct support)

- Staff organization (indirect support)

TABLE 7-6 Expense Allocation Process

Allocating Organization to	Recipient Organization	Allocations Review with Authority to Accept or Reject	Arbiter
Staff	Staff	Receiving organization	Department heads of each staff organization
Staff	Line	Receiving income center	Staff department head and income center head
Staff	General overhead	Chief financial officer (CFO) or chief executive officer (CEO)	CFO or CEO
Line	Line	Receiving income center	CFO or CEO

- Staff organization (general overhead)

- Income organization (line)

In such an arrangement as listed, the cost analyst would have to monitor closely those organizations that are allocating to general overhead. In essence they are claiming institutional status. Where this type of allocation process exists, procedures for review should be established. Table 7-6 illustrates such allocation.

The table clearly defines whose accountability it is to review, accept or reject, and to arbitrate the allocations. The cost analyst's job in this process is to convey the information, manage the system, and be available for requested changes. This will keep the analyst busy enough. The matrix in table 7-6 holds a particular department accountable in terms of justifying its expenses to other departments.

The Advantages and Disadvantages of Matrix Monitoring of Expenses

In most financial institutions, organizational expenses are reviewed on a vertical basis, either from the bottom up, in the organization hierarchy, or the top down. Sometimes certain benchmarks and guidelines are established on a top-down basis but are reviewed from bottom to top. The allocation system just described allows horizontal review of expenses, which means that an organization not only has to justify its expenses to its management, but it must justify its expenses to those organizations it claims to support. The review process is diagrammed in Figure 7-5.

Figure 7-5. Allocation Review Process

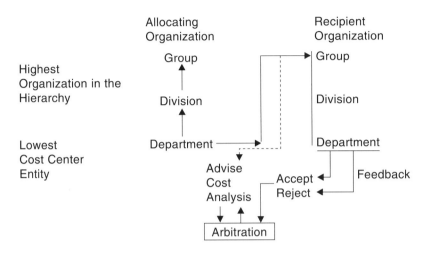

As you can see from the diagram, any recipient allocations below the group level have the effect of making the system more complex. An allocation system that is quite workable would be one that allocates from the lowest cost center level (department) to the highest organizational level (group) on the recipient side. An example of this would be a staff department allocating its expenses to a line group.

The disadvantages of matrix allocation and its consequent monitoring have to do with the review process. It is time consuming and somewhat disruptive. However, it does force dialogue, justification, and understanding of what is happening in each organization.

GENERAL AND ADMINISTRATIVE EXPENSE RATES (OVERHEAD)

An interesting byproduct of a well-designed allocation system is a rate structure for costing overhead. If the allocation system is not part of a cost transfer mechanism, it can be used for developing general and administrative (G&A) expense rates. Consider, for example, a system with the following design specifications:

1. Allocations are based on net expenses—that is, those remaining after transfers in and transfers out have been effected.

2. The line groups (income centers) are the ultimate recipients.

3. There is a category for allocations to G&A.

The results of the process are shown in table 7-7. The rate derived in the table is for use as a local G&A rate to be applied to cost studies performed for one of the specific line groups.

The next rate to develop is the institution's G&A rate. It would be an additional layer of overhead for all costings performed in the institution. Costings for the line groups would have two G&A type rates—the line group's rate and the institution's rate. The institution's rate would be developed as shown in table 7-8.

The application of the G&A rates for line organization X would be as in table 7-9.

In setting up the institution's G&A base there were several choices to be made. The choice made for this example was to assume that all G&A would be absorbed by the line groups. This is why the $8,000 allocated to general overhead was not included as part of the institution's expense base. The total institution expenses in this example are $72,700 ($64,700 + $8,000 = $72,700).

The G&A expense base comprised the following: $1,000 + $1,200 + $1,500 + $22,000 + 17,500 + $21,500 = $64,700. Therefore, it included the line groups' G&A plus their net expenses. Again it did not include the $8,000 general overhead allocation.

TABLE 7-7 Derivation of a Local G&A Rate for a Line Group

Allocating Organizations   *Recipient*

From staff and line   To line group

Formula:
    Allocations received ÷ Net expenses for line organization
= Line group's G&A rate.

Example:

Line Groups	Org. X	Org. Y	Org. Z	Total
1. Allocations received	$ 1,000	$ 1,200	$ 1,500	$ 3,700
2. Net expenses	22,000	17,500	21,500	61,000
Total	$23,000	$18,700	$23,000	$64,700
Derived Rate (line 1 ÷ line 2)	.04545 (4.545%)	.06857 (6.857%)	.06977 (6.977%)	

TABLE 7-8 Derivation of an Institution's G&A Rate

Allocating
Organizations   *Recipient*

From staff   To general overhead
(There would be no
allocations from
the line groups to
G&A here as their only
option is line to line
within this construct)

      Formula:
        Allocations received ÷ Net expenses
      for the Institution = Institution's G&A rate.

Example:

1. Allocations to general overhead	$ 8,000	(Accept the number as a given.)
2. Total line group expenses (This includes allocations they received from staff and other line groups.)	64,700	
Derived rate (line 1 ÷ line 2)	.1236 (12.36%)	

To carry this further there are several alternatives to consider. Before weighing the choices, let us look at the expense components listed in table 7-10. The combinations could continue beyond those shown in the table. The main idea to glean from this process is consistency and proper theoretical recoupment of allocated expenses. A priority must be to maintain the integrity of the data through proper allocations.

TABLE 7-9 Application of G&A Rates to a
Line Organization

Product 1

Unit cost	$1.2750	
Plus: Org. × G&A at 4.545%	0.0579	(.04545 × $1.275)
Subtotal	$1.3329	
Plus: Institution × G&A at 12.36%	0.1647	(.1236 × $1.3329)
Total unit cost	$1.4976	

TABLE 7-10 Expense Components

Component A	Component B	Component C	Total Institution Expenses
$3,700	$8,000	$61,000	$72,700
G&A allocations to the line organizations from staff and other line groups— called "line group G&A."	G&A allocations (to general overhead) from staff organizations only—called "Institution G&A." These are allocations to the whole institution.	Line organizations' net expenses before allocations	

Choices:	Assumptions:
A ÷ C =	Line group G&A rate. The assumption here is that the total $3,700 in allocations from other organizations is a function of the line organization's expenses.
(A + B) ÷ C =	A Hybrid G&A rate. Here the total $11,700 ($3,700 + $8,000) in allocation is a function of the line organization's expenses.
B ÷ C =	Institution G&A rate. Here the $8,000 allocation (total institution general overhead) is a function of the line organizations' expenses. The rate would not be multiplied against the line group G&A buildup. It would only be additive to it. In the example the rate would have been $8,000 ÷ $61,000 = 0.1311 or 13.11%. It would have been multiplied against the unit cost of $1.2750 rather than the subtotal of $1.3329.
B ÷ (A + C) =	Institution G&A rate. Here the $8,000 allocation is considered a function of the line organizations' allocations plus their net expenses. This is the choice used in the example.
B ÷ (A + B + C) =	Institution G&A rate. In this method the $8,000 allocation would be considered a function of all activity including itself. This would result in a lower institution G&A rate. However, some costings of activity within the $8,000 may necessitate adjustments to the $8,000 allocation. Also the use of the rate on the $8,000 portion of the base itself would require adjustments.

ALLOCATION ISSUES

Allocations establish accountability within and across organizational lines. Despite this some people take exception to the time consuming nature of any allocation process.

To be sure, allocations are somewhat arbitrary and subjective. The accuracy can range from guesswork to the use of empirical data, such as volume counts, along with subjective judgments. What is important is to focus on the intended use of the data and to design accordingly.

An allocation system should be a reflection of senior management's philosophy. It should also be flexible enough to accept change. Change comes from growth, refinement, and philosophical shifts. The idea is to be prepared for change.

Allocation bases should be developed with the thought of being fair, equitable, and relevant. Common bases or denominators are generally used in determining allocations. To this end such things as volume counts, space occupied, percentage of total expense, and staff counts are to be a fair representation of expenses being allocated. Such things as balances generated and time spent are to be used in determining revenue allocations. There must be an overall consensus and understanding of how the allocations are being calculated and the reasoning behind them before they can be accepted as valid indicators of expense and revenue apportionment.

CHAPTER 7 APPENDIX

- Simultaneous method of closeout

The simultaneous process is usually complex and requires using simultaneous equations. The process would be as follows:

Before Allocations

Cost center 1	Cost center 2	Cost center 3
$5 expenses	$7 expenses	$4 expenses

Recipient Centers

Profit center A	Profit center B
$30	$20

Step 1 - Cost Center to Cost Center
Allocation Process

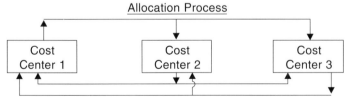

Step 2 - Cost Center to Profit Centers

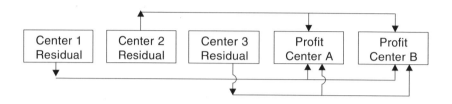

   Given that allocations go in two directions for cost centers the simultaneous method is more complex. Below are the allocation assumptions for each center.

Center 1

Allocates	40% of its expense to center 2
	20% of its expense to center 3
Receives	10% of center 2's expenses

Center 2

Allocates	10% of its expenses to center 1
	29% of its expenses to center 3

Center 3

Receives	20% of center 1's expenses
	29% of center 2's expenses

The allocation matrix setup for reciprocal allocations appears as follows:

Center 1	$5	+	.10	(center 2)
Center 2	$7	+	.40	(center 1)
Center 3	$4	+	.20	(center 1) + .29 (center 2)

These simultaneous equations can be solved algebraically:

$C1 = \$5 + .10\ C2$

$C2 = \$7 + .40\ C1$

$C3 + \$4 + .20\ C1 + .29\ C2$

Begin by substituting C1 into the C2 equation.

$C2 = 7 + .40\ (5 + .10\ C2)$

$C2 = 7 + 2 + .04\ C2$

$.96C2 = 9$

$C2 = 9.375$

Next substitute the value of C2 into the C1 equation.

C1 = 5 + .10   (9.375)

C1 = 5 + .9375

C1 = 5.9375

Next solve the C3 equation by plugging in these values of C1 and C2.

C3 = 4 + .20   (5.9375) + .29   (9.375)

C3 = 4 + 1.1875 + 2.71875

C3 = 7.90625

Allocate the costs as follows:

	Cost Center 1	Cost Center 2	Cost Center 3	Profit Center A	Profit Center B
Costs prior to allocation	$5	$7	$4	$30	$20
Allocation of center 1	(5.9375)	2.375[1]	1.1875	1.1875[2]	1.1875[2]
Allocation of center 2	0.9375[3]	(9.375)	2.71875	3.375[4]	2.34375[4]
Allocation of center 3			(7.90625)	4.4375[5]	3.46875[5]
Total	-0-	-0-	-0-	$39	$27

Notes: [1] 40% of center 1
         .4 × 5.9375 = 2.375
   [2] Assume 20% each of C1 to CA and CB
   [3] .1 × 9.375 = 0.9375
   [4] Assume 36% to CA and 25% to CB
   [5] Assume 56.12649% to CA and 43.87351 to CB

Allocation Process Complete

Profit center A	Profit center B
$39*	$27*

Note: *Depending on the algorithms the numbers between a sequential and a simultaneous process will no doubt be different. Also in practical usage, the simultaneous process may occur in several cycles as a means of further refinement and allocation of residual expenses.

The sequential method is best used when senior management wants an easy-to-explain process with an easy-to-follow audit trail. It is also best used when resources are limited and a high degree of sophistication is unnecessary. The simultaneous process is best used for a computer system that integrates and calculates a lot of data. Its drawback is the difficulty most people have in explaining or understanding how it works.

Organizational Profitability Reporting

Organizational reporting includes revenue, expense, and activity reporting on behalf of specific departments, divisions, or groups. If you were to ask the management of an organization to list their information needs, you would probably receive enough answers to compile a vast list. Certainly the needs could be ranked, with priorities ranging from "critical" to "nice to have." Obviously there are degrees of necessity when it comes to information. What is necessary is that the information reported be truly essential to management for making decisions. Unnecessary, nonessential information usually does not impel action. The following is a list of data that might be requested by institution management desiring organizational reports.

Revenue
  Interest income
  Fee income
  Internal transfer income

Expenses
  Compensation expense
  Other operating expense
  Cost of funds
  Internal transfer charges

Balances
   Funds provided
   Funds used
   Interest rate(s)/spreads

We sometimes see expenses divided between controllable and noncontrollable. The division may be based on a concept that holds the organization's managers accountable only for those things that they can control. Sometimes an organization is held accountable for all expenses it incurs, whether controllable or not.

Whatever the concept and methodology, organizational reporting must be relevant to the current management philosophy of the financial institution in order to be effective.

ORGANIZATIONAL REPORTING CONCEPTS

Organizations can be viewed as being in one of the following categories:

- Profit center

- Income center

- Cost center

If an organization is viewed as a *profit center* there will be a tendency toward reporting more information than if it were an income or cost center. A definition of what its bottom line includes must be made. Some organizations may wish to report data only down to the "contribution to overhead and profit" line. Others may have reporting on an artificial "after tax" basis. Others may make a distinction between controllable and noncontrollable expenses. Whatever the level, management is usually interested in measuring the institution's overall profitability performance by organization. In order to achieve this measurement objective, the reporting procedure must take into consideration an abundance of data, some of which is arbitrary.

In looking at an organization as an *income center* the idea is to measure the center more on its production rather than its profitability. This method occurs in those financial institutions that view some lower echelon line organizations as being production centers. Sometimes branches are viewed as such. If this is the case they are consolidated and eventually reported as a group, on a profit center basis. For example, some financial institutions with a branching network view each branch as an income center; but they view a region or geographic cluster of branches as a profit center. In this view the items leading to the bottom line for a branch are fewer than if each branch were reported as a profit center. The advantage of measuring organizations on an income center basis is the mitigation of questions over arbitrary allocations and transfers that may exist.

The view of reporting an organization as a *cost center* is less complex than are the profit center and income center methods. The emphasis is usually on measurement and containment of expenses. There may be a need to evaluate staffing levels and requirements, as well, and relevant activity counts may also be required.

In setting up an organizational reporting system, one must state the objectives of reporting. Some common objectives are more accurate planning, accountability of performance through measurement, cost control, and accommodation of expense transfers.

Once the need has been established for organizational reporting and the objectives have been stated, a strategy should be developed. The strategy outlines the overall approach on getting the job done. Parameters and specifications are worked out before development commences. To be determined in advance are such details as level of reporting, desired accuracy, acceptable expenditures, desired information, management philosophy, report formats and frequency, and procedures for reporting.

The ideal organizational report is one that compares performance to a criterion such as a budget, is easy to read and understand, and is consistent and timely.

DETERMINING PRODUCTS WITHIN AN ORGANIZATION

The cost analyst or managers setting up a reporting system for either a profit center or an income center must decide whether or not individual products will be reported. A complex report would show individual product profitability within a given organization. A report of less consequence would list only the revenues by product. At a simpler level yet, revenue would be pooled for any fee-based services under the heading of miscellaneous income. However, this simple method of reporting does not usually serve the needs of decision makers, because it does not include individual product revenue. Again, how this is to be done is a function of senior management's philosophy. In some financial institutions, organizational reporting by product is necessary to meeting management's objectives. In others it is nonessential, since the focus of attention is elsewhere. (More will be said on this issue later in this chapter when reporting formats are discussed.)

REPORTING FORMATS AND CONCEPTS

In conceptualizing reporting formats let's start with a group of summary level reports. We will build on this as we go to more detailed reports. The process begins with a summary of the highest echelon: the institution itself.

TABLE 8-1 Summary Financial Institution Report

X, Y, Z Financial Institution
Consolidated Financial Review[1]
($ millions)

Results	Plan	Actual	Percentage Variance
Revenue	$12.0	$13.5	12.5%
Net profit before tax	2.0	2.2	10.0%
Net profit after tax	1.2	1.4	16.7%
Average assets	300	325	—
Equity	26.0	26.0	—
Return on assets	1.33% / .80%	1.35% / .86%	—
(ROA) annualized[2] (before tax/after tax)			
Return on equity			
(ROE) annualized[3]	9.23%	10.77%	16.7%

[1] This example uses 6 months year-to date (ytd) actuals.
[2] The ROA formula for successive months are as follows:

$$\frac{\text{Net profit } \textit{before} \text{ tax (ytd)} \div (\text{months ytd}) \times (12)}{\text{Average assets (ytd average)}} = \frac{\$2.0\text{mm} \div 6 \times 12}{\$300\text{mm}} = 1.33\%$$

$$\frac{\text{Net profit } \textit{after} \text{ tax (ytd)} \div (\text{months ytd}) \times (12)}{\text{Average assets (ytd average)}} = \frac{\$1.2\text{mm} \div 6 \times 12}{\$300\text{mm}} = .8\%$$

[3] The formula for ROE for successive months is as follows:

$$\frac{\text{Net profit } \textit{after} \text{ tax (ytd)} \div (\text{months ytd}) \times (12)}{\text{Average stockholders' equity (ytd average)}} = \frac{\$1.2\text{mm} \div 6 \times 12}{\$26.0\text{mm}} = 9.23\%$$

A report such as table 8-1 gives senior management the results but little else. It is essentially a snapshot of what has occurred the previous month, quarter, six months, or year. This example is a six-month report.

Its advantage is that it provides the results in a simple and easy to understand format. The disadvantage is that further explanation of what has occurred is still needed. The purpose of such a report is to provide management with a flash report on the financial results of the institution.

A variation of this report follows as table 8-2. It provides additional data. It is more analytical and provides for trending projections. It lists the current month's results, last month's results, the current month's variation from plan, the year-to-date actuals, the year-to-date variance from plan, the year-to-date actuals as annualized to a full year, and the full year plan.

TABLE 8-2 Detailed Institution Report

X, Y, Z Institution
Consolidated Financial Results
for the Month of June ($ millions)

Category	Curr Month	Prev Month	Curr Month Var from Plan Fav/(Unfav)[1]	YTD Actual	YTD Var from plan Fav/(UnFav)	YTD Actuals Annualized to Full Year[2]	Full Year Plan
Revenue	2.2	1.8	0.4	13.5	1.5	27.0	24.0
Expense	1.8	1.5	0.3	11.3	(1.3)	22.6	20.0
Net profit before tax	0.4	0.3	0.1	2.2	0.2	4.4	4.0
Net profit after tax	0.2	0.1	0.0	1.4	0.2	2.8	2.4
Return on assets after tax.	.86%	.89%	.06%	.86%	.06%	.86%	.80%
Return on equity after tax	10.77%	11.08%	0.31%	10.77%	0.31%	10.77%	9.23%
Staff FTE	175.0	170.0	(5.0)	168.0	2.0	168.0	170.0

[1]Absolute amounts.
[2]Should exclude the trending of one time only and other exceptional items.
[3]Full time equivalent

The focus of this report is on the potential full year results given what has happened year-to-date. It is a way of flagging potential problems before they happen.

The next level of reports would represent the major line and staff organizations within the institution. Use of reports at this level assumes there is an adequate way of gathering data for responsibility reporting within the institution. Let's begin with a line organization. Its summary report could be like table 8-3. This report summarizes the results of eight detailed reports. It shows trend reporting of month-by-month actuals, a year-to-date total, a comparison of current month results to plan, and a comparison of year-to-date results to plan.

This report is useful as a high-level summary of results for an income-producing organization. As management reviews the results on this report they can find the detailed information according to the special categorical report as listed.

Next we have a series of detailed reports that serve as backup to the summary report. These detailed reports are presented here in tables 8-4 through 8-10.

TABLE 8-3 Line Organization A, Summary Report ($ thousands)

Report No.	Category	Jan	Feb	... Nov	Dec	YTD Total	Current Month Fav/(Unfav) to Plan	Ytd Fav/(Unfav) to Plan
	Revenue							
1	Net interest income	30	25	32	35	372	4	5
2	Product A fees	12	14	11	10	132	(1)	(8)
	Product B fees	7	9	8	7	96	2	6
	Product C fees	10	7	6	5	122	1	3
3	Income transfers (net of incoming and outgoing)	1	1	1	2	13	1	0
	Total revenue	60	56	58	59	735	7	6
	Expense							
2	Product A costs	10	11	10	9	123	1	2
	Product B costs	6	10	7	7	92	0	0
	Product C costs	9	7	6	6	120	(2)	(2)
4	Staff compensation	10	10	11	11	125	0	0
4	Other operating expenses	2	1	3	2	21	0	(2)
5	Expense transfers (net of incoming and outgoing)	1	1	1	2	14	0	0
6	Charge-offs/losses	0	3	0	5	12	3	(4)
	Total expense	38	43	38	42	507	2	(6)
	Net income before taxes	22	13	20	17	228	9	0
7	Staff FTE	4.8	4.7	5.0	5.0	4.9	0	0

Report 1 (table 8-4) is a detailed report on the net interest income of a revenue-producing organization.

Report 2 (table 8-5) provides specific profitability reporting on fee-based products.

Report 3 (table 8-6) provides information on internal funds transfers. It gives the balances, yields, and interest calculations for placings and takings.

Report 4 (table 8-7) lists all of the administrative operating expenses for an organization. It provides trends by month. The next level below this report would be a staff report listing hours paid and compensation for the reporting period, by staff member, and expense detail sheets showing item-by-item expenditures within each category such as subcategories of marketing or advertising.

TABLE 8-4 Line Organization A, Report 1: Net Interest Income (Rounded $000's)

Category	Jan	Feb ...	Nov	Dec	YTD Total/Avg	Current Month Fav/(Unfav) to Plan	Ytd Fav/(Unfav) to Plan
Funds placed							
Commercial loans							
Balances	11,613	11,613	11,613	11,613	11,613	0	0
Yield	15%	15%	16.5%	16%	15.8%	0.5%	0.8%
Interest income	150	135	160	160	1,835	5	93
Consumer loans							
Balances							
Yield							
Interest income[1]							
Intrainstitution							
Balances							
Yield							
Interest income[1]							
Total funds placed							
Balances							
Yield							
Interest income[1]							
Funds received							
Non-interest bearing							
Deposits							
Balances							
Yield (derived)[2]							
Cost of funds							
Interest bearing							
deposits							
Balances	11,613	11,613	11,613	11,613	11,613	0	0
Yield	12%	12.2%	13.2%	12.5%	12.6%	(0.01)%	(0.76)%
Cost of funds	120	110	128	125	1,463	(1)	88
Intrainstitution							
Balances							
Yield							
Cost of funds							

Note: Additional features that could be added to a report such as above could be a line for charge-offs or loss provisions; inclusion of administrative expenses and staff organization allocations; and taxes.
[1]Before cost of funds.
[1]There may be some form of an administrative cost that could be included here. However, if the decision is to do so then the other yield categories should be burdened likewise.

TABLE 8-4 Continued

Category	Jan	Feb	...	Nov	Dec	YTD Total/Avg	Current Month Fav/(Unfav) to Plan	Ytd Fav/(Unfav) to Plan
Capital								
Balances								
Yield								
Cost of funds								
Total funds received								
Balances								
Yield								
Cost of funds								
Net interest income/cost	30	25		32	35	372	4	5
Net yield								
(margin, spread)								
Net interest income/cost								

TABLE 8-5 Line Organization A; Report 2; Product Fee Income (Rounded $000's)

Category	Jan	Feb	...	Nov	Dec	YTD Total/Avg	Current Month Fav/(Unfav) to Plan	Ytd Fav/(Unfav) to Plan
Product A								
Volume	2,400	2,800		2,200	2,000	26,400	(200)	(1,600)
Fees	12	14		11	10	132	(1)	(8)
Costs	10	11		10	9	123	1	2
Profit/loss	2	3		1	1	9	0	(6)
Product B								
Volume	350	450		400	350	4,800	100	300
Fees	7	9		8	7	96	2	6
Costs	6	10		7	7	92	0	0
Profit/loss	1	(1)		1	0	4	2	6
Product C								
Volume	2,500	1,750		1,500	1,250	30,500	250	750
Fees	10	7		6	5	122	1	3
Costs	9	7		6	6	120	(2)	(3)
Profit/loss	1	0		0	(1)	2	(1)	0

Note: Including unit costs is optional here. In the product profitability reports they could be reported at the unit cost level.

TABLE 8-6 Line Organization A, Report 3: Income Transfers (Incoming and Outgoing)

Category	Jan	Feb ... Nov	Dec	YTD Total/Avg	Current Month Fav/(Unfav) to Plan	Ytd Fav/(Unfav) to Plan
From						
Organization B						
Balance						
Yield						
Interest income						
Organization D						
Fee income allocation (H)[1]	1	1	1	2	13	1	0
Total incoming transfer income	1	1	1	2	13	1	0
To						
Organization C						
Balance						
Yield						
Interest income						
Organization F						
Fee Income						
Total outgoing transfer income	0	0	0	0	0	0	0

[1] (H) is an example of a coded designator that would explain the basis or reason for the allocation. A reference table of coded explanations would greatly enhance a report like this.

Report 5 (table 8-8) serves as an invoice of organizational transfers-in and transfers out. It lists them on a monthly basis.

Report 6 (table 8-9) gives information on either loan loss provisions or loan charge-offs and on other losses incurred. It is up to management to decide whether they wish to see loss provisions or actual charge-offs in this report.

Report 7 (table 8-10) is a staff report. It provides information on hours paid and FTE staff.

The next report (table 8-11) is designed for those organizations that have a transaction cost accounting system for movement of cost data from processing or service centers to profit or income centers. It lists for each activity category the volume, unit costs, and their total cost for the current month, last month, and year-to-date. This report allows an income center to keep track of the volume, unit cost, and total cost of activities and products that flow to it.

TABLE 8-7 Line Organization A, Report 4: Administrative Expenses ($000's) [1]

Category	Jan	Feb ... Nov		Dec	YTD Total/Avg	Current Month Fav/(Unfav) to Plan	Ytd Fav/(Unfav) to Plan
FTE staff [2]							
Regular staff	4.0	4.0	4.0	4.0	4.0	0	0
Overtime	0.8	0	1.0	0.8	0.6	0	0
Temporary/agency	0	0.7	0	0.2	0.3	0	0
Total FTE staff	4.8	4.7	5.0	5.0	4.9	0	0
Regular salaries	7.0	7.0	7.5	7.5	87	0	0
Overtime	1.4	0	1.8	1.4	12.6	0	0
Fringe benefits	1.0	1.0	1.1	1.1	12.4	0	0
Temporary/agency	0	1.0	0	0.3	5.4	0	0
Bonuses/incentives	0.6	1.0	0.6	0.7	7.6	0	0
Total compensation	10	10	11	11	125	0	0
Other operating expenses							
Marketing/advertising							
Entertainment							
Travel							
Professional/community							
Contributions							
Recruiting/employee							
Subscriptions							
Postage/delivery							
Stationery and supplies	0	0	1	0	2	0	0
Telephone	1	0	1	1	7	0	(2)
Wires							
Data processing							
Equipment maintenance							
Equipment rent							
Insurance							
Legal	1	1	1	1	12	0	0
Premises							
Guards							
Consultants							
Service charges							
Miscellaneous							
Subtotal							
Depreciation							
Subtotal							
Incoming transfers							
Outgoing transfers							
Total other operating expenses	2	1	3	2	21	0	(2)
Total expenses	12	11	14	13	146	0	(2)

[1]This report could also be used by a staff organization for expense tracking.
[2]FTE = Full-time-equivalent staff based on hours paid.

TABLE 8-8 Line Organization A, Report 5: Expense Transfers (Incoming and Outgoing)

Organization	Jan	Feb ... Nov	Dec	YTD Total
Expense transfers from Organization E (J)[1]	1	1	1	2	14
Total incoming transfers	1	1	1	2	14
Expense transfers to Organization G					
Total outgoing transfers	0	0	0	0	0
Net	1	1	1	2	14

[1] J represents a code that could be tied to an explanation table. The explanation table would be based on some reason or allocation basis.

This completes a basic set of organizational reports. There are many possible variations to this. What are being presented here are basic formats for the cost analyst to absorb and then build upon.

The more basic the reports one begins with, the more probability there is of success in producing information. When you construct reports and begin the information gathering, apparent strengths and weaknesses in report structure and in information availability will surface. This is why it is suggested that you work with basic reports in the beginning and then build upon them in complexity as you realize successes.

TABLE 8-9 Line Organization A, Report 6: Loss Provisions/Experience

Category	Jan	Feb ... Nov	Dec	YTD Total	Current Month Fav/(Unfav) to Plan	Ytd Fav/(Unfav) to Plan
Nonaccruals charged-off						
Loan X	0	3	0	0	3	0	(3)
Loan Y	0	0	0	1	1	(1)	(1)
Loan Z	0	0	0	2	2	(2)	(2)
Subtotal	0	3	0	3	6	(3)	(6)
Operating losses						
Teller	0	0	0	0	2	2	0
Fraud (charge card)	0	0	0	1	2	3	2
Fraud (checks)	0	0	0	1	2	1	0
Subtotal	0	0	0	2	6	6	2
Total losses	0	3	0	5	12	3	(4)

TABLE 8-10 Line Organization A, Report 7:
Staff Report, December Current Report Month

Staff Member's Name	Social Security Number	Annual Salary	Current Month Hours Paid	YTD Hours Paid
B. Moya	000-00-0001	27,000	160	2,080
J. Pointe	000-00-0002	21,000	224	2,704
A. Hall	000-00-0003	21,000	192	2,288
G. Martin	000-00-0004	21,000	192	2,496
Agency	000-00-0005	—	32	624
Total	—	—	800	10,192

cols. (1 + 2) + 3 Current Month FTE Staff	Current Month 1 Reg FTE Staff	2 O.T. FTE Staff	3 Temp FTE Staff	ytd Total FTE Staff
1.0	1.0	0	0	1.0
1.4	1.0	0.4	0	1.3
1.2	1.0	0.2	0	1.1
1.2	1.0	0.2	0	1.2
0.2	0	0	0.2	0.3
5.0	4.0	0.8	0.2	4.9

TABLE 8-11 Line Organization A, Profit or Income Center Transaction Cost Report, December

Category	Current Month Per Unit Volume × Cost = Amount	Last Month Per Unit Volume Cost Amount	Year to Date Per Unit Volume Cost Amount
Demand deposit accounts (DDA's)			
Checks paid	11,000 × .05 = 550	8,000 × .05 = 400	106,800 × .05 = 5,340
Deposits accepted			
Proof processing, etc.			

FOCUSING ON MANAGEMENT INFORMATION

In setting up reports for organizational reporting, one must understand the potential uses for such information. The following list provides many of the reasons and justifications for having management information available on an organizational basis. Management reporting is usually for comparison of performance to a set of criteria. The following are performance measurement categories and suggested criteria for measurement. The use of each one is a function of what is being measured.

Profitability performance
Actual to plan variances
Actual to target objectives (those objectives that were set for the organization)
Explanation of key items affecting performance (an accounting of what occurred that affected performance)
Unusual occurrences
Time comparisons (this month versus last month, this year versus last year)

Activity performance
Volume and balance variances (actual to plan)
Capacity utilization
Organizational/staff effectiveness (measures of resources expended to results achieved)
Organizational/staff efficiency (the ratio of work performed to resources available)

Expense performance
Cost-of-funds measurement, interest spread management (income yield minus cost of funds = spread)
Staffing cost and equivalency; actual to plan variances; staff effectiveness; average compensation measurement per staff member; this year versus last year
Measurement of controllable and noncontrollable expenses
Exceptional, unusual, and one-time-only expense items
Trends of expense growth, stagnation, and contraction.
Details on questioned items

The focus in many financial institutions today is on control and containment of noninterest expense items. To deal with these effectively management needs to bring to light the nonessentials and low performing activities.

TABLE 8-12 Organizational Line Group X, Functional Profitability Report Year-to-Date Actuals ($ 000's)

Functional Product Groups	Revenue				Costs					General Services	Institution G&A	Net Profit before Taxes
	Fees	Net Interest Income	Other	Total	Direct Costs	Support Costs	Group G&A	Total Group Costs	Operating Profit/ Loss			
Product group A												
Product line 11	50	0	0	50	25	10	2	37	13	3	2	8
Product line 12												
Product line 13												
Total product group												
Product group B												
Product line 21												
Product line 22												
Product line 23												
Total product group												
Product group C												
Product line 31												
Product line 32												
Product line 33												
Total product group												
Other												
Total												

COMPLEX REPORTING FORMATS AND CONCEPTS

Having covered the basic essentials of organizational reporting earlier in this chapter, let us consider the more complex reporting formats. Because there are several variations on these formats, it is suggested you use these formats for ideas in formulating your own reporting formats.

Table 8-12 is an organizational profitability report by individual product. It could be produced monthly, quarterly, semiannually or annually. The advantage of this report is that an organization knows where it is making a profit and where it is not making a profit. The report also shows the various revenue, expense, and overhead items.

The format in table 8-13 is for reporting fees collected by each organization within a line group (income group). Similar reports could be set up that would track analysis charges (fees charged against a customer's deposit credits) and net interest income. The reporting is by organization and by product.

The report shown as table 8-14 is for either a profit center or an income center. It could go to the lowest responsibility level in an organization. An example of the lowest level would be a branch. The highest level would be a level that consolidates all the reporting of several branches.

The array of possible report formats is almost endless. Remember that the purpose of the report is to convey information to management regarding the performance and activity of a given organizationinformation they need to make sound decisions. To this end reports are designed, tested, tried, refined, and produced.

It is important for all financial institutions to have a formal mechanism for reporting costs and profitability. At a minimum it could be a report that lists average balances, yields, revenue, and expenses by organization. This information would be useful to management in making decisions such as where to concentrate organizational resources.

Responsibility Codes

Where there is organizational reporting there should also be a hierarchy of numerical codes designating organizations. In small financial institutions this can be relatively simple. However, if growth is anticipated, then a decision must be made early in the formatting of reports as to how the numerical designators are to be organized. Any time numerical codes are designed, future expansion or growth should be taken into consideration. Financial institutions have found themselves short of numerical designators for their departments a few years after installing a numerical system. Such occurrences are the result of insufficient planning. The alphanumeric coding system depicted in figure 8-1 should be able to accommodate any small to medium-size institution. It is a hierarchy that could be used in establishing a reporting system.

TABLE 8-13 Line Group X Fees Collected for the Month of December

Line Organization	Product Group A	Product Group B	Product Group C	Product Group D	Product Group E
Region A	10				
Region B	5				
Region C	8				
Region D	15				
Region E	12				
Total fees collected	50				

TABLE 8-14 Profit or Income Center Profitability: Willows Branch 010, December ($ 000's)

	Current Month Actual	Current Month Plan Variance Fav/(Unfav)	Year to Date Actual	Year to Date Plan Variance Fav/(Unfav)
Revenue				
Fees collected	8	1	90	10
Net interest income[1]	45	0	500	0
Other revenue	2	0	8	0
Intrainstitution funds credit	5	0	68	0
Revenue transfers incoming	4	0	12	0
Less revenue transfers outgoing	1	0	6	0
Total Revenue	63	1	672	10
Expense				
Branch expenses	23	(2)	260	(8)
General expenses	4	0	42	
Processing services	10	1	135	0
Admin./Support expenses	3	0	11	0
Intrainstitution funds expense	1	0	8	0
Expense transfers incoming	2	(2)	15	(15)
Less expense transfers outgoing	1	0	7	0
Subtotal	42	(3)	464	(23)
Overhead				
Group G&A @ 5%	2	0	24	0
Institution G&A @ 15%	6	0	72	0
Total expenses	50	(3)	560	(23)
Net income/(Loss) before tax	13	(2)	112	(13)

[1]Exclusive of intrainstitution funds credit/expense

Figure 8-1. Coding System

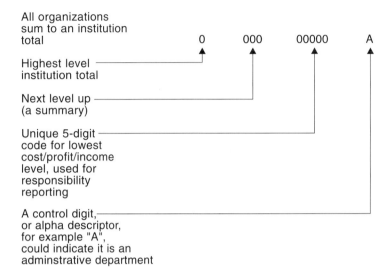

The main focus would be on the five-digit center code. It would be unique. A specific five-digit sequence could only be used once; an organization assigned a code of, say, "76823" would be the only one having that code. The code would be used for resource billing and management reporting. The "next level" codes would be used for hierarchy summaries of organizational data.

With the rapid increase in technology we see today there may be other forms of coding that are more efficient than what is being presented here. The cost analyst must aim to be consistent and logical, and to leave abundant room for organizational growth and change.

EXPENSE CATEGORIES

In setting up categories for expense reporting it is necessary to prepare a document that explains what is contained in each category. This will alleviate any questions that may arise regarding what goes where. Below are general explanations of major expense categories used in reporting. It must be noted that a specialized organization such as a data processing center or a retail branch may require a more detailed breakdown of expenses.

FTE regular staff Full-time equivalent regular staff counts based on the number of hours paid. (These hours are converted to staff equivalents. An example of this is a center that has accumulated 825 regular staff hours for a given month. Assume each staff member is paid based on 160 hours for that month. The staff count would be 5.16 FTE (825 ÷ 160 = 5.16). Of course, in months when there are five weeks, the 160 would become something else, such as 200.)

FTE overtime Full-time equivalent staff derived from overtime hours paid. (For example, if 220 actual overtime hours were paid in a one-month period this would equal 1.4 FTE (220 ÷ 160 = 1.4). This assumes a 160-hour work month, of course. It also assumes the 220 hours are actual rather than the result of a time-and-a-half multiplying factor.)

FTE temporary/agency Full-time equivalent staff derived from temporary and agency staff hours paid. (For example, if 320 hours were paid in a one-month period this could equate to 2.0 FTE (320 ÷ 160 = 2.0). Again this assumes a 160-hour work month.)

Regular salaries Hourly and salary wages paid to full-time and part-time staff

Overtime Wages paid for work classified as being outside of normal working hours

Fringe benefits Usually a derived rate, applied against regular salaries in order to determine the amount; includes medical coverage, retirement vesting, and provisions for vacation and sick pay

Temporary/agency A category for outside help working on a temporary basis as well as personnel working through an agency and on a temporary basis

Bonuses/incentives Nonfringe benefits attracting wages, including performance bonuses and incentives as well as severance pay

Total compensation The aggregate of regular salaries, overtime, fringe benefits, temporary, agency, and bonuses or incentives

Marketing/advertising Promotional gift items; radio, television, magazine, and newspaper advertising; billboard and campaign signs; and solicitations and advertising agency fees

Entertainment   Expenses incurred on behalf of entertaining customers, clients, and other business associates at lunch meetings and other social events of a business nature

Travel   Cost of transportation, meals, lodging, and incidentals on behalf of institution's business

Professional/community   Memberships in business associations

Contributions   Corporate gifts to nonprofit organizations

Recruiting/employee   Executive search and agency fees, employment advertising, relocation fees, educational expenses, and geographic location incentives

Subscriptions   The costs of newspapers, magazines, research publications, newsletters, and information services

Postage/delivery   Postage expense, package delivery, and mailroom services

Stationery and supplies   Office supplies of a general nature (daily business items such as pens, pencils, paper, and calendars)

Telephone   Rental and purchase of uncapitalized equipment, use of phone lines, and other related expenses are in this category

Wires   Cost of cablegrams, telegrams, and wire messages

Data processing   The cost of using data processing services. (In some financial institutions there are separate categories for data processing as follows: DP equipment rent, DP depreciation, DP equipment maintenance, DP supplies, DP data lines, and DP processing.)

Equipment maintenance   The cost of repairing and maintaining equipment

Equipment rental   The cost of leasing or renting equipment

Insurance   All forms of insurance with the exception of employee health and life insurance coverage

Legal   Fees paid for legal services

Premises   Rent and lease payments on buildings and offices, parking, minor building repairs (uncapitalized), and other period expenses associated with occupying a structure

Guards   The cost of protection

Consultants   The cost of utilizing the services of outside professionals who provide consultive services

Service charges   Fees paid for use of an activity or service other than a subscription or consulting engagement

Miscellaneous   Any cost that is not covered in the foregoing categories

Depreciation   The amortization of capitalized items

9

Product Profitability Reporting

"What are we to report and how are we to do it?" This is a question that one may ask when an organization is considering the viability of reporting product profitability information for the first time.

As with any subject it is best to start out with some basic concepts and build on them. Product profitability reporting covers earning assets, sources of funds, and services provided. This is basically what financial institutions are all about. Within this framework there is revenue, expense, and activity.

Begin by trying to isolate the revenue and expense associated with each product line. The goal is to ascertain the profitability of each product line. Data is constructed around each product line in order to identify and differentiate the revenue and expense attributable from one product line to another.

DEFINING PRODUCTS

The *product* level is the lowest level at which revenue is reported. Business checking is a product. For many organizations this is the lowest level at which product-related information is reported; that is, they do not report activities or tasks. Other organizations report on products at one level higher—the product line. A product line is a group of products such as demand deposits.

In setting up product reporting the analyst prepares a list of products, usually in collaboration with product management or marketing and other interested individuals. The initial list should not include items for which no revenue is being charged. These should be placed on an exceptions list for management review. When such a new or implied product emerges, however, it should be considered for inclusion on the list. This process of establishing a product reporting system can be a good exercise in organizing a systematic approach to managing products. This is especially true if no formal product management or marketing function exists. If the function already exists, then the exercise reveals opportunities for improvement.

Defining products may require several passes. What presently exists is often different from what is being prescribed or what is being planned for the future. The analyst can help close the gap by outlining an incremental framework for achieving reporting goals.

Armed with an agreed to list of products to include in the report, the analyst then goes about aligning revenue, expense, and activity measurements with each product.

Let's look first at *earning assets*. In putting earning assets on a product line reporting level, we find such product lines as commercial loans, consumer loans, leasing, credit cards, securities, and investments. The list will evolve if you begin listing the earning assets to be categorized and reported on a product line basis.

We then look at the *funding activities*. This includes such product lines as demand deposits, time deposits, borrowed money, and capital. Again, the list could certainly be longer and more detailed. The cost of funds for each of the product lines must be a known quantity in reporting the profitability of earning assets.

At this point we need to align the earning assets with the funding activities on a revenue or cost basis. The formula is as follows:

	Revenue	(from earning assets)
less	Cost of funds	(from funding activities)
less	Administrative or operating costs	(as identified by cost studies)
less	Actual charge-offs or loss provisions	(from charge-offs)
=	Net profit before tax	

Administrative and operating costs are usually a combination of direct, indirect, and allocated costs. Also included are such costs as the institution's overhead recoupment. Actual charge-offs or allocated provisions are listed as a deduction from the revenue of earning assets.

The list of fee-based *product offerings* of a financial institution can be lengthy. They occur in two categories—commercial services and consumer services and share two characteristics: they are essentially fee-based and are not listed on the balance sheet.

Commercial services could include account reconcilement, customer payroll, remittance banking, and accounts receivable. Consumer services are vast in number. They include but are not limited to exchange, escrow, and personal trust.

Product Reporting Concepts

There is a relation between product line profitability and financial institution's over-all profitability. The sum total of all product line profits should equal total institution profit. In order for this to occur there must be a means of allocating indirect and overhead kinds of expenses to the various product lines. Consider Figure 9-1, which illustrates how to account for all of a financial institution's revenue and expense on a product line basis.

Table 9-1 illustrates the various revenue and expense items for earning assets, funding activities, and fee services. The list is not all inclusive, but it does include enough items to give the essence of what belongs in each category. The table is based on the following formula.

Figure 9-1. The Relation between Total Bank Profitability and Total Product Line Profitability

Net Profit/(Loss) Before Taxes = Net Revenue from Earning Assets − Net Cost from Funding Activities + Net Profit/(Loss) from Fee Services

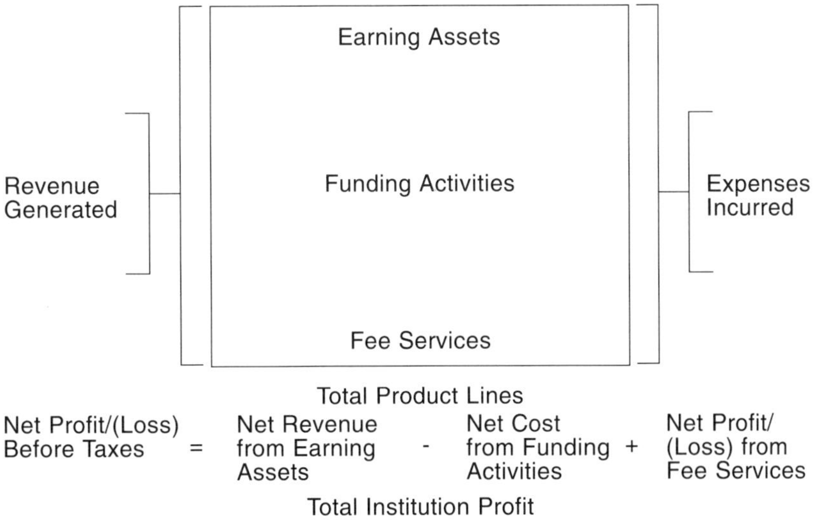

The core accounting (general ledger) system should be set up with a chart of accounts that will capture fees on a product or product line basis. This obviously facilitates product line profitability reporting on the management information side. If the fee revenue is readily discernible by product line, then there is a minimum of allocation required to isolate such revenue. Financial institutions need this kind of reporting on a quick turnaround basis in order to evaluate sales achievement goals.

In product-aligning expenses, the cost of funds, loan loss provisions, and certain operating expenses require allocation. A concept or basis is developed and used for each of these.

TABLE 9-1 Revenue and Expense Elements

	Earning Assets	Funding Activities	Fee Services
Revenue			
Fee revenue (fees and charges)	x	x	x
Interest income	x		
Loan fees	x		
Transfer fees	x		
Trading profits	x		
Lease financing revenue	x		
Equity income	x		
Charge cards	x		
Clearing fees	x		
Other	x		
minus			
Expenses			
Staff compensation	x	x	x
Other operating	x	x	x
Loan loss provisions	x		
Interest cost		x	
Clearing fees	x		
Other	x	x	x
equals			
Net profit before taxes			

The cost of funds can either be a pooled average or a matched resource according to risk, maturity, and application. As a matched resource there must be convincing logic as to the nature of the matching.

Loan loss provisions are usually assigned to earning assets on the basis of experience for that category. Some operating expense is directly identifiable, but a certain amount of operating expense needs to be allocated. The allocation is tied to some basis, concept, or justification.

In establishing product profitability reporting, a number of issues need to be raised and resolved. One thought should be kept in mind: The more that is allocated to product lines the less integrity there is of reported data. That is, the less directly identifiable data there is, the more reliability there is on subjective allocation techniques.

Your goal should be to have minimal allocations and mostly rely on directly identifiable revenue, expense, and activity.

A number of tasks need to be accomplished in preparation for reporting. First, you must decide on whether to distinguish controllable from noncontrollable expenses. Some financial institutions measure performance only for those expenses that are controllable. Other financial institutions subscribe to a philosophy of accountability for fully absorbed expenses, even if some are beyond the control of those being held accountable. It is suggested that a format be developed that would accommodate the reporting of both as separate line items when reports are being developed. Of course, the cost of doing this must be weighed against the expected benefit of having such information.

The next preparatory task is to establish a hierarchy of definitions; for example:

Product group (a common group of product lines)

Product line (a common line of products)

Product (the lowest level for counting revenue)

Activity (generally the lowest cost level)

Task

The remaining tasks are as follows:

- Identify revenue by product.

- Develop costs at the product level.

- Identify and select appropriate activity measurements (transactions, balances, and other volume measurements).

- Apply volume weights and frequency analyses to product reporting.

- Decide on the frequency of reporting (weekly, monthly).
- Identify who will receive the reports.
- Determine what level of reporting is needed summary or detail.
- Decide reporting formats.

Identification of revenue by product. For sales tracking it is essential to have a chart of accounts on the revenue side of the general ledger that will capture revenue on a product basis. This may involve subaccounts. It is important to distinguish fee income on a product basis so that profitability and sales information can be readily made available to those in decision-making positions.

Development of costs at the product level. The ability to determine profitability on a product-by-product basis is a function of being able to match product costs with product revenue for each product. Cost should be developed and reported in the same structure and framework as the revenue components. For example, if there is a charge (revenue) for "accepting a payment," then a cost should be developed for accepting a payment. This way the revenue can be aligned with the cost and a consequent profit or loss can be derived.

Identification and selection of appropriate activity measurements. The measurements that should be reported are those things that describe the business activity that is controllable. Again, it is what will help the decision makers who are accountable for a product that should be reported. This may include such things as transactions and balances.

Application of volume weights and frequency analysis to product reporting. As activities from various organizations flow into the production of a product, there may be differing volumes to account for. For reporting purposes the costs of the activities may have to be factored on a ratio basis in order to coincide with the reported product volume.

The frequency of reporting. It must be decided how often a product profitability report will be produced. Will it be weekly, monthly, quarterly, or annually? Whatever is necessary and makes sense should be the determinant. The frequency of production is usually decided on by the primary recipient(s).

The recipients of the reports. Who is to receive the reports is a question that involves organizational knowledge. The needs of each potential recipient organization in the financial institution must be known. Who will benefit most should be determined. The list of recipients should include those who have a need to know. However, some who would like to have the reports may also request such distribution. Generally those who will be making decisions based on the information being reported are those who should primarily receive the reports. Generally senior management decides who is to receive the reports and provides the list to the cost analyst.

The level of reporting. Some recipients like to go into the fine details of revenue expenses and activity information. Others want only a cursory glance at a profitability summary. If the reports are designed properly, the needs of both can be met. The top page of the report could be a summary, with detailed supporting schedules attached.

The needs of product management/marketing. Probably one of the most interested groups of recipients of product profitability reports are product management or marketing. They have a vested interest in what is being reported. Their needs are primary in that they want to know how products are selling, what their revenue is, and how profitable they are.

They also have a need to receive the product profitability reports in a timely manner. These reports must be complied with a high degree of accuracy and with relevant and useful information.

Though their main interest may focus on profitability they do have concerns elsewhere but in close proximity. They generally have a requirement for specific information on revenue, direct expense, allocated expense, overhead, item costs, activity measurement, and analysis of what has occurred.

Requests from product management or marketing for further justification of how the allocated indirect expenses and overhead were derived and applied are quite common. So be sure any allocations are well thought out in advance. Careful documentation should be available and the method must be explainable.

Product management or marketing has a need to know what is happening to specific products. Through the reports they receive, they may want to focus on any pressure points within the categories of revenue, expense, and activity and react accordingly. To do so they need solid data to make their decisions. Hence be sure to solicit input from product management or marketing when designing the report.

POSITIONING COSTS TO MATCH THE FEE ELEMENTS

Most financial institutions that have a pricing committee also have a detailed schedule of fees and charges. For pricing decision purposes and for product profitability measurement it is important to have item costs on a product-by-product basis. Wherever there is a defined fee element for a product unit, there should also be a matching cost element with the same definition. Costs should be aligned with the fee schedule. Consider, for example, a fee-based service called product A, funds transfer.

Product	Description	Fee
Product A (funds transfer)	Basic processing	$150 per Month
	Phone authorization	5 per Call
	Photocopy and send confirmation	7.50 per confirmation

This product comprises three fee elements, or "subproducts." The pricing committee prices these subproducts and decides as an overall strategy for this service that it would be most valuable to be able to see the cost of each subproduct so as to know the profitability of each one.

If the cost were aligned to each subproduct, the alignment would appear as in table 9-2.

At this juncture product management knows they will make $5 per month on the basic processing. This of course assumes all fees are collected or compensated for via balances. The phone authorization subproduct with a $5 fee will experience a loss of $1 per call. Photocopy and confirmation will lose $0.50 per confirmation. The capturing of profitability information such as this is a step in the right direction in product profitability reporting. It will provide data that will aid the pricing committee in formulating product A's strategy.

The next step is to attach volume counts to this structure, as shown in table 9-3. Assume the volume data is based on actual experience. The volume count will show product management the magnitude of profit or loss for each subproduct as well as the total profit or loss for the product.

TABLE 9-2 Costs Aligned to Subproduct

Product	Description	Fee	Cost	Potential Profit (Loss)[1]
Product A (funds transfer)	Basic processing	$150 per month	$145 per month	$5 per month
	Phone authorization	$5 per call	$6 per call	($1) per call
	Photocopy and send confirmation	$7.50 per	$8.00	($0.50) per confirmation

[1]The word *potential* is used as a qualifier in case of fee concessions and waivers that may be granted to specific customers.

TABLE 9-3 Profit Potential for Product A

Description	Fee	− Cost	= Potential Profit/(Loss)	× Volume =	Total Potential Profit/(Loss)
Basic processing	$150.00	$145.00	$5.00 per month	525	$2,625
Phone authorization	5.00	6.00	(1.00) per call	783	(783)
Photocopy and send confirmation	7.50	8.00	(0.50) per confirmation	498	(249)
Total potential profit/loss based on actual volume					$1,593

Revenue
  Basic processing $150.00 × 525 = $78,750
  Phone authorization $5.00 × 783 = $ 3,915
  Photocopy $7.50 × 498 = $ 3,735
    Total revenue $86,400
Costs
  Basic processing $145.00 × 525 = $76,125
  Phone authorization $6.00 × 783 = $ 4,698
  Photocopy $8.00 × 498 = $ 3,984
    Total costs $84,807
    Total potential profit $ 1,593   ($86,400 − $84,807 = $1,593)

This kind of a product report allows product management to see the details they need in assessing the elements and the overall structure of product A as it is being sold to the marketplace.

REPORTING FORMATS AND CONCEPTS

The report should begin with a simple, high-level summary. At the highest level, management is interested in seeing what the revenue, expense, profitability, and comparison to plan are for the period being reported. At the detailed level there may be interest in having activity measurements, allocations, and unit cost data.

Let us begin with a simple non-balance sheet product report and then build on it toward a more complex and detailed reporting format.

**TABLE 9-4 Report 1: Product Profitability
Summary for the month of January (and YTD)**

Product	Revenue	Expense	Profit/Loss	Variance from Plan, Fav/(Unfav)
A	58	49	9	1
—				
—				
—				
Total (all products)				

Report 1 (table 9-4) lists the revenue, expense, profit or loss, and variance from plan for each product. It is a basic summary level report. Its simplicity suggests there should be more detail available for each product.

Report 2 (table 9-5) is an expanded version of report 1. It shows more detail on what constitutes the revenue. It also shows any fee waivers. The expenses are broken down between direct, allocated, and institutionwide general and administrative (G&A).

**TABLE 9-5 Report 2: Product Profitability
Summary for the Month of January (and YTD)**

Product	Revenue			Memo
	Fees Collected	Applied against Balances[1]	Total Revenue	Waived Fees/ Concessions
A	58	0	58	0
—				
—				
—				

Expense				Profitability Variance From Plan, Fav/(Unfav)
Direct	Allocated	Institution G&A	Total Expenses	Profit/ Loss	
41	2	6	49	9	1
Total (all products)					

[1]Assumed revenue in this case would be an artificial deposit credit given for balances at a specified rate.

TABLE 9-6 Report 3: Product Profitability Report, Product A

	Revenue			Memo	Analysis of Revenue Example			Variance from Plan
Month	Fees Collected	Applied against Balances	Total Revenue	Waived Fees/ Concessions	Processing	Authoriz	Confirm	Fav/(Unfav)
Jan	58	0	58	0	50	3	5	1
Dec								
YTD total	58	0	58	0	50	3	5	1

Direct Expenses ($000's)

Month	Compensation	DP	Sales/ Marketing	Postage	Supplies	Telephone	Equipment	Premises	Misc.	Total Direct Expenses	Allocated G&A	Institution G&A	Total Expenses	Variance from Plan Fav/(Unfav)
Jan	18	4	5	1	1	2	8	2		41	2	6	49	0
Dec														
YTD total	18	4	5	1	1	2	8	2		41	2	6	49	0

TABLE 9-6 (continued)

Profitability

Month	Net Profit before Tax	Variance from Plan Fav/(Unfav)	Comparison to Last Year, Better/(Worse)	Profit Contribution To Allocations and Overhead	
Jan	9	1	2	17	(Revenue minus direct expenses) (58 – 41 = 17.)
... Dec					
YTD total	9	1	2	17	

Activity

								Example	
Month	No. of Customers	Variance from Plan, Fav/(Unfav)	Processing Volume	Variance from Plan, Fav/(Unfav)	Authorizations	Variance from Plan, Fav/(Unfav)	Confirmation	Variance from Plan, Fav/(Unfav)	
Jan	22	(2)	2,875	0	38	10	1,000	(200)	
...									
YTD total	22	(2)	2,875	0	38	10	1,000	(200)	

Report 3 (table 9-6) provides detailed information for individual products. There would be a report 3 for each product offered. It shows the revenue, expense, and activity on a month-by-month basis with a year-to-date total.

The total revenue is broken down by fees collected and by charges applied against balances in lieu of collected fees. There is a column for waived fees. The revenue sources are listed along with their associated revenue. By way of example, three sub-products are listed; they are processing, authorizations, and confirmations, but they could be anything. They should represent the major source categories of revenue for the product being reported.

The expense section should list those items that are relevant and significant to the product being reported.

Such expense items as compensation, data processing, marketing and sales, postage, supplies, telephone, equipment rental or lease, premises, allocations, and the institution's G&A are listed and totaled. They are then compared against plan. Again, the data is reported on a month-by-month basis.

The next section of the table focuses on profitability by month and year-to-date. It lists the net profit before tax, comparison to plan, comparison to last year, and the profit contribution to allocations and overhead.

The last section covers activity measurement. Listed are such things as the number of customers, with a comparison to plan; processing volume, with a comparison to plan; and selected revenue-producing categories.

For each of the segments in report 3 additional details could be provided either in an addendum to the report 3 or in a supplemental report.

TABLE 9-7 The Hierarchy of Reports, Monthly with YTD Totals

Detailed Reporting	Intermediate Reporting (Some Details)[1]	Summary Level Reporting[2]
For each product		
Revenue	Revenue	Revenue
Expense	Expense	Expense
Profitability	Profitability	Profitability
Activity		

[1]Several products are listed in the same report. This could be a product line or product group summary.

[2]Several products are listed in the same report. This could be a summary of several product groups.

TABLE 9-8 Product Profitability Balance Sheet, Product X, Consumer Loans—Automobile ($000's): Report 1

| Month | Revenue | | | Expenses | | | | | Contribution to Cost of Funds and Profits | @12% Pooled Cost of Funds | Net Profit before Taxes | Average Balances |
	@17% Interest Yield	Fees/ Charges	Total Revenue	Administrative	Allocated	Loan Loss Provision	Institution G&A	Total Expenses				
Jan	80	5	85	13	8	3	4	28	57	56	1	5,465
... Dec												
YTD Total	80	5	85	13	8	3	4	28	57	56	1	5,465

	Yield	Cost of Funds	Spread	Net spread Fav/(Unfav) to plan[1]
Current month	17%	12%	5%	0.3%
Year-to-date	17%	12%	5%	0.3%
Current month plan	17.5%	12.8%	4.7%	—
Year-to-date plane	17.5%	12.8%	4.7%	—

[1] 5.0% − 4.7% = 0.3%.

HIERARCHY OF REPORTS

Some accountants may suggest item costs be listed at this point in the reporting process. This is especially true if there is an automated delivery system based on standard costs. At such a point the reporting becomes complex.

The basic reporting process is summarized in table 9-7. It illustrates the hierarchy that begins with details and works upward to a summary.

Given the suggested hierarchy of detail, there are three reports that follow as examples. The first (table 9-8) has the most detail and it reports on a balance sheet product. The revenue categories consist of gross interest income and revenue from fees or charges.

The expenses comprise assigned administrative, allocated, loan loss provisions, and the institution's G&A. The next column is the contribution to cost of funds and profits. It is the result of revenue minus expenses. The cost-of-funds column that follows could be based on some arbitrary pool rate. This column is subtracted from the contribution to cost of funds and profits column to arrive at the net profit or loss before taxes. Any relevant balances are listed in the last column.

At the bottom of the report such things as current month yield, year-to-date yield, current month variance from plan, and YTD variance from plan are listed.

An alternative method of reporting this data would be to show earning assets on a net interest income basis using both dollars and percentages as shown in table 9-9.

TABLE 9-9 Earning Assets, on Net Interest Income Basis

	Jan. Feb.....Dec. Total	
	$ Amount	Percentage of balances
Interest	xx	xx
Fees	xx	xx
Total income	xx	xx
less: Cost of funds	xx	xx
Net interest income	xx	xx
Less:		
Provision for loan losses	xx	xx
Direct expenses	xx	xx
Allocated expenses	xx	xx
Income before taxes	xx	xx

TABLE 9-10 Product Profitability For the Month of January (and YTD): Report 2

	Revenue		Expenses				
Product	Interest	Fees/Charges	Expenses and Administrative	Allocated	Loan Loss Provis.	Institution G & A	Total Expenses
Consumer loans—auto	80	5	13	8	3	4	28

Contribution to Cost of Funds and Profits	Variance from Plan, Fav/(Unfav)	Gross Revenue Yield before Cost of Funds	Net Yield after Expenses but before Cost of Funds	Balances
57	2	17%	12.11%	5,465

TABLE 9-11 Product Profitability For the Month of January (and YTD): Report 3

Product	Revenue	Expense	(col. 2 – col. 3) Contribution to Cost of Fund and Profits	Variance from Plan Fav/(Unfav)	Net Yield before Cost of Funds	Balances
Consumer loans—auto	85	28	57	2	12.11%	5,465

An intermediate level of detail is shown in table 9-10. This example is only for one month. Several balance sheet products can be listed at one time on this report.

The third report (table 9-11) is summary providing management with a brief overview of each product's results. As are the other reports in this sample hierarchy, this one also is designed for balance sheet products.

Reporting Balance Sheet Products

This nature of their balance sheet products is such that allocations play a key role in applying administrative and operating expenses to these product lines. It is important to make a list of the key elements to report for balance sheet products. Key elements are:

Interest revenue	Loan loss provision
Fee revenue	Average yields
Cost of funds	Average spreads
Direct administrative expenses	Average balances
Indirect allocated expenses	Variance from plan data
Institution overhead	Monthly trending

The reporting format could continue in complexity. This is a function of the type of product being reported and the needs of management. There is a need to have flexibility for change and expansion.

10

Customer Profitability Reporting

Customer profitability is the third component of the profitability triad. The bottom-line profitability tie of organizational, product, and customer profitability must be kept in mind as one looks at the issues and concepts of customer reporting.

In some financial institutions there is no customer reporting system. In others it exists but is manually prepared. In still others it is part of a system that regularly captures and reports data. The trend in financial institutions today is toward some form of reporting no matter how rudimentary it is.

As financial institutions diversify their business activities they need to be aware of opportunities for cross-selling products to their customers. A well-designed and well-executed customer information system is needed. Financial institutions also need to be aware of unprofitable relationships and uncollected fees.

In order to meet the tactical and strategic challenges ahead, financial institutions need an adequate customer data base. Profitability reporting is just one segment. An overall system should include the following:

Customer profitability reporting

Customer fee reporting

Customer balance reporting

Customer activity reporting

Customer billing

Customer profile reporting

In this broader view, customer profitability reporting is a subset of a customer information data base. However, many financial institutions simply refer to the whole system as "customer profitability reporting."

The possibilities are vast and can range from simple to complex. In analyzing a financial institution's need for customer information there are at least two good reasons to justify the need: to improve relationship with customers and to sell them additional services.

Customer relationship management is geared toward maintaining a profitable relationship. It involves reviewing and taking action relative to services used, balances maintained, service charges collected, and overall activity.

New sales opportunities come as a result of a financial institution's diversity of product offerings and selling more than one product to a customer. Studying customer profiles in determining market needs are important. In some institutions just having an idea of which relationships are profitable and which are unprofitable is a very important step.

In this chapter we will cover the essentials of customer profitability reporting and the "how to's" of setting up a system that will provide management with useful data for improving customer management and sales.

THE ELEMENTS OF A CUSTOMER INFORMATION FILE

If you were to make a list of the types of the institution's customers, your list would probably include the following:

Domestic and international
Commercial (wholesale)
   Corporate—Large, medium, and small
   Small businesses

   Correspondent institutions

Consumer (retail)

Governmental

Based on this brief list you might wish to classify the commercial customers according to some form of code such as the Standard Industrial Code (SIC). This would allow for industry segmentation. Then you would probably want to classify them according to size based on some criterion. Market segmentation according to geographic location would be next. Market clustering and the like could be studied as you look at the geographic distribution of your customers. All of this could be captured with an alphanumeric coding system.

A correspondent institution relationship usually involves some form of reciprocity. If the optimal effects are to be realized, it is important to keep track of activity, balances, income, and expenses entailed in this kind of relationship.

The consumer base is much larger and possibly more diverse than is the commercial base. The most sought after information would probably be product utilization patterns and personal customer profiles. The opportunities to be gained from such a system are vast. Also geographic and demographic information on the consumer customer base can be very useful.

Most institutions do not have a customer information data system that covers their consumer customer base. By choice they concentrate on commercial customer activity and profitability. The reason is clear. Commercial customers are assigned account officers and are managed on an individual basis—hence the need for customer information. Therefore, on the customer side, the major use would be for optimizing cross-selling opportunities. The reasons are different for having a commercial customer information data base than for a consumer base. However, development and maintenance cost and intended use are important in establishing either of these bases.

Let us now look at the specific elements to consider for inclusion when constructing a customer information file (CIF).

Commercial (wholesale)

Customer balances—deposits (by account type)

Customer balances—loans (by category)

Services/products utilized (including volume)

Revenue (interest income, fees collected, fees charged against balances, and waived fees)

Cost of funds

Administration expenses

Cost of Services/products provided

Profitability

Float

Credit commitments and customer utilization

Deposit earnings (actual and implied)

Industry type

Size of corporation

Number of accounts/master relationship link

Geographic location

Master relationship link

Contact names/account

Assigned account officer

Based on this data internal institution reports can be developed as well as external reports that would go to the customers.

Correspondent Financial Institutions

Customer (correspondent) balances—their deposits at your institution

Institution (your bank) balances—your deposits at their institution

Net position (your institution)

Services/products utilized (including volume)

Revenue (interest income, fees collected, fees charge against balances, and waived fees)

Cost of funds provided

Customer deposit earnings (actual and implied)

Administrative expense

Cost of services/product provided

Profitability

Float

Credit commitment and utilization (for correspondent)

Credit commitment and utilization (for your institution)

Correspondent size (assets)

Geography

Contact names

Assigned account officer

Next would be a retail customer base. There are a vast number of items that could be included in such a data base.

Consumer (retail)

Customer balances—deposits (by account type)

Customer balances—loans (by category)

Fee services/products utilized (including volume)

Revenue (interest income, fees collected, fees waived)

Cost of funds provided

Customer deposit earnings (actual and implied)

Number of accounts/master relationship link

Geographic location and profile

Household profile (number in family, household income, net worth, credit experience, ages, gender, and occupation)*

Profitability

As you think of all that occurs in the process of providing products to customers, you will find more items to add to the list of information to be gathered.

TWO MANAGEMENT PHILOSOPHIES

On the commercial side there are two basic philosophies on the reporting of customer information for customer relationship management purposes. One philosophy says all that an account officer needs to see is revenue, balances, and activity information—no profitability data. This philosophy uses the strategy that account officers are to sell and manage whatever is being offered by the institution and let the higher level managers in the organization concern themselves with profitability. This philosophy suggests there are reasons for selling that are above the scope of the account

---

*Obviously the legality and disclosure ramifications of such a profile would need to be explored prior to implementation. This type of information could be a valuable tool for cross-selling.

officer. The main thrust in this philosophy is to push what is being sold and to make sure there are adequate balances and collected fees to cover any charges. At the account officer's level costs are not an issue here.

A system that is predicated on this philosophy should have cost data available, however, even though it may be suppressed from any reports. The theme in this philosophy is fee revenue generation, interest income generation, and balance management and fee collection.

The second philosophy centers on profitability. Under this philosophy the account officer is held accountable for the profitability of the customer relationship. Hence the account officer needs access to a full range of information. Profitability information, of course, includes costs and is therefore not shown to customers. Under this philosophy the account officer needs customer information relative to revenue, balances, activity, and costs. This philosophy generally gives the account officer more autonomy regarding what to sell. The primary emphasis is on the bottom line. The main theme is the profitability of a customer relationship. Either method has its merits.

USING A CIF TO COLLECT FEES

There is an increasing trend to charge and account for services or products on an individual, stand-alone basis. This necessitates distinguishing products purchased by customers. The comingling of large customer deposits and a host of institution-provided services at no charge is a thing of the past. In many institutions, balances may still be used to offset services provided, but with a separate and distinct accounting.

A well-designed customer information file (CIF) could double as an accounts receivable system. The trend is to collect fees for products used rather than require specified compensating balances. This is a consequence of the unbundling of services. With this trend of collecting fees, there needs to be a invoicing mechanism. One of the reasons for this trend is the volatility of interests rates. As interest rates change, so do the requirements for balances. If balances of a certain size are required in lieu of collected fees, then balance requirement changes could occur frequently. For the same service at the same price there could be a different balance level requirement given an interest rate change. (Balance requirements will be discussed in more detail later in this chapter.)

THE ESSENTIALS OF CUSTOMER COST DATA

If a customer information file is to include customer cost data, a procedure and philosophy must be agreed upon in advance. Such things as the degree of overhead absorption must be agreed upon in principle. Some systems include product item costs on a fully absorbed basis. That is, they include the institution's G&A. The cost data may appear as in the following example:

Product Number	Product Name	Volume	×	Cost	=	Total Cost
D 200 253	Checks deposited	850		$0.02500		$21.25

Depository services	Product Line	Product number
D	200	253

The product numbering arrangement suggests a detailed tracking system. However, this is not necessary unless there is an automated tie-in of one system with another as a means of capturing the total customer relationship. Some form of alphanumeric designation for each product or a simple three-digit numerical code system with no prefixes can be used. The complexity of the designation depends on the institution's size, number of customers, and number of products.

A uniform product numbering system would be helpful in the customer information data system, in a product fee schedule, and for identifying item costs.

TRACKING COMMERCIAL CUSTOMER PROFITABILITY

A viable customer profitability reporting system requires that current revenue, cost, balance, and activity data be available. It also requires a systematic and logical approach to capturing and reporting data. All ingredients must represent the same reporting time frame.

If the cost data is static it should be updated annually or with an agreed upon frequency. Static cost data is data that is not derived from a system that calculates and reports actual costs on a frequent basis. A system that tracks and reports cost data on an actual basis is complex and usually prohibitively expensive.

Customer profitability reporting is dependent upon accurate and timely input of data. This may involve in manual effort. If such is the case there should be cut-off points for inputs.

There may be certain legal restrictions regarding the inclusion of trust profitability and nonfinancial institution business profitability reporting with that of financial institution business profitability. This is something to explore in viewing a customer's overall relationship. There are, however, three basic profitability areas in financial institutions to measure: loans, deposits, and fee-based services.

In loan activity, yields and spreads are measured. They may be compared against a plan. However, there must be a cost-of-funds pool that is applied in order to derive spreads and hence profitability.

In deposits the net available balances are derived after deductions for float, services, and compensating balances. The deposit balances could be given an overall cost-of-funds rate based on any interest paid and administrative and operating costs to retain these balances. This could be measured against actual pooled funds costs and given a hypothetical profit or loss. It would not tie to the other members of the bottom-line triad of organizational and product profitability, however.

Fee-based services are measured by total product revenue minus total product costs. The revenue side is elusive at times. It is important, therefore, to count charges against balances as well as collected fees. Waived fees and uncollected revenue should be reported as well.

There may be an overall profitability objective for each customer. This would suggest a comparison of actual profitability to planned profitability.

Deposit Credit Rates

Deposit credit rates are usually developed for establishing the worth of a customer's available balances. As previously mentioned, rates may be used in establishing the "profitability" of a customer's deposit relationship. They are also used in determining the worth of deposits as an offset to charges for financial institution services used by the customer. This will be covered by example later.

Questions arise such as: What rate is to be used? Should it be an outside market rate? Should it parallel an internal pooled cost of funds concept, or should it be an arbitrarily set rate that is not tied to anything? These questions may be difficult to answer.

The *outside market rate driven* rate is competitive in the marketplace. For example, the rate of a certificate of deposit (CD) could be used. The maturity days to use for parity would have to be decided on. But market rates are volatile. During periods of uncertainty and monetary restraint they may fluctuate widely.

This volatility can affect the institution's profitability to the extent of applying balances against charges. When interest rates are high, the customer gets a higher deposit credit. Hence, a smaller balance is needed to cover services utilized than during lower interest rates. The following example illustrates this effect.

Assume a CD rate of 9.1 percent is normal and that 12.5 percent is relatively high. Also assume a customer has $150,000 in available balances and has utilized the financial institution's remittance banking services over the previous period. The charges for this product were $850.00. The customer has elected to pay for any services utilized via available balance credits. The credit is calculated using the formula $I = PRT$, where $I =$ the deposit credit, $P =$ the net average available balance, $R =$ the deposit credit rate, and $T =$ the number of days in the reported month. Using $I = PRT$ and the rule of 360 days, the calculation for a 30-day month is thus

$$I = \frac{\$150,000 \times .091 \times 30}{360}$$

$$I = \$1,137.50$$

This would be the deposit credit at 9.1 percent (0.091). There would be a surplus credit of $287.50 ($1137.50 − $850.00 = $287.50) after the $850.00 in utilized services is deducted. This surplus of $287.50 is neither given to the customer nor counted as income to the institution. It is implicitly an income to the institution in the form of interest-free funds. However, it is not directly accounted for as income.

At the 9.1 percent rate, how much is really needed in deposits to cover the $850.00 in service charges? Using the formula:

$$P = \frac{I}{RT}$$

$$P = \frac{\$850}{\frac{.091 \times 30}{360}}$$

$$P = \$112,088.$$

Thus, it takes $112,088. at 9.1 percent to compensate the institution for $850.00 in service charges. What happens when the deposit credit goes up to 12.5 percent? Using $I = PRT$:

$$I = \frac{\$150,000 \times .125 \times 30}{360}$$

$$I = \$1,562.50.$$

This would be the deposit credit at 12.5 percent.

Given the 12.5 percent rate, we will look at the balance required to compensate the bank for $850.00 in services. Using $P = I/RT$, we find

$$P = \frac{\$850}{\dfrac{.125 \times 30}{360}}$$

$$P = \$81,600.$$

The balance requirement is now $81,600. This is $30,488 less than the earlier requirement of $112,088.

The lower balance requirement is tantamount to a change in the pricing level for services rendered by the institution. The prices have not really changed though. The value of the customer's funds has changed. The object is to recognize the market value of the funds provided by the customer. This is particularly true since customers usually do not leave large amounts of cash uncommitted and idle in an account that doesn't attract interest. Customers tend to be sensitive to interest rates.

Let's now look at an institution's *pooled cost of funds*. Assume an institution at year end calculates its weighted average cost of funds for all resources, including paid-in capital. Also assume the institution plans to use this rate for customer deposit credit for all of the forthcoming year. The philosophy behind using a rate structure such as this is to ensure stability and consistency in providing deposit credits. It is arbitrary, especially during periods of wide rate fluctuations. If, for example, the rate were 8.75 percent, the institution would require $116,572 in balances for 30 days to cover $850 in service charges. This rate would ensure deposit credit stability throughout the year. However, there could be a wide gap, at times, between this rate and the marketplace rate. A modification would be a monthly change in the deposit credit rate based on the institution's previous month's cost-of-funds experience.

The last scenario to consider is a totally arbitrary rate that would be considered as part of the pricing structure. It is a rate that would assist the institution in optimizing the trade-off from receiving compensating balances in lieu of collecting fees for services rendered. Assume the institution sets its arbitrary deposit credit rate at 8 percent. Perhaps they base it on what they believe would be a low rate yet acceptable to the institution's customers. This lower rate would obviously translate into a requirement of more compensating balances than the previously mentioned 8.75 percent, 9.1 percent, and 12.5 percent bases. Assuming the same $850 in service charges for a 30-day period we calculate the following. Using $P = I/RT$,

$$P = \frac{\$850}{\dfrac{.08 \times 30}{360}}$$

$$P = \$127,501.$$

The balance requirement is now $127,501. This is appreciably higher than the other required balances with their concomitantly higher rates. The higher balance requirements that are driven by lower rates need to be considered as the institution decides on its deposit credit structure.

To be used in a customer information data system, deposit credit rates must be defined philosophically and be easily understood by those who must manage to them. Customer understanding and acceptance is essential.

FLOAT

Float may be defined as an uncollected balance. It is basically uncollected funds. It can either be beneficial to the institution or it can be a costly nonavailability of funds. The side of float that adversely affects an institution's profitability are those items it receives for processing that are uncollected. This includes such things as noncash item deposits or payments, such as checks that have not been processed for collection. Float that is favorable to an institution's profitability are noncash items it issues that either have not been presented for payment or have been processed and presented for collection.

In an effort to optimize availability of funds institutions have increased the effectiveness and efficiency of their operations. Some financial institutions have also developed informational reports that provide them with data on float, from both an operational and a customer standpoint. Float management is an important aspect of financial institutions. The first step toward float management is to know where the float is occurring and why it is occurring.

Some of the following practices result in reducing float and thereby enhance a financial institution's profitability:

- Identifying high dollar transit items

- Monitoring of float through float category tracking and investigation

- Reducing holdovers by processing late deposits

- Clearing out-of-state checks as soon as possible

- Expediting items to the proof operations

- Resolving out-of-balance deposits on a priority basis if they occur just prior to the weekend

- Maintaining awareness of amounts in prioritizing rejected items

Float management can be a profitable venture in an institution. It requires a systematic evaluation of the factors causing float and implementation of consequent remedies.

The type of float that is beneficial to an institution is checks and other items drawn on the institution that have not been presented for collection. The type of float that is not beneficial to an institution is checks and other items deposited at the institution, and drawn on another institution, and not presented for collection. Float management places its emphasis on the latter.

Float factors can be developed through a study of each major corporate customer. This would be in lieu of a more sophisticated float capturing system. A customer's float activity is studied for a specified period of time. Through the study it may be determined, for example, that a customer's deposits average two days for collection. This becomes the factor in giving a customer's account credit for available balances in a customer data system. For example, as each noncash deposit is made, a two-day clearing factor is applied against it. Therefore, the balance is not counted as available until the third day. This is illustrated in figure 10-1.

Figure 10-1. Recording a Float

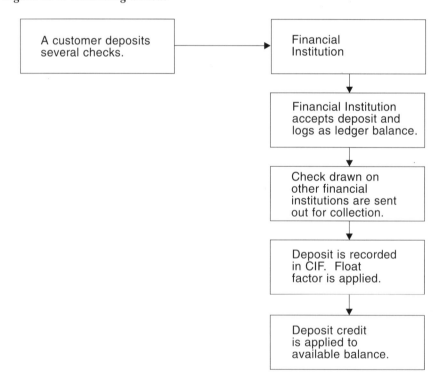

As we look at managing a customer relationship, float becomes an important consideration. It must be accounted for in looking at the total profitability relationship. Both the financial institution and the customer need to think in terms of collected and available funds. Collected funds are ledger balances minus float. Available funds are collected funds minus reserves and commitments. Reserves must be deducted from a customer's collected balance before credits for funds can be applied. Reserves are unavailable to the financial institution for its use. Hence, reserve balances do not attract funds credit.

REPORTING CONCEPTS AND FORMATS

A good customer profitability reporting system is one that is timely and accurate in evaluating the performance of a customer relationship. Behind it there should be a customer information data base that provides a vast array of possibilities for the segmentation of information. Some financial institutions build a system that allows them to review the following information either on a regular basis or on call as needed:

- Individual customer profitability

- Total customer relationship reporting (revenue, cost, activity, balances)

- Market segmentation by size, geography, or some other criteria

All of these allow a financial institution to cross sell and more effectively manage their customer relationships. Marketing research for tactical and strategic planning purposes benefits from the ability to extract and position customer data given a special requirement. An institution that can do this will realize more sales opportunities.

It should be noted here there is a difference in reported information between the internal reports and those that are given to customers. Customer profitability analysis reports are for internal use only. They are used by the account officer and institution management as tools for decision making and customer monitoring. The external report that is given to the customer is essentially a demand deposit analysis statement. It can, however, show loan activity and fee service utilization. It reports to the customer his or her balances, activity, and charges for the period being represented. External reports that are given to customers should not include the institution's cost data.

Reports that come out on a regular basis must convey timely and accurate information that an account officer can act on either for account management or for cross selling. We begin with a simple report format that can be done on a manual basis. Reports related to the commercial (wholesale) side of financial services will be presented first.

TABLE 10-1 Report 1 (Internal)

X, Y, Z Company
Account Officer Worksheet
for the Month of _____

Fee Services

Column #	1	2	3	4	5	6	7
Product	Volume	Unit Price	Total Implied Revenue (Col.1 × Col. 2)	Unit Cost	Total Cost (Col.1 × Col.4)	Waivers and Price Concessions	Total Implied Product Profit (Col.3 – Col. 5 – Col. 6)
Total							Line 10

Accounting of total implied revenue

Amount of waivers and price concessions $ _____   Approval _____
Amount of revenue to be collected in fees $ _____   Date invoice sent _____
Amount of revenue to be compensated for in balances $ _____   Line 15

Deposit credit rate _____ Line 20
Total implied revenue — fee services _____ (Same as line 10, col.3)
DDA balances for month reported (average ledger balance, noninterest bearing)

Account #	Balance
Total	_____ Line 30
Less loan compensating bals.	
Less float	
Less reserves	_____
Net average available balance	_____ Line 40 (For deposit credit purposes)

Deposit Credit

From line 20   deposit credit rate
From line 40   net average available balance

using $I = PRT$

$$\text{Deposit Credit} = \frac{Line \times Line\ 20 \times \#\ days\ in\ month}{100 \times 360} \quad (\text{"Banker's Rule"})$$

or

$365/366$ ("Exact Interest")

Line 45

less   Deposit credit
       revenue to be compensated
       for in balances   (from line 15) line 50
       Surplus credit/(deficiency   line 55
       to be collected)   (line 45 minus line 50)

Interest bearing deposit balances

1	2	3	4
Acct #	balance	rate	interest paid
Total			Line 60

Loan Balances

Column #1	2	3	4	5	6	7	8	9	10	11	12	13
Loan Number	Balance	Rate	Interest Revenue	Pool COF Rate	Pool Cost of Funds	Net Int. Income	Net Yield/ Spread	Loan Fee Revenue	Admin. Exp.	Loan Loss Provis.	G&A	Net Loan Profit
			$I = PRT$ P = Col. 2 R = Col. 3		$I = PRT$ P = Col. 2 R = Col. 5	(Col. 4 Minus Col. 6)	Col. 3 Minus Col. 5					(Col. 7 + Col. 9 – Col. 10, Col. 11, and Col. 12)
Total												Line 70

Total customer relationship profit/loss _____ Line 80
(Line 10 Col. 7 + Line 55 if positive plus Line 70, Col. 13)

Report 1 is a basic customer profitability worksheet report. It can be filled out either manually or via computer. The report is for one month's activity. Each element is explained in the following list. The totals for all products appear on line 10.

Product Each product utilized during the report month is listed by name and number if applicable.

Volume When appropriate the product activity volume is listed. Some products do not have a volume count per se. They may be packaged and sold as service modules. In the event of such occurrences a count of 1 is appropriate.

Unit price The standard price as approved by the pricing committee or other official delegation is listed in this column. This is the approved and published unit price for the product listed.

Total implied revenue This is the extension of volume times price. It is implied because no balance requirements and no collected fees accruing to this activity have been accounted for to this point.

Unit cost The unit cost, as provided by cost analysis, is included in this column. In order to maintain consistency and uniformity, this must be the approved and published unit cost for the product listed. It should be fully absorbed to include the institution's G&A.

Total cost This is the result of multiplying the volume times the unit cost for a specific product.

Fee waiver and price concessions A waiver occurs when the standard price is ignored and thereby not charged to a customer. Price concessions occur when the standard price is discounted or lowered. In effect, this occurs when the institution charges less than the standard price. A dual control procedure should be established such that at least two officers must approve price waivers and concessions before they can be effected.

Total implied product profit To arrive at this figure the total cost and all waivers and price concessions are subtracted from the total implied revenue. It must be kept in mind that we now have an implied profit as there is no verification of collected fees or adequate compensating balances at this point.

In order to maximize the profit potential of each product, close scrutiny should be given to fee waivers and price concessions. In the example form, there is an approval line. This would require a signature approval of an officer above the level of account officer. In the process of bringing a new customer onto a service, it is usually decided in advance whether the fees by specified product used will be collected or will be offset with compensating balances. A listing is provided of how much is to be collected in fees and how much if any, is to be offset by balances when the invoice is sent. A billing system, either manual or computer driven, is assumed to exist in tandem with customer profitability reporting. This is not a requirement of customer reporting and is mostly a philosophical and procedural issue. In any event there must be some follow-up mechanism in place to determine who is paying and who is not. Listing the date an invoice was sent is a way of establishing a base in the event follow-up action becomes necessary.

The amount of revenue to be compensated for in balances is to be agreed upon when the service is signed for by the customer. Sometimes this is an occasion for negotiating requested fee waivers and price concessions. Obviously any service performed by a financial institution costs money. Therefore, free and discounted services are a potential loss to the financial institution.

The deposit credit rate is a philosophical and procedural issue. The line on the form is blank so that one rate can be inserted or adjusted by the account officer as often as is necessary.

The average ledger balance for noninterest demand deposits is listed for each account by number. From the total, which appears in line 30, such things as committed compensating balances, reserves, and float balances are subtracted. This provides net average available balance (for deposit credit purposes). The deposit credit is calculated using the formula $I = PRT$.

An issue to be resolved is which annual base to use — the 360 or 365/366. The 365/366 base will produce a lower yield (deposit credit).

The deposit credit is recorded on line 45. From line 45 the amount of revenue to be compensated for in balances is subtracted (line 50). It is carried from line 15 to line 50 for this purpose. This results in one of the following: a surplus credit, for which usually no action is taken; a deficiency, for which fees are to be collected or balances are to be deposited in amount and duration so as to yield an equivalent to the deficiency; or a perfect balance of zero. One of these three must occur.

The next section of the report has to do with interest bearing deposit balances. The account number(s), balance(s), rate(s), and interest paid are recorded. There could also be additional items such as maintenance costs. For purposes of example we will assume the earning potential of the balance(s) offset the interest paid and any maintenance costs. Hence, there is neither a profit nor a loss to consider in this section.

Loan balances would be listed by loan number, balance, rate, interest revenue, fee revenue, total revenue, pool cost of funds rate, pool cost of funds amount, net interest income, net yield, administrative or maintenance expense, loss provision, institution G&A overhead, net spread and lastly assumed loan profit. Let's take each item separately and cover the specifics.

Column 1 is the loan number. This is optional, but most financial institutions find it advantageous to use loan numbers in customer reporting. It makes referencing easier.

Each column in the "loan balances section" is explained as follows:

Column 2 balance would be the average loan balance for the reported month.

Column 3 is for the loan rate to be applied against the balance. This rate may be flexible as many loans are prime rate, London Interbank Offered Rate (LIBOR), or money market indexed.

Column 4 is the result of multiplying column 2 times column 3. The result is the interest revenue.

In column 5 the pool cost of funds rate would be the agreed upon rate for use in customer profitability reporting. It could be the financial institution's experience in terms of average cost of funds for the previous quarter or year.

Column 6 reflects the multiplication of column 2 times column 5, the average loan balance times the pool cost-of-funds rate.

In column 7 the net interest income is derived by subtracting the pooled cost of funds (column 6) from the interest revenue (column 4).

Column 8 shows the net yield or spread percentage before operating and overhead expenses. The net yield or spread percentage is used by many financial institutions in planning their profitability. They try to manage to a predetermined spread. Essentially this is the revenue percentage yield minus the cost of funds percentage rate.

Column 9 is used for listing loan fees such as commitment and origination fees.

Column 10 is for administrative expense. This would include account officer time and other expenses deemed appropriate. This could be based on an hourly rate as developed through a cost study of account officers' expenses and other departmental expenses.

Column 11 is reserved for a loss provision. The provision is usually a factor based on experience of the loan type listed and any special circumstances that may be known.

Column 12 is for bank G&A overhead. The basis for allocating this must be determined so as to be consistent with the institutionwide allocation of overhead.

Column 13 is the net loan profit. It is arrived at by adding the net interest income (column 7) to the loan fee revenue (column 9) and then subtracting the administrative expense (column 10), the loan loss provision (column 11), and the institution's G&A (column 12).

The last item on the form is the overall customer relationship profitability (line 80). It is the culmination of adding fee-based services profitability plus any surplus deposit credits plus loan profitability.

This form can either be used as an account officer pro forma worksheet (in setting up a new customer) or as a regular report on the profitability of an existing customer relationship.

It is important to look at a customer's overall profitability relationship to avoid double counting such things as balances. That is, one needs to be careful to not count the same demand balances to support noncredit services from various areas of the institution plus having these balances form the basis for the rate of interest charged on loans.

It is important to note that in such a system as this, the deposit credit of $125.67 will have to be offset by an expense to demand deposits on a product reporting basis. If this is not done the revenue figures, and hence the internal institution profitability reporting, will be inflated in the amount of customer deposit credits given. If you choose not to expense DDA for the deposit credits given, then there should be a reconciling pool taking the offset.

Let's now move to a more detailed customer report format. The one shown in table 10-3 has sections for fee services revenue, fee services cost and profitability, billing, balance deficiencies, loan profitability, activity and deposit balances, and a profitability summary. Therefore, it is a comprehensive internal report that is used for the management of a customer relationship.

Section 1 is for reporting revenue from fee services. It covers such detailed information as product number, product name, standard unit price, applicable volume, implied revenue, waived fees, net revenue, revenue to be collected, and revenue to be applied against balances. The following list gives a brief explanation of each column.

Product number   A number assigned to a product based on a family or group of products, identical to number assigned for the same product in product and organizational reporting.

Product name   A one- or two-word literal designation of a product.

Standard unit price   The universal price as determined by a pricing committee or management team.

Volume   Applicable volume counts showing customer utilization of a particular product.

Total implied revenue   The result of multiplying the standard price times the volume. It is implied at this point because of the potential for price concessions.

TABLE 10-2 X, Y, Z Company Account Officer Worksheet for the Month of January ____

Fee Services

Column #	1	2	3	4	5	6	7
Product	Volume	Unit Price	Total Implied Revenue	Unit Cost	Total Cost	Waivers and Price Concessions	Total Implied Product Profit
Money transfer	1	$7.00	$ 7.00	$4.00	$ 4.00	$7.00	$(4.00)
Deposits	23	1.50	34.50	1.20	27.60	0	6.90
Checks paid	819	0.15	122.85	0.10	81.90	0	40.95
Total	—	—	$164.35	—	$113.50	$7.00	$43.85 Line 10

Accounting of total implied revenue

Amount of waivers and price concessions $ ____ 7.00 ____   Approval ____ XX ____

Amount of revenue to be collected in fees $ ____ 122.85 ____   Date invoice sent ____ Feb. 8

Amount of revenue to be compensated for in balances

$ ____ 34.50 ____   Line 15

Total $164.35   Line 20

Deposit credit rate ____ 7.0% ____   Line 30

Total implied revenue — fee services $ ____ 164.35 ____   (Same as line 10, col. 3)

DDA balances for month reported (Average ledger balance, noninterest bearing)

Account #	Balance	
D020500	$27,500	
Total	$27,500	Line 30
Less loan compensating bals.	2,500	
Less float	968	(3 × $10,000 [given] ÷ 31 = $967.74)
		# days float × Amount of float ÷ # days in month)
Less reserves @ 12%	3,184	(.12 × 26,532) (27,500 − 968 = 26,532 net demand)
Net average available balance	$20,848	Line 40 (For deposit credit purposes)

Deposit Credit

From line 20   deposit credit rate _____ 7.0%

From line 40   net average available balance _____ $20,848

Using $I = PRT$

$$\text{Deposit credit} = \frac{\text{line } 40 \times \text{line } 20 \times \text{\# Days in Month}}{100 \times 360 \text{ or } 365}$$

$$\text{Deposit credit} = \frac{\$20,848 \times 7 \times 31}{100 \times 360}$$

$$= \$125.67$$

Deposit

credit $125.67 _____ Line 45

Less Amount to be compensated

for in balances $ 34.50 _____ (From line 15) line 50

Surplus credit/deficiency

to be collected) $ 91.17 _____ Line 45 minus line 50) Line 55

Interest bearing deposit balances

1	2	3	4	
Account #	*Balance*	*Rate*	*Interest Paid*	
T 020500	$8,000	5.50%	$37.89	
	$8,000		$37.89	Line 60

$$I = \frac{\$8,000 \times 5.5 \times 31}{100 \times 360}$$

$$I = \$37.89$$

(continued)

TABLE 10-2 Continued

Loan Balances

Column #1	2	3	4	5	6	7	8	9	10	11	12	13
Loan Number	Balance	Curr Rate	Interest Revenue	Pool COF Rate	Pool Cost of Funds	Net Int. Income	Net Yield/ Spread	Loan Fee Revenue	Admin. Exp.	Loan Loss Provis.	G&A	Net Loan Profit
CLO20500	$50,000	12%	$516.67	9.5%	$409.03	$107.64	2.5%	—	$50.00	$25.00	$15.0	$17.64
		Prime +1										
Total	$50,000		$516.67		$409.03	$107.64	2.5%		$50.00	$25.00	$15.0	$17.64

$$I = PRT$$
$$I = \frac{50{,}000 \times 12 \times 31}{100 \times 360}$$
$$I = \$516.67$$

Column 6:
$$I = PRT$$
$$I = \frac{50{,}000 \times 9.5 \times 31}{100 \times 360}$$
$$I = \$409.03$$

Column 7:
$$I = PRT$$
$$P = \text{Col. 2}$$
$$R = \text{Col. 3}$$

$$I = PRT \quad (\text{Col. 4}$$
$$P = \text{Col. 2} \quad \text{minus}$$
$$R = \text{Col. 5} \quad \text{Col. 6})$$
$$= \text{Col. 5}$$
$$= \text{Col. 7} = \text{Col. 8}$$

Column 8: (Col. 3 minus Col. 5)

Column 13: (Col. 7 + Col. 9 minus Col. 10, Col. 11, and Col. 12)

Line 80 (Col. 7) — Line 70 (Col. 13)

Total customer relationship profit/loss _____ $152.66 _____ Line 80
$43.85 + $91.17 + $17.64 = $152.66
(Line 10, col. 7 + line 55 if positive plus line 70, col. 13)

TABLE 10-3 Report 1 (Internal), Page 1 of 6: Section 1

X, Y, Z Company
for Internal Account Officer Use Only
for the month of: January

*Commercial Master Account
Number:* 5712-020-500

Revenue (Fee Services)

*Contact: J. Boyd
Phone: 842-3786*

*Account officer: F. Gribbs
Phone: 683-4791*

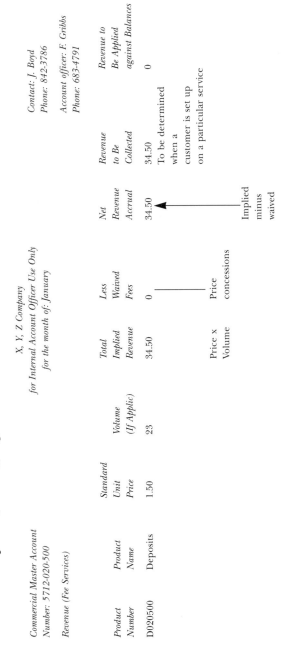

Product Number	Product Name	Standard Unit Price	Volume (If Applic.)	Total Implied Revenue	Less Waived Fees	Net Revenue Accrual	Revenue to Be Collected	Revenue to Be Applied against Balances
D020500	Deposits	1.50	23	34.50	0	34.50	34.50	0
		Price x Volume			Price concessions	Implied minus waived	To be determined when a customer is set up on a particular service	

Waived fees Price concessions. This reduction from implied revenue is a tool for managing waivers.

Net revenue accrual The remainder after waived fees have been subtracted from the total implied revenue. This is the accountable revenue in terms of making sure there are sufficient balances to compensate for this revenue or the revenue has been invoiced to the customer for collection.

Revenue to be collected Determination, when a customer is set up on a new service, as to whether to use fee basis and collection or a compensating balance basis.

Revenue to be applied against balances A default category for revenue accounting purposes. (That is, if a customer utilizes a financial institution's service and has not made a provision for how the service is to be paid for, it would default to this category. Obviously, if there are deficient balances then an invoice billing should be sent out. This would be done in order to collect the fees due or ask for compensating balances for a specified amount and number of days.)

Section 2 of this detailed report (shown in table 10-4) has to do with cost and profitability reporting by product for fee services. The idea is to report the net profit to the institution of a specific relationship with a commercial customer. The information being reported includes: product number, product name, unit cost, applicable volume, net revenue, and net profit.

The unit cost is developed as a result of a cost study. Generally, it should include bank G&A when being used in a customer profitability report. The total cost is the extension of the unit cost times a volume.

The net revenue is taken from the previous section. That is, it represents the actual charges for the services being provided. It is the implied revenue minus any price concessions. The net profit is the net revenue minus the total cost.

TABLE 10-4 Report 1 (Internal), Page 2 of 6, Section 2

Fee Services Cost and Profitability

Account Number	Product Name	Unit Cost	Volume (If Applic)	Total Cost	Net Revenue	Net Profit
D020500	Deposits	1.20	23	27.60	34.50	6.90 (Net revenue) minus total cost)
Total	—	—	23	27.60	34.50	6.90

TABLE 10-5 Report 1 (Internal), Page 3 of 6, Section 3

Billing

Accounts Receivable Aging

	This Month	*Last Month*	*60 to 90 days*	*90 to 120 days*	*120 to 180 days*	*180 days and Over*	*Total to Be Collected*
Revenue to be collected	34.50	55.00	0	0	0	0	89.50
Total	34.50	55.00	0	0	0	0	89.50

Section 3 of report 1 (shown in table 10-5) is a recap of any billings to the customer and the aging of receivables regarding that customer. The revenue to be collected is accounted for by the following columns: this month, last month, 60 to 90 days, 90 to 120 days, 120 to 180 days, and 180 days and over. The idea is to segment the receivables according to how long they have been on the books as a collectible revenue. A policy question to be resolved is whether the institution should charge interest on accounts receivables that are outstanding for greater than a reasonable period of time such as 30 days.

TABLE 10-6 Report 1 (Internal), Page 4 of 6, Section 4

Balance Deficiencies to Be Collected

Invoice Reference	*Month of Deficiency*	*One-Day Equivalency Balance*	*30-Day Equivalency Balance*	*Fee Equivalency*	*Interest Rate*
020500-5712	November	450,045	15,000	150	12%
.					
.					
.					
Total	—	↑	↑		

Fee equivalency
$I = PRT.$
where I = the fee
to be compensated
for with balances
or collected fees.

1-day equivalency
I = Fee equivalency
P = Balance to be determined
R = Deposit credit rate
T = 1 day,
where $P = I/RT$

$$P = \frac{150}{.12 \ \times \ \frac{1}{360}}$$

$$P = \frac{150}{.0003333}$$

$$P = 450,045$$

30-day equivalency
I = Fee equivalency
P = Balance to be determined
R = Deposit credit rate
T = 30 days,
where $P = I/RT$

$$P = \frac{150}{.12 \ \times \ \frac{30}{360}}$$

$$P = \frac{150}{.01}$$

$$P = 15,000$$

Section 4 of report 1 (table 10-6) is devoted to accounting for balance deficiencies. This goes back to the revenue that is accounted for via compensating balances. Revenue to be collected via compensating balances is called analysis charges. The balance deficiencies to be collected section includes the following columns; invoice reference; month of deficiency; a one-day balance equivalency; and a 30-day balance equivalency. The columns are explained as follows:

Invoice Reference   The reference number of the invoice that was sent out requesting compensating balances fees be remitted

Month of deficiency   The month when the deficiency occurred (an audit trail for keeping track of deficiencies by chronological occurrence)

One-day equivalency balance   How much the customer would have to deposit with the bank for one day in order to satisfy the deficiency (using formula, $I = PRT$, where P (principal balance) is the unknown to be solved and I = the fee to be recovered

30-day equivalency balance   How much would have to be deposited by the customer in order to satisfy the deficiency (using the formula $I = PRT$)

Fee equivalency   The accrued fees for services provided that were to be compensated for via customer deposit balances (the amount the customer would have to pay in cash if the customer decided to do so)

Interest rate   The deposit credit interest rate that is in effect for each individual deficiency being reported

In section 5 of the detailed report (table 10-7) the focus is on loan profitability. The column headings are as follows:

Loan number   Identifier providing an audit trail showing where the information came from and which loan is being reported

Balance   The average balance for the period, of each loan being reported, with an asterisk to signal past due balances

Current rate   The rate being charged the customer for each loan

Interest revenue   The gross interest income charged for the loan for the reported month

TABLE 10-7 Report 1 (Internal), Page 5 of 6: Section 5

Loan Profitability

Loan Number	Balance	Current Rate	Interest Revenue	Pool COF Rate	Pool Cost of Funds	Net Interest Income
CL020 500	50,000	12%	$516.67	9.5%	$409.03	$107.64
:						
:						
Total						

Net Yield/ Spread	Loan Fee Revenue	Admin Expenses	Loan Loss Provision	Institution's G&A	Net Loan Profit
2.5%	—	$50.00	$25.00	$15.00	$17.64

Pool COF rate   The institution's pool rate for cost of funds, used for internal funds allocations

Pool cost of funds   The amount charged internally or allocated for funding the loan; the result of multiplying the balance times the pool COF rate for the period of time specified by the report, usually one month

Net interest income   An amount derived by subtracting the pool cost of funds from the interest revenue

Net yield or spread   The percentage yield derived by dividing the net interest income by the average loan balance, using the formula $I = PRT$ where R = the unknown rate to be solved for

Loan fee revenue   Any loan fees accruing to the loan for the reporting period e.g., commitment fees and origination fees

Administrative expense   Any direct or allocated expenses involved in originating, booking, and administering a loan are included here, e.g., out-of-pocket expenses, account officer's time, and overhead allocations

Loan loss provision   An allocation based on experience for each loan category listed, usually is multiplied by the outstanding balance as a percentage factor

Institution's G&A   An allocation to each loan of the institution's overhead, sometimes based on outstanding balances

Net loan profit   The amount that results from adding the net interest income to the loan fee revenue and then subtracting administrative expense, loan loss provisions, and the institution's G&A

Section 6 of report 1 (see table 10-8) is an internal reporting of an individual customer's deposit balances. The columns are explained as follows:

Type of account   A literal description of the account type, e.g., non-interest-bearing and interest-bearing

Account Number   The checking account number

Ledger (book) balance   The average book or ledger balance for the reporting period

Less float   The average amount of uncollected balances, using either actual float or a factor based on experience, to be subtracted from the ledger balance

Less compensating   Required compensating balances either for specific loans or for services provided, subtracted from the ledger balance

Less reserves   Any applicable regulatory reserves, subtracted from the ledger balance to arrive at the net available balance

Net available balance   The balance that is used in calculating deposit credits; the net balance after float, compensating, and reserve balances have been subtracted from the ledger balance

Interest rate   The rate for payment of interest on interest-bearing deposits

Interest paid   The amount of interest paid on interest-bearing deposits

Deposit credit rate   An internal rate assigned by the institution, used to determine the value of non-interest-bearing deposits—an artificial rate determined by the institution's management

Surplus deposit credits   The hypothetical interest amount for the surplus deposits, a benefit to the institution, included as a profit item if it is positive

An institution policy question to be resolved regards interest-bearing deposits. There are assumed profits if the institution is paying, for example, 5 percent and is able to place the surplus on the market for 12 percent. The difference between what the institution pays the depositor for interest and what it could receive on the open market could be assumed as a profit. Of course the deposit credit rate may be lowered to account for such things as administrative expenses.

Section 7 of report 1 (table 10-8) is a profitability summary. It is the aggregate of the net profit for fee services in section 2; the net loan profit in section 5; and the surplus deposit credits minus interest paid in section 6. It shows the customer relationship profitability for the month being reported and for year-to-date. It also has columns for actual-to-plan comparisons.

TABLE 10-8 Report 1 (Internal), Page 6 of 6: Section 6 (January) and Section 7

Deposit Balances

Type of Account	Account #	X Ledger (Book) Balance	Less Float	Less Compensating	Less Reserves	Net Available Balance	Interest Rate	Interest Paid	Deposit Credit Rate	Surplus Deposit Credits
DDA Non-interest-bearing	D020500	72,000	1,500	20,000	8,460	42,040	—	—	8 %	289.61
Total		72,000	1,500	20,000	8,460	42,040	—	—	—	289.61
									Interest rate	Pseudo interest credit (surplus) amount
Interest-bearing deposits	0	0	0	0	0	0	—	—	—	—
Total	0	0	0	0	0	0	—	—	—	—

Section 7

Profitability summary

$$I = PRT$$

$$I = \frac{\$42{,}040 \times .08 \times 31}{360}$$

$$I = \$289.61$$

	Actual	Plan
Total profit/loss for the month	314.15	200
Total profit/loss YTD	314.15	200

6.90	section 2
17.64	section 5
289.61	section 6
314.15	

Report 1 is detailed and provides much information to the account officer. It is not to be shown to the customer. However, something must be made available to the customer. Report 2, shown in tables 10-9 to 10-13 is designed to mirror the internal report while leaving out proprietary cost and profitability data.

Report 2 has five sections. None of them lists any cost or profitability data. Section 1 list the fee services used by the customer; section 2 is a billing statement; section 3 lists the balance deficiencies to be paid; section 4 shows the customer loan activity; and section 5 lists the deposit balances.

Section 1 of report 2 (shown in table 10-9) is similar to section 1 of report 1 except that the term *fees* is used instead of *revenue*, as in "fees to be paid" rather than "revenue to be collected." It is a detailed listing of the services used by the customer during the period being reported.

Section 2 (table 10-10) is a billing invoice with an accounts receivable aging feature. It is similar to section 3 of report 1. The difference is it describes the revenue to be paid rather than the revenue to be collected.

Section 3 of report 2 (table 10-11) is the balance deficiencies to be paid rather than the balance deficiencies to be collected as in report 1.

Section 4 of report 2 (table 10-12) lists the customer's loan activity. It has the following columns:

Loan number   The number assigned to a specific loan

Previous balance   The outstanding loan balance at the beginning of the reporting period.

Current interest rate   The current interest rate being charged on the loan

Interest accrued   The amount of interest accrued for the reporting period for each loan listed

Date last payment received   An acknowledgment to the customer of receipt of payment

Amount of last payment   The amount of the last payment

Amount applied to principal   The portion of the payment received that has been applied to the principal

Amount applied to interest   The portion of the payment received that has been applied to interest

New balance   The remaining balance after the payment has been deducted from the principal and interest accruals

TABLE 10-9 Customer Report 2 (External), Page 1 of 5: Section 1

Commercial Master Account
Number: 5712-020-500

X, Y, Z Company
for the month of January

Contact: J. Boyd
Phone: 842-3786

Account officer: F. Gribbs
Phone: 683-4791

Revenue (Fee Services)
(Incurred)

Product Number	Product Name	Standard Unit Price	Volume (If Applic.)	Total Implied Fees	Less Waived Fees	Net Fees Accrual	Fees to Be Paid	Fees to Be Applied Against Balances
D020500	Deposits	1.50	23	34.50 (Price × Volume	0	34.50	34.50 (To be determined when a customer is set up on a particular service)	0
					Price concessions)	(Implied Minus Waived)		

TABLE 10-10 Customer Report 2 (External), Page 2 of 5: Section 2

Billing

Accounts Receivable Aging

	This Month	*Last Month*	*60 to 90 Days*	*90 to 120 Days*	*120 to 180 Days*	*180 Days and Over*	*Total to be Paid*
Fees to be paid	34.50	55.00	0	0	0	0	89.50
Total	34.50	55.00	0	0	0	0	89.50

TABLE 10-11 Customer Report 2 (External), Page 3 of 5: Section 3

Balance Deficiencies to Be Paid

Invoice Reference	*Month of Deficiency*	*One-Day Equivalency Balance*	*30-Day Equivalency Balance*	*Fee Equivalency*	*Interest Rate*
020500-5712	November	450,045	15,000	150	12%
Total					

Fee equivalency: $I = PRT$,
Where I is the fee to be compensated for with balances or collected fees.

1-Day Equivalency	30-Day equivalency
I = Fee equivalency	I = Fee equivalency
P = Balance to be determined	P = Balance to be determined
R = Deposit credit rate	R = Deposit credit rate
T = 1 day,	T = 30 days,
Where $P = I/RT$	Where $P = I/RT$

TABLE 10-12 Customer Report 2 (External), Page 4 of 5: Section 4

Loan Activity

Loan Number	*Previous (Beginning) Balance*	*Current Interest Rate*	*Interest Accrued*	*Date Last Payment Received*
CL020500	$50,000	12%	$516.67	12/31

Amount of Last Payment	*Amount Applied to Principal*	*Amount Applied to Interest*	*New Balance*
$516.67	0	$516.67	$50,000

TABLE 10-13 Customer Report 2 (External), Page 5 of 5: Section 5

Deposit Balances

Type of Account	Account #	Ledger (Book) Balance	Less Float
DDA non-interest bearing	D020500	72,000	1,500
Total		72,000	1,500
Interest-bearing deposits			
Total			

Less Compensating	Less Reserves	Net Available Balance	Interest Rate	Interest Paid
20,000	8,460	42,000		
20,000	8,460	42,000		

Section 5 of report 2 (table 10-13) does not list deposit credits for non-interest-bearing accounts as is done in report 1. this is a debatable issue. Some financial institution managers believe that you should show customers the amount of credit bearing given to them for the net collected balances they have maintained with the institution. Any amount of credit in excess of that required to compensate the institution for fee-based services rendered could be shown as being available to support other services provided the customer for which no specific charges was made.

CONSUMER REPORTING

The next area to cover in reporting is the consumer customer base. The capability of calling out special reports is of interest here. There is one segment on the consumer side that may impel a financial institution toward regular reporting—individuals with high net worth. Given their discretionary assets, such customers are a market segment that provides unique opportunities to an institution in terms of cross-selling and specialized individual services.

A household profile of service utilization will provide the institution with much needed information for coordination in cross-selling. In some financial institutions individual customers are known personally even though there is no customer information system. However, as an institution grows, so do the number and complexity of relationships. When we combine this fact with the fact that financial institutions traditionally experience measurable turnover in their consumer base and staff annually, we see the need for systematic tracking of customers. Customer turnover is costly both in forgone future revenue but also in organization and closeout processing costs.

The reasons for customer turnover vary. Of course some leave because they move out of town, but the institution wants to avoid losing customers because of misunderstandings or dissatisfaction with the institution's services. Customers have a tendency to expect everyone at their institution to know everything about their relationship with the institution and their specialized needs, and to understand their personal finances.

For example, a customer may wish to purchase traveler's checks. He or she may mention to the teller that he or she would like to have the fees waived. The teller may not know the customer. Unless the teller can verify the customer has a deposit that is significant enough to offset the waived fees, that teller will have to rely on good manners and some guessing. Of course the teller may know the customer and that person may be a customer of long standing and hence may be known. If this is the case there is no problem. Good judgment, institution policy, community relations, and the like come into practice in such situations. Knowledge of the customer's profile would give the teller a distinct advantage of being informed. Continuing with the example, what if the customer had a $100,000 certificate of deposit with the institution? Further, what if the teller doesn't know about it? This is one of the reasons customer relationship information is important.

The financial institution needs to be able to look at a report on paper or on a computer terminal screen that describes the customer's accounts. The institution's managers also need to be able to call up profile reports for segmenting the customer base. This is particularly important in product sales campaigns. Table 10-14 is a sample design for a consumer customer report.

The consumer customer profile report as illustrated by table 10-14 can be a valuable marketing tool.

Household/family names(s), social security numbers, ages and gender   The given names of each known member in the family and their respective ages and gender.

Street address and city   The primary residence of a household or family, multiple residences.

Phone   Home and/or work phone number(s).

Maiden name   Mother's maiden name or some other authentication (personal identification code).

Credit rating   The household's rating for creditworthiness.

Date of last rating   Date of the last credit rating.

Customer date   Date the customer initiated a relationship with the institution, important in ascertaining stability.

TABLE 10-14 Consumer Customer Relationship Profile, Customer Number 020829

Household/Family Names:	*Social Security #*	*Age:*	*Gender:*
• *Jones, Dale H.*	*000-00-0001*	*32*	*M*
•			
•			
•			

Address: 214 Consumer Avenue, Local city USA

Phone: 842 -3769   Maiden Name: _____ Credit Rating: A+

Date of Last Rating: 8/1/xx   Customer Since(Date): 2/4/xx

Commercial Account Relationship#: _____

Deposits (Checking, Savings, Certificates)

Origination Date	*Account Number*	*Household/Family Name(s)*	*Today's Balance*	*Highest Balance Last 30 Days*
2/4/xx	DD020829 (Alphanumeric code includes account type designator.)	Jones	2,876 (Asterisk indicates overdrawn or hold.)	3,912

Loans

Origination Date	*Account Number*	*Household/Family Name(s)*	*Current Balance*
8/5xx	AL020829	Jones	8,295 (Asterisk indicates past due account.)

Credit Lines/Charge Cards

Origination Date	*Account Number*	*Household/Family Names*	*Current Balance Owned*	*Current Line*
8/9/xx	CC020829	Jones	150 (Asterisk indicates past due/lost card.)	2,500

Services Utilized (last 12 months)

Date Used	*Product Name*	*Fees Paid*	*Fees Waived*	*Volume* (If applicable)

Historical (Previous Loans, Deposits, Business)

Origination Date	*Account Number* (Alphanumeric code includes Account type designator.)	*Highest Balance*	*Date Closed* (If applicable) (Double asterisk indicates an early payoff.)

Household Income Range: 35,000
Narrative: (15 words or less)

Commercial account relationship number Should the customer have a business account, the business relationship number would be listed here. (Some financial institutions even go further and assign master relationship numbers to cover multiple companies and linkages to individuals.)

Deposits The organization date of the deposit account(s); the account number (with account type described); account holder name(s); today's balance; and the highest balance in the last 30 days. This provides information on what types of deposits the customer has with the institution and how much. There could also be warning flags on overdrawn conditions or holds on funds.

Loans The origination data of each loan; the account number (with type of loan descriptors); borrower's name(s); and current balance (with asterisk for a past due account)

Credit lines/charge cards Origination date; account number (with type of credit line); account/cardholder name(s); and current balance (with asterisk for a past due account or a lost card)

Services utilized Services the customer has used during the past 12 months. As important as deposit, loans, and credit lines/card information, it gives a profile of the customer's financial services needs. In cross-selling the more you can profile a customer the more exacting you can be in identifying cross-selling opportunities. Each service utilized is listed by data used, product name, fees paid, fees waived, and volume (if applicable).

Historical Information on a customer's previous relationships with the institution, may be useful in making decisions about the granting of future loans and waived fees. Include origination date of account; account number (with description code); highest balance; and date closed (with a double asterisk for early payoff on loans).

Household income Either a range or a coded system designator of a more exacting number.

Narrative Brief special relationship instructions.

These are just some examples of information that can be gathered on the consumer customer base. With the proper systems the data on individual customers and households can be aggregated by various geographic and demographic groupings for marketing analysis. What is important is to gather information that is useful to the institution and will enhance its relationship with the customers in addition to providing further selling opportunities and therefore more profit.

Essential Decision Information

A financial institution's management must make decisions daily that affect its direction, image, goals, and profitability. In order to make these decisions they need accurate and representative information. The information must be presented in a format that is easily understood. The approach used to derive the data must be easily understood. It must make sense. The format should make all aspects apparent.

MEASURING PROFITABILITY

Earlier in this book the concept of the profitability triad was introduced. You will recall organizational, product, and customer profitability must all tie in on the bottom line of the institution's profitability. Table 11-1 conceptually shows how the same

TABLE 11-1 The Three Dimensions of Profitability

Category	Organizational Profitability				Product Profitability					Customer Profitability					
	Organizations			Total	Products				Total	Customers					Total
	X	Y	Z		A	B	C	D		1	2	3	4	5	
Revenue	15	20	65	100	20	35	15	30	100	5	4	25	42	24	100
Expense	17	15	43	75	15	25	17	18	75	3	4	18	33	17	75
Net Profit	(2)	5	22	25	5	10	(2)	12	25	2	(0)	7	9	7	25

data is arrayed in three dimensions. The table illustrates an oversimplified example of an institution that has only four products being sold by three organizations who have only five customers. What is important is to report aggregates for each of the three that either tie or reconcile. This concept is similar to H_2O being presented in three forms—water, ice and vapor.

This triad reporting assists management when it seeks out information on the causes of decline in profits. It is also valuable when management wishes to improve profitability, even when the operation is already healthy. Note that methods used to allocate indirect costs to organizational units, products, and customers can influence their indicated profitability.

On a cross-matrix basis it is possible to sort out products, organizations, and customers that are less than profitable. For example in table 11-1 two loss situations are apparent; Organization X, and product C reflect losses for the institution. The data for customer 2 may reveal that certain controllable factors in organization X and product C are contributors to this breakeven only situation. This suggests that the obvious factors be dealt with first, but one need not stop there. Often there are hidden factors that decrease the profit potential of an organization, product, and customer.

In analyzing these factors one may well find a common denominator throughout the triad that is affecting the profitability. Are there other factors that are in need of improvement? There may be.

Certainly everyone would agree customer 1 is highly profitable on a revenue to expense ratio. But are there further opportunities for profit in this relationship?

It is this kind of cross-matrix analysis that allows an institution to improve its profitability.

MANAGEMENT'S INFORMATION NEEDS

The decisions management must make can be wide and vary in complexity. This is particularly true as management seeks to optimize the profitability and operational posture of the institution. This decisions may be categorized as follows:

Staffing
   Staff reductions
   Hiring additional staff
   Salary administration changes
   Organizational realignments

Operations
   Automation
   Work flow changes
   Centralization/decentralization
   Introducing/discontinuing/changing a product

Balance Sheet
Asset/liability management, decisions on funding, loans, futures, float and rate change, volatility/vulnerability
Asset/liability pricing

Marketing
Advertising/solicitation campaigns
Fee pricing changes

This is only a partial list of what management needs from cost analysis for decision making. It does point out the ever increasing need for cost and profitability data, whether it be historical, planned, or a pro forma sensitivity analysis. Later in this chapter a brief overview of analytical constructs will be presented.

Available Information versus Ideal Information

There may be requests for information that does not exist. Consider how the information is to be used. You may find the information is available but in a format or combination other than that requested. When data is limited the cost analyst must be imaginative in discerning the actual needs of the requestor.

Some requests take too long to fulfill. Be sure to weigh the potential benefits of the information against the cost of obtaining it. The person requesting the information may have no idea how much effort would be required to obtain it and may be willing to do without it. Management needs to be aware that some requests may be superfluous or not cost effective to carry out.

Unique Information

One of the biggest challenges in cost analysis is meeting requests for one-time-only, highly specialized, and nonroutine information. This type of information is usually directed toward a unique decision. The analyst may have to synthesize the information based on similar activity or situations. Such requests demand urgent response. The quickest solution may be to work with aggregates on a summary level and then draw inferences toward a more detailed level.

The goal is to derive data that will provide management with data representative enough so as to give them correct decision information. When time is short and information difficult to obtain, the creative skills of the analyst are invoked. Information inferred can usually be tested within the context of simulation. A good hedge is to provide "what if" kinds of analyses. These can provide probable ranges as a protection against the diminished accuracy caused by insufficient data and lack of time.

Staffing Information

In staff reductions the cost of current staff versus the cost of planned residual staff needs to be measured. It is important that staff equivalencies and their related compensation be accounted for. The impact measurement of staff reductions is dependent upon this. (The measurement and impact analysis of staff changes are extensively covered in chapter 13.)

An issue that needs to be resolved is normal attrition versus layoffs or displacements. This will no doubt determine the timing of any departures. The issue of internal migration needs to be reviewed as well. How many of the staff will simply do other work and remain on payroll? How many will transfer elsewhere in the institution? The bottom line usually is the difference between soft dollar reductions (reallocated elsewhere) and hard dollar reductions (terminations).

In staff additions the hiring of additional staff should be weighed against the benefit of their production or income generation. (This should also be done with existing staff.) Each addition should have measurable benefits to the institution. In some areas this may be difficult to ascertain. In such cases measurable objectives should be set forth. That is, the desired production or income generation should be stated as an objective and then measured. The impact of staff additions should be quantified both in compensation and in staff count. The impact should be determined for "this year" and "next year."

Organizational realignments of staff usually involve functional realignments. Often these are done in order to reduce redundancies, streamline efficiency, and compress the layers of reporting. A before and after analysis should include their quantification.

Operations Information

The cost/benefit of a proposal for automation must be carefully considered. Automation often results in a future benefit of not having to hire as much additional staff as previously planned.

Automation usually involves significant development costs and an appreciable outlay for hardware, software, and training. The benefits of automation generally are in the area of more efficient operations and increased capacity. Some of the beneficial quantification will therefore fall into the soft dollar category.

Work flow changes are similar to automation in that improved efficiency is the overall objective. Any time savings may produce added capacity. Staff savings may also result when efficiency is improved. Sometimes this means reallocating staff to other activities that have been in need of additional attention. Staff reductions should be measurable and defined as either "managed to" hard dollars or simply soft dollar reallocations.

Centralization/decentralization migrations are interesting to analyze. In the latent stages of a decentralized environment there may be several redundancies to quantify. This is particularly true if an institution has experienced significant change. A growing institution that is decentralized may find itself with a headquarters staff that is redundant in relation to a decentralized staff. An institution that is decentralized and is retrenching may find itself with too much staff all the way around. It is probably easier to quantify the benefits of migration from decentralization to centralization than it is from centralization to decentralization. This is because the benefits are usually qualitative in nature when an institution is decentralizing its functions.

Introducing/discontinuing/changing a product entails looking for the incremental changes. "What will go away or appear as a result of the proposed action?" needs to be looked at. The quantitative impact of increased production or lower production should be analyzed in terms of additional resources, idle resources, or obsolete resources.

Balance Sheet

Asset/liability management decisions require a microcosm analysis of maturities, funding needs, interest rate gaps, core deposit mixes, the impact of float, and downside risk. The basic analyses required for this function are immense. It is imperative that one be aware of the need for much analytical support in a function that has such a heavy impact on the liquidity and net interest income of the institution.

Pricing balance sheet products comes in the form of asset pricing and liability pricing. On the (asset) loan side, the analysis focuses on the expected spreads versus a benchmark cost of funds. On the (liability) deposit side, interest rates are viewed in terms of market competition and regulatory statutes. In calculating the benefit of additional deposits, one offsets the cost of those deposits against their placement value in the marketplace (interest revenue minus cost of funds and administrative costs). Core deposit cost and retention are usually the key issues on the liability side.

In pricing balance sheet items it is important to conduct sensitivity analyses on potential changes as a result of pricing changes. A scale of possible changes in balances given specified levels of change in interests rates is produced. The changes in balances are set as a function of changes in pricing. For example, on the asset side the risk of revenue loss for asset pricing changes is quantified along with the potential for revenue gains.

Marketing Information

Advertising and direct mail solicitation campaigns are quantified in terms of market response. Aside from institutional advertising, special campaigns can be quantified in terms of response and success. What is analyzed is the cost of bringing in new business. The cost is compared to the value of the resultant new business.

Decisions on pricing changes for fee-based services are clarified by sensitivity analyses. They show the profitability impact of proposed changes. Two important things are affected: revenue and customer response. As prices are raised, the customer attrition rate may increase. In addition to projecting this attrition, the potential net change in revenue must be reasonably known.

EXAMPLE DECISIONS

Staffing

Suppose there is a request from a processing area for an additional staff member. No industrial engineering data is available, but there is historical data on activity volumes and staffing. The data for the previous twelve months is listed in table 11-2.

Before we look at the cost aspect of this study, let us review the hours worked to see if a valid inference can be drawn. The per month volume ranged from a low of 16.08 in month 1 to a higher 23.61 in month 10. The center was at full complement of staff in month 1. The volume was also at its lowest. In month 10 the center was down one person. This meant they had only 75 percent ($3 \div 4 = 0.75$) of their normal staffing. Here, the hours worked is the important variable. For three persons there was a combined 478 hours of work. If each person were scheduled to work 160 hours

TABLE 11-2 Activity Volumes and Staffing

		1	2	3	4
		Staff Count	Staff Hours Worked	Volume	Average Volume per Hour
Month	1	4	625	10,050	16.08
	2	4	630	11,000	17.46
	3	4	627	10,800	17.22
	4	3	480	10,500	21.88
	5	4	629	12,000	19.08
	6	4	633	11,200	17.69
	7	4	642	11,100	17.29
	8	4	644	11,800	18.32
	9	4	641	12,350	19.27
	10	3	478	11,285	23.61
	11	4	625	11,890	19.02
	12	4	643	12,400	19.28
(most recent)					
Monthly average		3.83	608.08[1]	11,364.58	18.69[2]

[1]12-months total ÷ 12.
[2]Col. 3 avg ÷ col. 2 avg.

that month, the gross available hours would be 480 hours (160 × 3 = 480). The total is just two hours short of this. We can assume that essentially the workload did not cause an overtime condition, since we see the overall hours aggregating to slightly less than the gross available. It would be helpful to have overtime data available in order to determine if the 478 hours involved any overtime during peak processing.

With the available data we do not know what the upper limits are. We do know the center can take a capacity of 23.61 units per hour per staff member. May be each person can do more. The data suggests the center is possibly overstaffed at this point. It may be that quick turnaround during peak processing is the reason for having that fourth person.

Let's assume the average compensation for each staff member is $12 per hour. Aside from considering other operating costs we see the following costs occurring for the previous twelve months:

	1	*2*	*3*
Cost	*$ Per Hour*	*Volume Per*	*Per Unit Cost*
Ranges	*Compensation*	*Staff Member*	*(col. 2 ÷ col. 1)*
High	$12	16.08/hour	$0.7463
Low	12	23.61/hour	0.5083
Average	12	18.69/hour	0.6421

If a fifth person were added the average compensation cost per unit would obviously increase because of the resultant decreases in average volume per staff member. This of course, assumes there is no significant increase in business planned in the near future.

Unless there are additional factors affecting the center, the data suggests an additional staff member is not warranted. This is particularly true as one looks at months 4 and 10. It even suggests the center is overstaffed.

Operations

Assume that management wishes to introduce a new product. There are many factors to consider such as research and development, marketing campaigns, future earnings, and earnings per share impact. The format for such a profit-and-loss impact analysis appears in table 11-3. It allows management to see a project's impact on revenue, expenses, taxes, and earnings per share over a four-year period. This type of analysis can be used for projecting the profitability impact of any proposed or ongoing project.

TABLE 11-3 Proposed Product's Projected Profit/Loss

Category	Year 0	Year 1	Year 2	Year 3	Year 4	Total
Revenue						
Fee revenue	$ —	$ xxx	$ xxx	$ xxx	$ xxx	$ xxx
Balance earning	—	xxx	xxx	xxx	xxx	xxx
(credit for surplus funds)						
Total revenue						
Expenses						
Research and Development	xxx	—	—	—	—	xxx
Compensation		xxx	xxx	xxx	xxx	xxx
Marketing		xxx	xxx	xxx	xxx	xxx
Depreciation	xxx	xxx	xxx	xxx	xxx	xxx
Other operating expense		xxx	xxx	xxx	xxx	xxx
Institution G&A	xxx	xxx	xxx	xxx	xxx	xxx
Total operating expense						
Cost of funds	xxx	xxx	xxx	xxx	xxx	xxx
Total expense	xxx	xxx	xxx	xxx	xxx	xxx
Profit/Loss before taxes	(xxx)	xxx	xxx	xxx	xxx	xxx
Assumed taxes (benefit)						
Income tax (benefit)	(xxx)	xxx	xxx	xxx	xxx	xxx
Total taxes (benefit)	$(xxx)	$ xxx	$ xxx	$ xxx	$ xxx	$ xxx
Net profit (loss) after taxes	$(xxx)	$ xxx	$ xxx	$ xxx	$ xxx	$ xxx
Cumulative net profit/						
(loss) after taxes	$(xxx)	$ xxx	$ xxx	$ xxx	$ xxx	—
Earnings per share impact	$(xxx)	$ xxx	$ xxx	$ xxx	$ xxx	$ xxx

Each line item in table 11-3 is explained as follows:

Fee revenue   Projected fee revenue accruing as a result of the new product. (A separate detailed schedule showing fees and volumes should be attached.)

Balance earnings   Any applicable earnings credit from balances that may be attracted by the product

Total revenue   Fee revenue plus any balance attracting earnings (assumes the product is a fee-based service as distinguished from a balance sheet product such as a loan)

Research & development   Systems development, compensation, other operating and premarketing research attributable to the product (assumes a policy of expensing R&D as it is incurred)

Compensation   All soft dollar and hard dollar compensation associated with the ongoing production and delivery of the product (a separate detailed schedule could be produced)

Marketing   The cost of advertising, solicitation, and product information preparation

Depreciation   Straight line, reflects the amortization of capital expenditures incurred on behalf of the product

Other operating expense   All other operating expenses incurred in the production and delivery of the product. (Significant line items should be detailed on another schedule.)

Institution G&A   The associated overhead allocation in order to ensure proper accounting for Institution G&A

Cost of funds   The cost of carrying balances for unrecouped expenditures. This includes R&D, capital expenditures, and operating expenses.

Total Expense   The aggregate of all expenses

Profit (loss) before taxes   Total revenue minus total expense

Income tax (benefit)   Applicable city, state, and federal taxes or benefits

Total taxes (benefits)   Income tax/benefit plus investment tax credit

Net profit (loss) after taxes   Profit/loss before taxes minus total taxes/benefits

Cumulative net profit/(loss) after taxes   The cumulative aggregate of net profit (loss) after taxes, used in calculating the payback period

Earnings per share   The net profit (loss) divided by the number of common shares outstanding

The summary schedule shown in table 11-4 is just as important as the previous one. It aligns the profit or loss impact to a cash flow impact. This allows for a number of financial analysis techniques to be applied against the results. The following are explanations of each line item in table 11-4.

Net profit (loss) after tax   Carryover from the previous schedule

Cash flow adjustments   Additions and subtractions to the net profit/loss after tax that will bring it to a cash flow basis

TABLE 11-4 Proposed Product's Projected Cash Flow Impact

Category	Year 0	Year 1	Year 2	Year 3	Year 4	Total
Net Profit (loss) after tax	$(xxx)	$ xxx	$ xxx	$ xxx	$ xxx	$ xxx
Cash flow adjustments						
Add depreciation straight line	xxx	xxx	xxx	xxx	xxx	xxx
Add tax impact of accelerated depreciation	xxx	xxx	xxx	xxx	xxx	xxx
Subtract ( ) capital expenditures	(xxx)					(xxx)
Add cost of funds	xxx	xxx	xxx	xxx	xxx	xxx
Subtract tax impact of cost of funds	(xxx)	(xxx)	(xxx)	(xxx)	(xxx)	(xxx)
Total adjustments	$(xxx)	$ xxx	$ xxx	$ xxx	$ xxx	$ xxx
Net after tax cash flow	$(xxx)	$ xxx	$ xxx	$ xxx	$ xxx	$ xxx
Cumulative net after tax cash flow	$(xxx)	$ xxx	$ xxx	$ xxx	$ xxx	—
Net discounted after tax cash flow	$(xxx)	$ xxx	$ xxx	$ xxx	$ xxx	$ xxx
Earnings per share impact	$(xxx)	$ xxx	$ xxx	$ xxx	$ xxx	$ xxx

Payback period _____ years

Discounted payback period _____ years

Internal rate of return (IRR) _____ %

ROA impact _____

ROE impact _____

Depreciation (straight line)   Adding back of straight line depreciation that was used as an expense in the projected profit and loss

Tax impact of accelerated depreciation   The adding of the tax consequences of using accelerated depreciation, assuming the calculation is carried out elsewhere.

(The obvious impact is an additional tax benefit, the advantage of which is smoothed in later years. If it is carried out far enough the net advantage is zero.)

Capital expenditures   The actual cash flow attributable to capital purchases is reflected on this line as an outgoing cash flow.

(In the previous P&L, only the amortization (depreciation) of it had been reflected. This is why depreciation is added back in on this schedule in setting up the cash flow items.)

Total adjustments   All adjustments totaled; ( ) net outflow.

Net after tax flow   The net profit/loss after tax is added to the total adjustments; reflects the overall cash flow; ( ) net outflow of funds.

Payback period   The number of years and/or months it takes to recoup a negative cash flow; the point at which the negative cash flow has been brought to zero

Net discounted after tax cash flow   The cash flow as discounted by a specified interest rate, usually a desired rate of return or cost of funds rate or a specified benchmark rate

Discounted payback period   Takes into account the cash flow discounting and reflects the number of years and/or months it takes to recoup the negative cash flow; overcomes the drawback of "payback period" which ignores the dollar value of future benefits

Internal rate of return (IRR)   The interest rate that equates the present value of the expected future receipts (cash flow) to the cost of the investment outlay (year of investment); also the discount rate that causes NPV to equal zero.

Earning per share impact   The net profit/loss after tax, divided by the number of shares outstanding, done for each of the years listed in the projected P&L

ROA IMPACT   The projected impact on the return on assets performance.

ROE IMPACT   The projected impact on the return on equity performance.

Balance Sheet

In times of rapid interest rate changes, the cost of funds becomes unpredictable and has a tendency to change without notice. Two major concerns the institution may have are erosion of core deposits during high interest rates (a migration to money market instruments) and the consequent higher cost of funding assets.

What needs to be avoided is having to borrow funds on the open market at a high rate in order to fund low-yielding assets. The institution's management either restricts the bank's asset growth or prices at a level that will ensure a breakeven profit. The analysis may appear as follows:

Loans	$ 90 million	Core deposits	$ 70 million
Other	7 million	Other	25 million
Overnight	3 million	Overnight	5 million
Total assets	$100 million	Total liabilities and capital	$100 million

This oversimplified balance sheet shows this financial institution has an overnight exposure of $2 million ($3 million minus $5 million). This of course assumes the same rate for the placings (assets) as exists for the takings (liabilities). This overnight position may be an aberration. But what if it were a daily occurrence? The funding gap could be costly. Should the institution allow assets to roll off until the $2 million shortfall is balanced or should they price incrementally at the money market rate?

In order to make this decision management must be informed about the maturity of the assets. What if, for example, all new loans (assets) are priced at the money market rate and $60 million of the loans matured next week? If the money market rate was 20 percent, they may find few takers at that price. It would not be a prudent pricing policy for them to price all loans at 20 percent when they have 70 percent of their funding source from a relatively low-interest core deposit pool.

What the institution needs to know is the maturity schedule of the assets in order to set a rate that will on the average absorb the higher cost of funds they are absorbing on an overnight basis.

The institution must strive toward minimizing its exposure to the overnight market while at the same time pricing for stability in the marketplace at a profit.

Marketing

In some organizations there may be a philosophy of the more you sell the more profit you will receive. This is true if the product is profitable to begin with. But what about a service that is a loss on a fully absorbed basis? Consider the example shown in table 11-5.

TABLE 11-5 Product A (Business Service)

Monthly Average per Customer

Revenue	$510
Expense (direct)(1)	500
Expense (allocated)	120
Profit/loss before taxes	($110)

(1)Including amortized conversion costs.

TABLE 11-6

	Per Month		Number of Month		Expected Average Profit/Loss for 12 Months
Revenue	$510	×	12	=	$6,120
Expense (direct) (1)	500	×	12	=	6,000
Expense (allocated)	120	×	12	=	1,440
Total Profit/Loss					($1,320)

(1)Including amortized conversion costs.

The average fully absorbed loss is $110 per customer per month. On a direct basis the profit is $10 per month per customer ($510 - $500). Since the data is based on averages, the analyst at this juncture would probably find it prudent to seek further data on customer profiles. The analyst may wish to determine if there are some significantly profitable relationships and some very unprofitable ones. Reasons would need to be explored. What if it costs $1,500 to sell the service and convert a customer to this new business service from a former one? Also what if the average customer lasted only 12 months with the service? Let's assume this $1,500 is included in the direct expense of $500 per month and is amortized at $125 per month for profitability measurement. Then the profile of the service would look a little different. The analyst would probably position the data at this point as shown in table 11-6.

We see a loss of \$1,320 for the 12 months. But if the conversion cost of \$1,500 were subtracted out, the \$1,320 fully absorbed loss would turn into a \$180 profit for the 12 months. The idea here is twofold. Management needs to know that the conversion costs are inordinately high and the retention rate is only 12 months. Decisions would then focus away from selling more and hence losing more to a concentration on improving the service quality and reducing costs. The result would hopefully be a higher customer retention rate. Charging conversion fees to the customers is not an uncommon occurrence; it is actually a motivator to remain as a customer longer than the average.

The Cost Study Process from Start to Finish

Up to this point in the book we have covered the many aspects of cost analysis methodology and cost and profitability reporting. It is now appropriate to focus on a project approach to performing a cost study. The example selected is an income-producing group in a self-contained environment similar to a small financial institution.

PLANNING THE PROJECT

The first step in conducting a cost study is to develop a plan. In analytical projects there are four phases to consider:

1. Assignment of the project
2. Research of available information
3. Analysis of the information
4. Presentation of the results

The following outline may help you to develop a useful project plan.

   I. Assignment of the project
      a. Determine the purpose of the study.
         Pricing
         Transfer charges
         Organizational profitability reporting

Product profitability reporting
Customer profitability reporting
Management decision making
b. Determine time constraints and lead time needed.
When is the study due?
Where are the information dependencies?
What is the lead time needed?
c. Determine the objective(s) of the study.
Is it a feasibility study?
Is it a cost study?
Is it an alternative choice study?
II. Research
a. Reconnaissance
Use introductory conversations with concerned personnel to obtain an overview of their needs.
b. Reading of documents bearing on the project
Review any data that is submitted with the request. From this comes a clearer definition and understanding of the project and an indication of relevant factual material that must be gathered.
c. Game plan—approach model
Determine data sources (reports and other documents).
Establish basic assumptions and document them.
Determine constraints (time, breadth, and depth).
Identify alternatives.
Structure your choice (draw a map of what you are going to do and how you intend doing it).
Design methodology (standard, nonstandard).
Establish accountability (assume responsibility and assert yourself).
d. Detailed gathering of all relevant facts.
Obtain or prepare an organizational chart of the unit being studied.
Conduct carefully planned interviews with appropriate personnel.
Gather data sources (through research, compilation, and documentation of written information).
III. Analytical process
a. Develop the analytical framework to meet the purpose and objectives.
Arrange the data in a meaningful format for interpretation.
Sort out and identify relevant data.
b. Develop results.
Sum up the data.

c. Analyze the results.
   What does the data mean?
d. Develop conclusions and recommendations.
   Summarize conclusions.
   Be specific on what has occurred and what should be done.
IV. Presentation
   a. Compose a written memorandum stating the purpose, assumptions/methodology, results, conclusions, and recommendations.
   b. Orally present results and analysis to primary recipients.

If the framework outlined is followed, the project should be manageable. You will know where the project is going and how the pieces are to come together. Having a map of where you are going is essential in setting out on a costing project.

The Need for Review

It is important to keep people informed about what you do in your cost study and how the project is progressing. Apprising key personnel on the direction of the project is essential.

AN EXAMPLE COST/PROFITABILITY STUDY

Let's take an example of a request for an organizational cost/profitability study of an income-producing group. The instructions are that functional cost and profitability relationships be established and that item costs are to be developed. Basically the request is to develop functional profitability data within the constraints of an income-producing organization and to develop product costs where applicable. Figure 12-1 depicts the normal flow of activity in a cost and profitability study.

Before we cover each module it may be useful to review the hierarchy we are working with in this study. We begin with an income group. The (line) income group in this example is a commercial services group. The group's data (revenue and expense) is distributed to the various departments in the group. By example the hierarchy is illustrated as follows:

Group	Departments	Functions	Products
Commercial services	Credit	Loans & Acceptances	Acceptances discounted

In this example the credit department's expenses would be spread to the functions it serves. Loans and acceptances functional data would be broken down by product. A product in this example is acceptances discounted. The product data is unitized; that is, volume data is brought into the analysis and unit revenue, cost, and profitability data is developed. This is the objective of the study.

Figure 12-1. The Flow of Activity in a Cost Study

Module

I.
| Review of total group's P&L | Define period of study. Identify exclusions. |

II.
| Staff allocation | Based on interviews with managers, allocate staff equivalencies and associated mid-point compensation to responsibility centers (RCs). |

III.
| Other operating expense alignment to responsiblity centers (RCs) | Align or allocate expenses to RCs. Include any local overhead allocations. |

IV.
| Allocation and alignment of departmental expense to functions | Allocate expenses to functions. This is a realignment of departmental expenses to functions. |

V.
| Identify products | Identify all products by function. |

VI.
| Allocation and alignment of direct and indirect expenses to products | Allocate direct and indirect functional expenses to the products. |

VII.
| Identify product volume | Identify appropriate product volume data. |

VIII.
| Develop product costs | Divide total product expense by total product volume. |

IX.
| Identify and allocate revenue to each function and product | Isolate and identify revenue on an individual product basis. |

X.
| Develop a product profitability report | Align product revenue with product costs. |

XI.
| Develop functional P&L report | Align functional revenue with functional expense. |

XII.
| Write summary of findings and conclusions | Write a report on the entire study, covering the main points. |

We will now walk through the study module by module, beginning with a review of the total group's profit and loss (table 12-1). In this study we will assume the data gathered is for 12 months. Phase I entails creating an income statement for the department being studied. It also involves making adjustments to the reported data. Exclusions are an example of this.

TABLE 12-1 Cost Study Module I: Total Group's Income Statement for the Year Ended 19xx ($ 000's)

	Per Books	Exclusions/ Adjustments	Net
Revenue			
Net interest	$751		$751
Net interest — inter-company	0		0
Loan fees	321.6		321.6
Fee services	715.4		715.4
Other revenue	618		618
(Line 100) Total revenue	2,406		$2,406
Compensation			
Salaries	600	(100)	$500
Fringe benefits	180	(30)	150
Bonuses	35		35
Overtime	10		10
Temporary	17		17
Agency/other	8		8
(Line 200) total compensation	850	(130)	$720
Other operating expenses			
Premises (rent)	200		200
Premises (depreciation)	100		100
Equipment (depreciation)	16		16
Provisions for loan loss	0		0
Miscellaneous	2	(2)	0
Marketing	40		40
Entertainment	90		90
Equipment maintenance	15		15
Postage and delivery	20		20
Stationery and supplies	100		100
Professional and community activities	15		15
Telephone/telegraph	85		85
Travel	85	(15)	70
Utilities	20		20
Cleaning and maintenance	10		10
Charitable contributions	10		10
Regulatory fees/insurance	3		3
Consultants	27	(7)	20
Equipment rent/lease	10		10

(continued)

TABLE 12-1 Continued

	Per Books	Exclusions/ Adjustments	Net
Insurance/protection	15		15
Credit reports	2		2
Legal Fees	12		12
Recruiting	3		3
Operating losses	0		0
Subscriptions	5		5
Intracompany transfers	150	(10)	140
Line 300 total other operating expenses	1,035	(34)	1,001
Line 400 total expenses	1,885	(164)	1,721
Line 500 group's profit/loss before taxes	521	164	685

Exclusions/Adjustments Explanation

Exclusions

Salaries—To adjust for management trainees on a personnel training program

Fringe benefits—To adjust for management trainees on a personnel training program

Misc.—To adjust for a one-time-only fee

Travel—To adjust for unusual travel requested in order to assist the domestic group

Consultants—To adjust for project requested by legal department

Intracompany—Transfers to adjust for DP project requested by credit review department

The purpose of any exclusions/adjustments is to normalize the data being reported. Unusual expenses such as those that are beyond control of the group's management and one-time-only occurrences are treated as exclusions. These exceptional items have to be judged on a case-by-case basis.

At this point we have normalized the group's income and expense for the period being studied. Module I of the cost study is now completed. We are now ready to go to module II, staff allocations, shown in table 12-2. We need to allocate staff compensation to the various organizations/departments. For purposes of this study we will not allocate the associated staff count (equivalency). The complete column heading literals are as follows: staff member, total compensation, general administration, operations administration, credit department, foreign exchange trading, foreign exchange processing, teller window, accounting, letters of credit, paying and receiving, telecommunications, loans and acceptances, mail room, reconcilement, investigations, data processing, marketing and business development, collections. The rows are labeled employee, temporary, or agency. The totals are transferred to module III (table 12-3).

TABLE 12-2 Cost Study Module II: Commercial Services Group. Distribution of Employee Compensation ($000's)

Staff Member	Total Comp[1]	Gen'l Admin	Ops Adm	Credit	FX Trad	FX Proc	Teller Window	Acctng	Letters of Credit	Paying and Recing	Tele- Comms	Loans and Accepts	Mail Room	Reconcil	Investig	DP	Mkting and Bus. Dev	Coll
		$	$	$	$	$	$	$	$	$	$	$	$	$	$	$	$	$
Empl 1	$65	$65																
2	42	42																
3	40		40															
4	32			32														
5	36				36													
6	31				31													
7	28				28													
8	22					22												
9	12					12												
10	10						10											
11	11							11										
12	11							11										
13	14							14										
14	15								15									
15	13								13									
16	10								10									
17	10									10								
18	11									11								
19	12										12							
20	11										11							
21	33											33						
22	25											25						

[1]The alignment of total compensation by employee assumes the details of accruing salary, fringe benefits, bonus, and overtime for each employee were worked out on a separate schedule along with an organization chart.

(continued)

TABLE 12-2 Continued

Staff Member	Total Comp[1]	Gen'l Admin	Cps Adm	Credit	FX Trad	FX Proc	Teller Window	Acctng	Letters of Credit	Paying and Recing	Tele-Comms	Loans and Accepts	Mail Room	Reconcil	Investig	DP	Mkting and Bus. Dev	Coll
Temp 23	25											25						
24	13											13						
25	11						3					8						
26	10												10					
27	12													12				
28	13													13				
29	14														14			
30	28															28		
31	17															17		
32	11															11		
33	30																30	
34	27																27	
35	15																	15
Total	$720	$107	$40	$32	$95	$34	$13	$36	$38	$21	$23	$104	$10	$25	$14	$56	$57	$15

[1]The alignment of total compensation by employee assumes the details of accruing salary, fringe benefits, bonus, and overtime for each employee were worked out on a separate schedule along with an organization chart.

TABLE 12-3 Cost Study Module III: Departmental Expenses ($000's)

Expense Category[1]	Total	Ovrhd & Genr'l[2] Admin	Ops Adm	Credit	FX Trad	FX Proc	Teller Window	Acctng	Letters of Credit	Paying and Recing	Tele-Comms	Loans and Accepts	Mail Room	Reconcil	Investig	DP	Mkting and Bus. Dev	Coll
Compen	720	107	40	32	95	34	13	36	38	21	23	104	10	25	14	56	57	15
Premises (Rent)	200	59	5	5	15	8	4	9	9	8	8	20	6	8	5	15	11	5
Premises (Deprec)	100	23			30					5	7		2			33		
Equip. (Deprec)	16	1		1	3	1		2	1	3	2					2		
Marketing	40	8															32	
Entertain	90	20	5														65	
Equip. (Maint)	15	2								2	3	2				6		
Postage	20												20					
Staitnry	100	48	1	1	2	1	1	2	3	5	7	3	2	1	1	18	2	1
Prof&Cmty	15	4	5		2												6	
Telephone	85	2	1	1	20	1	1	1	2	3	26	3	1	2	3	15	3	1
Travel	70	23	5	2	3											3	34	
Utilities	20	5.9	0.5	0.5	1.5	0.8	0.4	0.9	0.9	0.8	0.8		0.6	0.8	0.5	1.5	1.1	0.5
Clean&Mnt	10	2.5	0.3	0.3	0.8	0.4	0.2	0.5	0.5	0.4	0.4		0.3	0.4	0.3	0.8	0.6	0.3
Charitable	10	10																
Regl Fees	3	3																
Consults	20	3		2	7						1					10		
Equip (Rnt/Lse)	10				3													
Insur/Pro	15	15									2					5		
Cred Rpts	2		2	2														
Legl Fees	12		3	3					2			4			2			1
Recrtng	3	3																
Subscrpts	5			1	1											2	1	
Transfers	140	53	25	20	15												27	
Total	$1,721	$386.4	$87.8	$70.8	$199.3	$46.2	$19.6	$51.4	$56.4	$48.2	$80.2	$139	$41.9	$37.2	$25.8	$167.3	$239.7	$23.8

[1] For each allocation there should be a schedule detailing how the allocations were calculated and on what basis. For purposes of brevity only the concept is mentioned here.

[2] Common areas and institutional items are accounted for in overhead.

TABLE 12-3 continued

Expenses Category	Comments/Allocation Bases[1]
Compensation	From module II
Premises (rent)	Square footage occupied
Premises (depreciation)	Leasehold improvements
Equipment (depreciation)	Asset listing
Marketing	Invoices and organizational reporting
Entertainment	Same
Equipment maintenance	Same
Postage/delivery	Same
Stationery and supplies	Same
Professional and community activities	Same
Telephone/telegraph	Same
Travel	Same
Utilities	Percentage of premises rent to total
Cleaning and maintenance	Same
Charitable contributions	Allocate to administration
Regulatory fees/insurance	Allocate to general overhead
Consultants	Invoices and organizational reporting
Equipment rent/lease	Same
Insurance and protection	Allocate to general overhead
Credit reports	Direct allocation to credit department
Legal fees	Invoices and organizational reporting
Recruiting	Same
Subscriptions	Same
Transfers	Same

[1]The designation "Invoices and Organizational Reporting" denotes the information as either coming from invoices or some form of internal departmental expense reporting procedure.

ALLOCATION ISSUES

Examining the expense tracking at our example institution for allocation purposes, we find that the bulk of the *entertainment* category was incurred by the marketing and business development department. Therefore, this expense will be spread to the functions on the next schedule according to some predetermined basis. FX (Foreign Exchange) trading incurred a direct expense of $3 thousand, as did operations administration. A decision needs to be made as to how much each of these two departments will receive as allocations in addition to their directly incurred expenses.

TABLE 12-4 Cost Study Module IV: Functional Expenses (Department Expenses Aligned to Function)($ 000's)

Department	Total	Foreign Exchange	Lobby Teller	Letters of Credit	Paying and Receiving	Loans and Acceptances	Collections	Comments
Credit	$ 70.8	$	$	$ 10.2	$ 4.0	$ 54.3	$ 2.3	Allocation based on interview w/dept. mgr and recipients (users)
FX trading	199.3	197.0	2.3					Allocation based on estimate provided by chief trader and teller
FX processing	46.2	45.7	0.5					Allocation based on % FX trading to total expenses
Teller window	19.6		19.6					Direct allocation
Accounting	51.4	9.8	0.5	12.8	9.2	12.7	6.4	Allocation based on survey conducted by accounting supvr.
Letters of credit	56.4			56.4				Direct allocation
Paying and receiving	48.2				48.2			Direct allocation
Telecommunications	80.2	20.9	0.3	6.8	41.9	8.5	1.8	Message survey (incoming and outgoing)
Loans and accepts	139.0					139.0		Direct allocation
Mailroom	41.9	6.0	0.2	9.7	10.6	14.5	0.9	Allocation based on survey conducted (incoming and outgoing)

(continued)

TABLE 12-4 Continued

Department	Total	Foreign Exchange	Lobby Teller	Letters of Credit	Paying and Receiving	Loans and Acceptances	Collections	Comments
Reconciliation	37.2	7.4	0.5		29.3			Allocations based on activity log
Investigation	25.8	1.5			24.3			Allocations based on staff member's estimate
Data process	167.3	32.5	0.3	10.1	106.6	15.8	2.0	Allocations based on reports indicating resource usage
Mkting and bus. development	239.7	27.2	0.5	50.5	71.3	88.5	1.7	Allocations based on advertising and calling officers' time estimates
Collections	23.8						23.8	Direct allocation
Subtotal	$1,246.8	$348.0	$24.7	$156.5	$345.4	$333.3	$38.9	
Ops Admin	87.8	24.5	1.7	11.0	24.3	23.5	2.8	Allocation based on % expense to subtotal
O.H./Gnrl Adm	386.4	107.8	7.7	48.5	107.0	103.3	12.1	Allocation based on % expense to subtotal
Total	$1,721.0	$480.3	$34.1	$216.0	$476.7	$460.1	$53.8	

The entire amount of postage expense was paid through the mail room. There was no recordkeeping as to the usage of mail. An allocation base will have to be developed for spreading these expenses to the major functions.

The next step, module IV (table 12-4) is to align the departmental expenses with the major revenue-producing functions of the group.

Module V (table 12-5) identifies all products by function. It is interesting to note that this process sometimes uncovers products that have not previously been identified separately and sold to customers. The list in module V is abbreviated; some of the more detailed products one may find in this type of group have been omitted. What is being presented is a summary of the major product offerings.

TABLE 12-5 Cost Study
Module V: Product Listing

Foreign exchange
   Trading
   Other
Lobby teller
   Currency trading
   Other
Letters of Credit
   Import L/C
   Export L/C
   Export L/C reimbursement
   Standby L/C
Paying and Receiving
   Electronic payments
   Paper payments
   Electronic receives
   Paper receives
Loans and acceptances
   Loans booked
   Loans maturing
   Acceptances discounted
   Acceptances nondiscounted
Collections
   Documentary incoming
   Documentary outgoing
   Clean — incoming
   Clean — outgoing

TABLE 12-6 Cost Study Module VI: Allocation/Alignment of Direct and Indirect Expenses to Products ($000's)

Foreign exchange	
Trading	$ 472.0
Other	8.3
Subtotal	$ 480.3
Lobby teller	
Currency trading	$ 28.5
Other	5.6
Subtotal	$ 34.1
Letters of Credit	
Import L/C	$ 75.6
Export L/C	50.7
Export L/C reimbursement	68.8
Standby L/C	20.9
Subtotal	$ 216.0
Paying and Receiving	
Electronic payments	$ 177.3
Paper payments	130.9
Electronic receives	128.3
Paper receives	40.2
Subtotal	$ 476.7
Loans and acceptances	
Loans booked	$ 165.4
Loans maturing	121.2
Acceptances—discounted	122.2
Acceptances—nondiscounted	51.3
Subtotal	$ 460.1
Collections	
Documentary—incoming	$9.0
Documentary—outgoing	14.0
Clean—incoming	10.4
Clean—outgoing	20.4
Subtotal	$ 53.8
Total	$1,721.0

Once the major products are identified the expenses can be allocated to each product. In the transition from module V to module VI there is considerable work to be done. It involves tracking the processing work flow of each product within a function. That work is assigned a value, which in turn translates into a cost. For purposes of brevity this step is not included. However, there is considerable treatment of this concept in the earlier chapters of this book. (See table 12-6.)

TABLE 12-7 Cost Study Module VII: Identify Product Volumes ($000's)

	Product Expense	Product Volume
Foreign exchange		
Trading	$472.0	9,391
Other	8.3	
Total	$480.3	
Lobby teller		
Currency trading	$ 28.5	3,630
Other	5.6	
Total	$ 34.1	
Letters of credit		
Import L/C	$ 75.6	2,137
Export L/C	50.7	1,575
Export L/C reimbursement	68.8	3,179
Standby L/C	20.9	385
Total	$216.0	
Paying and receiving		
Electronic payments	$177.3	20,356
Paper payments	130.9	2,236
Electronic receives	128.3	31,500
Paper receives	40.2	4,379
Total	$476.7	
Loans and acceptances		
Loans booked	$165.4	1,135
Loans maturing	121.2	1,008
Acceptances—discounted	122.2	923
Acceptances—nondiscounted	51.3	535
Total	$460.1	
Collections		
Documentary—incoming	$ 9.0	202
Documentary—outgoing	14.0	273
Clean—incoming	10.4	247
Clean—outgoing	20.4	424
Total	$ 53.8	

TABLE 12-8 Cost Study Module VIII:
Develop Product Costs ($ 000's)

	1 Product Expenses	2 Product Volume	3 Derived Product costs (col. 1 + col. 2)
Foreign exchange			
Trading	$472.0	9,391	$50.26
Other	8.3		
Total	$480.3		
Lobby teller			
Currency trading	$ 28.5	3,630	7.85
Other	5.6		
Total	$ 34.1		
Letters of credit			
Import L/C	$ 75.6	2,137	35.38
Export L/C	50.7	1,575	32.19
Export L/C reimbursement	68.8	3,179	21.64
Standby L/C	20.9	385	54.30
Total	$216.0		
Paying and receiving			
Electronic payments	$177.3	20,356	8.71
Paper payments	130.9	2,236	58.54
Electronic receives	128.3	31,500	4.07
Paper receives	40.2	4,379	9.18
Total	$476.7		
Loans and acceptances			
Loans booked	$165.4	1,135	145.73
Loans maturing	121.2	1,008	120.24
Acceptances—discounted	122.2	923	132.39
Acceptances—nondiscounted	51.3	535	95.89
Total	$460.1		
Collections			
Documentary—incoming	$ 9.0	202	44.55
Documentary outgoing	11.0	273	51.28
Clean—incoming	10.4	247	42.11
Clean—outgoing	20.4	424	48.11
Total	$ 53.8		

The next phase of the project is to gather volume statistics for each product (see table 12-7). In actually doing such a project this could have already been done in the preparation of expense allocations to products for module VI.

We are now ready to calculate product costs. The costs are simply derived by dividing the product expenses by the product volume. Table 12-8 reflects this calculation for each product listed.

The next step is to identify the revenue attributable to each product. This is dependent upon the reporting system in place at the branch. Where only minimal reporting capabilities exist, probably only revenue information on the major functions will be available. On the other hand if a detailed reporting system exists, then the revenue associated with each product may be listed separately. In the case of paying and receiving and collections, there will be credit for funds added as a soft revenue. The hard dollar income for paying and receiving usually comes from net penalty fees accrued. The more astute the processing management, the more there will be hard dollar profits. One usually finds the bulk of the revenue for paying and receiving is from soft dollar credit for surplus funds, which is a reduction to cost of funds.

It is appropriate at this time to reconcile the product revenue listed in table 12-9 with the revenue listed in table 12-1 for the total group:

Other revenue (FX)	$ 618.0
Fee services	715.4
Loans fees	$ 321.6
Subtotal	1,655.0
Plus net interest	$ 751.0
Total	$2,406.0

The fee (noninterest) product revenue is therefore reconcilable to the reported revenue of the group.

The next step is to develop per item noninterest product profitability. Therefore, in module X (table 12-10) we align product revenue with product costs on a total and a per item basis. The only exclusion to this is the net interest on loans and the deposit credits.

TABLE 12-9 Cost Study Module IX:
Products (Noninterest) Fee Revenue
($ 000's)

	Noninterest Fee Revenue
Foreign exchange	
Trading	$ 618.0
Other	23.4
Subtotal	$ 641.4
Lobby teller	
Currency trading	$ 16.2
Other	1.9
Subtotal	$ 18.1
Letters of Credit	
Import L/C	$65.3
Export L/C	55.4
Export L/C Reimbursement	43.2
Standby L/C	28.6
Subtotal	$ 192.5
Paying and Receiving	
Electronic payments	$91.2
Paper payments	14.6
Electronic receives	84.2
Paper receives	4.1
Subtotal	$ 194.1
Loans and acceptances	
Loans booked	$321.6
Loans maturing	—
Acceptances—discounted	152.5
Acceptances—nondiscounted	63.4
Subtotal	$ 537.5
Collections	
Documentary—incoming	$ 11.5
Documentary—outgoing	17.8
Clean—incoming	15.9
Clean—outgoing	26.2
Subtotal	$ 71.4
Total	$1,655.0

**TABLE 12-10 Cost Study Module X: Product Profitability
Fee-Based Noninterest**

	1 *Revenue* *Noninterest* *($000's)*	*2* *Expense*	*3* *Net Profit/Loss* *(col. 1 – col. 2)*	*Volume*	*Per Item* *Profit/Loss* *(col. 3 ÷ col. 4)*
Foreign exchange					
Trading	$ 618.0	$ 472.0	$ 146.0	9,391	$ 15.55
Other	23.4	8.3	15.1	—	—
Subtotal	$ 641.4	$ 480.3	$ 161.1	—	—
Lobby teller					
Currency trading	$ 16.2	$ 28.5	$ (12.3)	3,630	$ (3.39)
Other	1.9	5.6	(3.7)	—	—
Subtotal	$ 18.1	$ 34.1	$ (16.0)	—	—
Letters of credit					
Import L/C	$ 65.3	$ 75.6	$ (10.3)	2,137	$ (4.82)
Export L/C	55.4	50.7	4.7	1,575	2.98
Export L/C reimbursement	43.2	68.8	(25.6)	3,179	(8.05)
Standby L/C	28.6	20.9	7.7	385	20.00
Subtotal	$ 192.5	$ 216.0	$ (23.5)	—	—
Paying and receiving					
Electronic payments	$ 91.2	$ 177.3	$ (86.1)	20,356	$(4.23)
Paper payments	14.6	130.9	(116.3)	2,236	(7.29)
Electronic receives	84.2	128.3	(44.1)	31,500	(4.57)
Paper receives	4.1	40.2	(36.1)	4,379	(8.24)
Subtotal	$ 194.1	$ 476.7	$(282.6)	—	—
Loans and acceptances					
Loans booked	$ 321.6	$ 165.4	$ 156.2	1,135	$137.62
Loans maturing	—	121.2	(121.2)	1,008	(120.24)
Acceptances—discounted	152.5	122.2	30.3	923	32.83
Acceptances—nondiscounted	63.4	51.3	12.1	535	22.62
Subtotal	$ 537.5	$ 460.1	$ 77.4	—	—
Collections					
Documentary—incoming	$ 11.5	$ 9.0	$ 2.5	202	$ 12.38
Documentary—outgoing	17.8	14.0	3.8	273	13.92
Clean—incoming	15.9	10.4	5.5	247	22.27
Clean—outcoming	26.2	20.4	5.8	424	13.68
Subtotal	$ 71.4	$ 53.8	$ 17.6	—	—
Total	$1,655.0	$1,721.0	$ (66.0)	—	—

We now go to module XI (table 12-11), which is a functional profit and loss report for one group. The product revenue data in column 1 comes from module IX. The product expense data in column 2 comes from module VI. The product volume information in column 3 comes from module VIII.

The profitability data for the paying and receiving and loan and acceptances and collections functions is incomplete as deposit credits and loan net interest are not included. But what we have in module X is product profitability on a fee basis only.

One can readily see that revenue is not covering the cost of providing some of the services on a fee basis. We can exclude the paying and receiving functions, as fees per se are not usually charged. The areas of focus are then the lobby currency trading and letters of credit. Do the fees need to be raised? Is cost cutting the issue? What is management's strategy? Are they willing to have a "loss leader" in order to attract other business? These issues must surely be addressed as the data is reviewed.

TABLE 12-11 Cost Study Module XI: Commercial Services Group Functional Profitability Report (000's)

	1 *Revenue* *from Modules* *I and IX*	*2* *Expense* *from Module* *VI*	*3* *Net Profit/Loss* *before Taxes* *(col. 1 − col. 2)*
Foreign exchange			
Trading	$ 618.0	$ 472.0	$ 146.0
Other	23.4	8.3	15.1
Subtotal	$ 641.4	$ 480.3	$ 161.1
Lobby teller			
Currency trading	$ 16.2	$ 28.5	$ (12.3)
Other	1.9	5.6	(3.7)
Subtotal	$ 18.1	$ 34.1	$ (16.0)
Letters of credit			
Import L/C	$ 65.3	$ 75.6	(10.3)
Export L/C	55.4	50.7	4.7
Export L/C reimbursement	43.2	68.8	(25.6)
Standby L/C	28.6	20.9	7.7
Subtotal	$ 192.5	$ 216.0	$ (23.5)

TABLE 12-11 Continued

	1 *Revenue from Modules I and IX*	2 *Expense from Module VI*	3 *Net Profit/Loss before Taxes (col. 1 − col. 2)*
Paying and receiving			
Electronic payments	$ 91.2	$ 177.3	$ (86.1)
Paper payments	14.6	130.9	(116.3)
Electronic receives	84.2	128.3	(44.1)
Paper receives	4.1	40.2	(36.1)
Deposit credit[1]	$ 696.4	—	696.4
Subtotal	$ 890.5	$ 476.7	$ 413.8
Loans and acceptances			
Loans booked	$ 321.6	$ 165.4	$ 156.2
Loans maturing	—	121.2	(121.2)
Acceptances—discounted	152.5	122.2	30.3
Acceptances—nondiscounted	63.4	51.3	12.1
Net interest	$ 751.0	—	751.0
Subtotal	$1,288.5	$ 460.1	$ 828.4
Collections			
Documentary—incoming	$ 11.5	$ 9.0	$ 2.5
Documentary—outgoing	17.8	14.0	3.8
Clean—incoming	15.9	10.4	5.5
Clean—outcoming	26.2	20.4	5.8
Deposit credit	$ 20.0	—	20.0
Subtotal	$ 91.4	$ 53.8	$ 37.6
Total	$3,122.4	$1,721.0	$1,401.4

[1]An arbitrary calculation for management information purposes only. The deposit credit is not reflected in the general ledger. It is an artificial credit given in recognition of balances provided for the institution's use by the function. An arbitrary credit rate is used in conjunction with the formula $I = PRT$.

We now reconcile the functional report to the group's ledger figures that appeared in module I.

	($000's)
Functional profitability	$1,401.4
less deposit credits	716.4
Net profit before tax	$ 685.0
(Per cost/profitability study)	
(exclusive of deposit credits)	
Per group's ledger (books)	685.0

The last thing to be done is module XII, writing a summary of findings and con-clusions. The main points that would be important to mention for this sample study would be the lack of profitability for certain products. The most obvious issue to be confronted is the lack of pricing levels to cover costs in certain products. Other issues to cover may include such areas as inefficiencies, identified information availability, and opportunities for further product segmentation.

13

Cost Control and Expense Planning

Many financial institutions look at cost containment as a means to improve profits. Some use it as a means of remaining profitable. Whatever the case, there is no escaping the necessity of having cost control in one form or another.

This chapter will cover cost control from a planning standpoint and also from the perspective of an ongoing review of actual expenses. Often in planning the impact of staff additions becomes a confused issue as the numbers are presented. Management may find themselves unable to determine the impact of this year's changes on next year's plan. These issues are dealt with in this chapter.

Suggestions for implementing cost control programs will be presented and explored. In financial institutions that already have cost control programs, it is a good idea to assess the adequacy of the program.

Noninterest expense containment is the focus of this chapter. There are many opportunities for savings through the identification and reduction of redundant and otherwise unnecessary expenses.

Opportunities for Profitability Enhancement

In some institutions, cost control may just be a matter of passing all purchase orders and invoices through the controller for approval and payment. It may also be a monthly exercise of reviewing variances from plan. This all may be quite adequate in some settings. But things become more complex as organization grow. What may have been a handshake understanding must now be a formal procedure due to organizational growth.

As an organization grows it becomes apparent that controls must become more formalized. The faster the growth the more profound the need. Noninterest expense can erode profits. For optimal profitability it must be controlled. This is not to suggest the stifling of growth and technological improvements. It is, however, a suggestion that the process of incurring expenses be controlled.

Major candidates for cost control are as follows.

Capital purchases/leasing
   Automobiles
   Processing equipment
   Computers
   Building/real estate ("brick and mortar")
   Office equipment (word processors, typewriters)

Major Projects
   New products
   New systems (automation, methods, changes)
   New functions

Compensation
   Salaries (regular and temporary)
   Overtime
   Fringe benefits
   Agency

Other operating expenses
   Postage and delivery
   Stationery and supplies
   Telecommunications
   Data processing
   Equipment rent/lease
   Depreciation
   Premises
   Marketing/advertising
   Entertainment
   Travel
   Professional/community activities
   Charitable contributions

Recruiting
Employee
Subscriptions
Equipment maintenance
Insurance
Legal
Protection
Collections
Consulting
Miscellaneous

In reviewing the total expenses of a financial institution, there are ratios that can be calculated for comparison. Some of the ratios that can be calculated are

- Total number of staff to asset size

- Total number of support staff to asset size

- Average salary per staff member institutionwide

- Total expenses to asset size

- Total expenses to revenue

- Total compensation expense to revenue

- Data processing expenses to total institution expenses

- Compensation expense to total institution expense

- The percentage mix of specific line item other operating expenses to total expenses

An example of the last item would be the mix of premises, travel, supplies, postage, and advertising to total expenses. There are some industry studies available that provide averages of what various financial institutions have experienced as a mix in each of these line items. Those items that stand out as large variances then become areas that should be looked into as candidates for cost reduction. Let us now review the possibilities of cost control for each of the items listed.

Capital Purchases/Leasing

Generally a lease-versus-buy analysis should be conducted on major purchases. Obviously the overall corporate tax ramifications need to be considered. Also the controller's approval should be required for all capital purchases before they are consummated.

Automobiles. Keeping track of what kinds of new cars are low maintenance and relatively trouble free can save a lot of money in repairs. Consumer reports detail experience with new cars. Some extras will enhance a car's resale value and, therefore, may be cost justified. Others may be unnecessary and add little to resale value.

Processing Equipment. Cost, reliability, comparability, efficiency, maintenance, and service quality need to be considered in purchasing equipment. Compare from several manufacturers before buying.

Computers. Compatibility, technological displacement, capacity, reliability, cost, standardization, efficiency, and applications are just a few of the things to consider. There should be a demonstrated need or purpose for the computer.

Building/Real Estate. The long-term effects of fixed costs are always something to weigh when considering owning versus leasing real estate. A need for a building today may change in the future as the business environment changes or shifts.

Office Equipment. In some organizations the need for typewriters is readily apparent. However, in other organizations there may be a surplus of equipment in one department and a shortage in others and the two are not brought together. A demonstrated need for office equipment may be difficult to discern. This suggests a policy of reassigning equipment that is surplus. Financial incentives could be made that would encourage this. It may reduce outside purchases. Also there should be a policy of discouraging redundancy of equipment.

Standardizing certain types of equipment throughout an organization can save money. It also facilitates training, transfer of personnel, and standardizes maintenance and supply needs.

Table 13-1 is a suggested capital purchase lease approval form. The form is basic. Certainly there are special needs at individual Institutions that could be incorporated in the form. The approval form guides the requestor through the process of making sure the request is a need and it fits into the overall plans of the organization.

The section that asks for this year's and next year's financial impact is really an assessment of what additional expenses will be incurred as a result of the proposed acquisition. Let's take a simple example of this. Suppose a $600 typewriter is being requested for purchase effective 1 November. The depreciation expense of this would affect this year for two months (November and December). Next year's impact would be a full year of depreciation. If the expected useful life of the typewriter is three years with no salvage value then we have $200 per year depreciation ($600 ÷ 3 = $200). This amounts to $16.67 per month depreciation ($200 ÷ 12 = $16.67).

Hence, this year's impact is $33.34 ($16.67 × 2 = $33.34). The financial impact is then $33.34 for this year and $200 for next year.

TABLE 13-1 Capital Purchase/Lease Approval Form

Name of Requestor _____   *Organization Name* _____

Title _____   *Organization Number* _____

Phone Number _____   _____ *Purchase* _____ *Lease*
                                                          Please attach lease/buy analysis if over $15,000.

Item	*Model*	*Unit*		
Description	*Number*	*Price*	*Quantity*	*Total*

Briefly state the need(s) that justify this purchase or lease.

Is this in your organization's approved plan?   _____ YES _____ NO

If no then provide this year's financial impact $ _____

Next year's financial impact $ _____

(e.g. Depreciation/Lease Payments)

Is any equipment being replaced by this acquisition?   _____ YES _____ NO

If yes then what is its intended disposition?

Requestor's Signature _____ Date _____

Approvals:

Department Head _____ Date _____ Data Processing _____ Date _____
                                      (If applicable)

Plan Verification _____ Date _____ Controller _____ Date _____

Major Projects

Projects that will require significant resources should be submitted to a management committee for approval. This should include proposed product offerings, systems changes, and new functions or organization. This allows for a strategic review of the proposal to ensure it is consistent with the financial institution's overall direction. Approval for major software purchases should also be part of this committee's authority. Data processing management should be involved as well.

Compensation

Later in this chapter there is a section on compensation and staffing control during planning. Salary administration guidelines should be established . In times of low inflation and earnings decline, the percentage and timing of increases should be slowed down. Salary administration must be designed as an incentive toward higher productivity while at the same time not adversely affecting earnings.

Staff additions and replacements should be controlled with a requisition approval process. (Table 13-2 is a sample form). Some departments incur overtime on a regular basis due to peaks occurring in their processing. Overtime that is incurred by an organization on a sustained basis is indicative of either a staffing problem, an unmanageable workload, or some other problem. Sustained overtime should be investigated. For example, it may be that temporary staff is needed in lieu of paying the premium of overtime.

The use of agency personnel should be approved by one or two levels above the requestor. This will ensure the need is recognized. It will also eliminate the element of surprise when the invoice arrives.

One of the items that can be significant in fringe benefits is medical coverage for employees and their families. There should be an annual review of the coverage and cost to the financial institution in conjunction with one's insurance carrier. Such things as raising deductibles, limiting coverage of some types of nonsurgical treatment, and setting up an audit program to prevent duplicate payment, overpayment, and fraud may help.

Let's assume a staff member resigned on August 30 of the current year and had an annual salary of $20,000. The requisition is filled out and shows a higher salary of $22,000 and a proposed starting date of October 1. In terms of staff count there is a favorable impact. We have one month of the position being vacant. This equates to an impact of 0.083 staff (1.0 ÷ 12 = 0.083). This is approximately 8 percent of a full-time-equivalent staff.

The impact would be determined by the proposed new hire's salary, the month of hire, and the net difference from the salary of the person being replaced if applicable.

From this, one can see the staff equivalency impact if a favorable 0.083 for this year. It is debatable whether this 0.083 equivalency should then be carried over as an unfavorable impact for next year for this form. Next year's impact is important when hiring a staff member for a newly created position.

The salary impact is calculated with two processes in mind. The first is the favorable salary impact of having no incumbent for one month, exclusive of benefits. This amounts to a favorable $1,666.67 ($20,000 ÷ 12 = $1,666.67).

The next is the salary increase of $2,000. This amounts to an unfavorable impact of $166.67 ($2,000 ÷ 12 = $166.67). Adding a favorable $1,666.67 to the unfavorable $1666.67 gives an overall favorable impact of $1,500 for this year.

What if this were a newly created position? With a proposed start date of October 1 we would have an unfavorable three-month salary and staff equivalency impact on this year.

The impact would be calculated as follows:

$$\$22,000 \div 12 = \$1,833.33 \text{ per month.}$$
$$\$1,833.33 \times 3 \text{ months} = \$5,499.99.$$

The impact is $5,499.99 for the current year. The reciprocal of this would be the impact for next year, exclusive of any merit increases. Next year's salary impact for this newly created position would be $16,500.01 (22,000 − $5,499.99 = $16,500.01).

TABLE 13-2 Personnel Requisition Form

Position _____ Level/Grade _____

_____ Nonexempt _____ Exempt _____ Officer Salary (weekly or annual) _____

Organization/Department _____

Brief description of accountabilities:

Job-related skills needed:

Shift _____ Hours per week _____

Effective date of opening _____

_____ Staff addition _____ Replacement   (If replacement name of person being
                                                replaced _____ Date of departure _____)
                                                _____

Requesting officer _____ Phone _____

In the approved plan _____ YES _____ NO

(If answer is no, then what is the $ impact and staff equivalent impact for this year and next year?)

Impact of variance from approved plan and impact on next year favorable/(unfavorable):

This Year	Next Year
Staff Equiv.	Staff Equiv.
Impact _____	Impact _____
$ Impact _____	*$ Impact* _____

Approvals:

Requestor _____ Date _____ Manager _____ Date _____

Executive Approval _____ Date _____

The staff impact would be calculated as follows:

$$3 \text{ months this year} \div 12 \text{ months} = 0.25$$

This is an unfavorable impact equivalency of 0.25 staff. The reciprocal of this would be the impact for next year. The staff increase for next year attributable to the hiring in October of this year then is 0.75 staff (1.0 − 0.25 = 0.75.)

Postage and delivery.   Unless there is a charge-back system or some way to monitor postage, it can be a difficult thing to manage throughout the institution. Guidelines on such things as personal mail and express delivery could help to achieve more effective use of this category. Also presorting outgoing mail can save money. Additional savings can be realized by using the four-digit zip code suffix.

Stationery and supplies.   Volume discounts for the institution as a whole could be realized. Organizations within the institution could order from a central supply room. Cost may tend to be higher than they should be if the individual organizations stockpile a cache of such things. If the organizations are made aware of the austere availability of goods they will tend to be more judicious in their use.

Telecommunications.   Occasional reminders on keeping personal phone calls to a minimum are helpful in keeping both productivity and message unit costs down. An annual review could be made of telephone and other communication configurations to ensure there are no redundancies or cost inefficiencies in the system's use and design. Line and equipment use and configurations should be strategically planned and implemented.

Data processing.   An adequate charge-back system will allow the user's visibility on their costs. They would then be in a position to determine the cost incurred versus the value of service received.

Equipment rent/lease.   As mentioned earlier, an approval procedure should screen out unnecessary proposals.

Depreciation.   An asset tracking system that would show each organization the book depreciation of its capital items, which would allow them to be aware of what they have and its cost of depreciation.

Premises.   A charge back to each department or organization will cause them to manage to a certain level of premises costs. When organizations are charged for premises they have a tendency to be more judicious in their use of space.

Marketing/advertising.   Any expenditures in this area should be well planned and centrally coordinated. It should be part of a financial institution's overall strategy.

Entertainment.   Income-generating organizations have a tendency to incur entertainment expenses in greater amounts than do staff organizations. For those in commercial lending it is part of their function to entertain potential customers. This category could be occasionally monitored for its effectiveness in business development.

TABLE 13-3 Travel Authorization Form

Name of Requestor: _____

Organization/Department: _____

Planned Itinerary:

	From/To	Carrier	Date	Leave/Arrive	Hotel

Purpose of trip:

Benefit(s) to the institution as a result of the trip:

Estimated cost:

Transportation _____

Lodging _____

Meals _____

Other _____

Total _____

Is this in the approved plan? ____YES ____NO

Signature and approvals:

Requestor _____ Date _____ Manager _____ Date _____

Executive _____ Date _____

Travel. Most institutions have established guidelines on travel expenses. To begin with, some financial institutions require an authorization form be filled out that requires that an itinerary, mode of travel, estimated cost, and business purpose be stated. Some also ask whether the travel cost is within the current year's approved plan. Some institutions establish maximums on daily food and hotel accommodations. Some also specify the allowable seating class on flights. (Table 13-3 is a sample form.) Some travel agencies will provide you with centralized recordkeeping facilities to help monitor travel costs.

Professional/community activities. There are many outside organizations that are beneficial to financial institutions. The question of how many staff members in one's institution can join an outside organization is usually a function of what the budget can absorb in conjunction with what is deemed judicious. This should be controlled with a measurement of potential beneficial value to the financial institution. On the more costly memberships, the value of information coming in to the financial institution and the potential for business development should be weighed against the cost of the membership. As a control mechanism there should be some form of preapproval process before application for membership.

Charitable contributions. One of the most effective ways to handle charitable contributions is to centralize the approval and disbursement of funds. The tax deductibility of each charitable gift should be verified. The total amount of charitable gifts could then be planned centrally on an annual basis. A centralized disbursement also would facilitate tracking.

Recruiting. This category includes the cost of advertising job openings and interviewing prospective employees. It also includes executive search and employment agency fees incurred. This category can become significant, especially if a number of higher level positions are being filled. Some organizations have instituted programs of charging user organizations directly when search and agency firms are used. Recruiting costs can be controlled by charging each organization for the costs it has incurred in recruiting staff. Having them include this in their budget may be helpful, but often the timing of hiring needs is unpredictable. If a budget level is established for each level of staff being sought, the hiring (recruiting) department could be encouraged to stay within the budget levels established as they recruit staff by charging them for the recruiting expenses. The idea is to bring all hidden costs of recruiting to light and to manage them.

Employee education.   Tuition reimbursement, training programs, workshops, and seminars are all part of employee education. Each planned attendance should be preapproved. Before training programs, workshops and seminars are initiated, there should be a demonstrated need. Also a competitive comparison for price and quality should be made. Sometimes bringing workshops and seminars in-house via outside vendors is more cost effective than sending staff to the outside or hiring in-house educational staff.

Subscriptions.   Multiple subscriptions of the same publication should be kept at a minimum. Those that are discretionary could be recognized as such. Group rates on subscriptions can also be a cost saving measure.

Equipment maintenance.   Some equipment requires frequent repair. Items that seem to break down all the time should be investigated. Sometimes the equipment is faulty. Also the repair bills should be verified with the individual who requested the repairs. They should be checked for reasonableness. Repair contracts sometimes are less costly than paying for individual calls. Also a preventative maintenance program can reduce repair costs in the long run.

Insurance.   In managing risk there is a challenge to be adequately covered by not having any blind spots, or overlooked areas of exposure. The challenge is also not to be overinsured. In financial institutions that have subsidiaries there is potential for redundancies of coverage.

Legal fees.   Legal fees are a function of some activity in the institution that requires outside counsel. The hours billed should be closely checked for reasonableness.

Protection.   The cost of guards and alarm devices is accounted for in this category. The cost of having an internal guard force should be weighed against the cost of a guard service. There are times in the growth of an institution when one clearly is more cost effective than the other.

Collection.   The costs incurred in order to collect on delinquent accounts could be reviewed occasionally for cost effectiveness. The factors that produce results most effectively, while at the same time maintaining community relations, could be emphasized in order to optimize the expenses being incurred in this category.

Consulting.   The services of consultants are used for many purposes in keeping a financial institution current and effective. It may be appropriate to keep a central project log that lists any engaged consultants, the project, expected target date, and the contracted or expected fees. If project approval is sought before hand the benefits of engaging consultants can be weighed and decided by more than one person.

TABLE 13-4 Expense Claim Form

Name: _____ Date: _____

Organization/Dept.: _____ Org. Number _____

Date	Description/Purpose	Enter-tainment	Lodging	Staff Meals	Trans-portation	Total Other	Amount
Total		$					

Signature of person submitting claim: _____ Date: _____

Supvr/Mgr. Approval: _____ Date: _____

Department Head _____ Date: _____

Please attach all receipts. Any claims amounting to $25 or more must be accompanied by a receipt.

If this is a travel-related claim, please attach a copy of the approved itinerary.

Miscellaneous. This category traditionally becomes a catch-all for anything that is non-descript or unexplainable. A good control for this is to obtain explanations for all items that appear in this category.

Table 13-4 is an example of a basic expense claim form. The special needs and nature of one's organization will require additions to this form. The idea is to control costs through accountability.

REVIEWING OPERATING EXPENSE PLANS

Most financial institutions go through an annual planning cycle. As part of this exercise the plans are submitted and reviewed. In some organizations they come under close scrutiny. In others the review may be cursory because of timing. Some organizations do not review their plans in depth because they don't have the tools or framework that allows for a systematic review of their budgets.

Those organizations that have an annual planning exercise go through a process that involves a "test of reality." That is, the plans are checked for reasonableness given previous experience. With this in mind the following benchmarks may serve as focus points for comparison.

- Last year's actual expenses
- This year's approved expense plan
- Year-to-date actual (this year)
- This year's probable estimate
- Next year's proposed expense plan

Let's take a look at what each of these points represents. Last year's actual expenses is a historical account of last year's expenses and should not necessarily be accepted as the norm. Year-to-date actual (this year) is an up-to-date accounting of this year's expenses. This year's expense plan is the official approved plan for this year. This year's probable estimate, given the year-to-date actuals, is a derivation and projects the most likely outcome for the year. It is based on this year's plan and actuals. Some call this year's probable estimate *revised forecast.* Next year's expense plan is the proposed exercise plan for next year.

Zero-based Budgeting

If an organization were to plan using a zero-based budgeting they would challenge the necessity of all expenses. Historical expenses are not used as benchmarks in zero-based budgeting. This concept zeroes out all previous expense levels and causes each organization to cost-justify its existence from ground up. The focus of this method is to create a new expense base that relies on establishing know needs.

In the expense plan illustrated here only a few selected expense items have been listed. Assume the plan has been constructed based on actuals as of September 30 of a given year.

The first thing to look at is the staffing. Staff equivalents are derived. If a staff member were to either join an organization or leave it in the middle of the month they would affect that organization as a 0.5 staff equivalent for that month. A way of looking at this is the person would only be in the organization for one half of the month. Hence the calculation ($1/2 \times 1 = .5$).

In the following example the organization has a year-to-date average staff equivalency of 16.8 persons. The following table illustrates how this was derived:

Monthly FTE Staff

Jan.	16.1
Feb.	17.0
Mar.	17.0
Apr.	17.3
May	16.8
Jun.	16.8
Jul.	16.8
Aug.	16.7
Sep.	16.7

151.2 ÷ 9 = 16.8 average FTE

Later in this chapter a staff impact guide will be presented. The guide will help you to determine the impact on next year of any staff changes that occur this year and next year. (See table 3-5.)

In order to meet this year's probable estimate of 18.0 ± persons, the 12-month total must reach 216.0 (12 × 18.0). Subtracting 151.2 from 216.0 gives a 64.8 total for the last 3 months. That means an average of 21.6 (64.8 ÷ 3) staff must be present during the last 3 months of the year. However, the estimate as submitted shows 19.0 staff in December. This prompts a question. Is this organization hiring regular staff additions for just two months (October and November) and managing down to 19.0 in December? The reasons for this would need to be reviewed further. This illustrates how staff equivalency tracking can surface discrepancies during the planning exercise.

The next item to review is salaries, temporary help, overtime, bonuses, and fringe benefits. For this example only regular salaries, overtime and fringe benefits, are included. Let's review each item as presented.

Regular salaries. The plan called for salaries to average $18,000 per staff member ($306,000 + 17.0 = $18,000). However, the average salaries for the year to date indicate $18,492. This is calculated by dividing the $233,000 incurred year to date by the 9 months YTD. The result is divided by the average equivalent staff YTD. The result is a monthly average salary per staff equivalency. This is then annualized by multiplying with a factor of 12. The calculation is as follows.

$$\$233,000 \div 9 = \$25,889.$$
$$\$25,889 \div 16.8 = \$1,541.$$
$$\$1,541 \times 12 = \$18,492.$$

TABLE 13-5 Partial Expense Plan ($000's)

	Last year's actual expenses	This year's expense plan	This year's YTD actual as of 9/30/xx	This year's probable estimate (as submitted)	Next year's expense plan (as submitted)
Staff (Average equivalent)	15.4	17.0	16.8	18.0	19.5
December equivalent staff	16.0	17.0	—	19.0	20.0
Compensation					
Regular salaries	$231	$306	$233	$366	$400
Overtime	10	12	7	11	15
Fringe benefits	40	55	42	69	80
Total Compensation	$281	$373	$282	$446	$495

TABLE 13-5 Continued

	Last year's actual expenses	This year's expense plan	This year's YTD actual as of 9/30/xx	This year's probable estimate (as submitted)	Next year's expense plan (as submitted)
Other operating expenses:					
Marketing	127	150	160	160	170
Entertainment	34	55	42	60	66
Travel	18	27	30	35	38
Consulting	13	4	4	4	11
Depreciation	10	10	10	10	10
Miscellaneous	315	390	215	385	400
Total other operating	$517	$ 636	$461	$ 654	$ 695
Total expense	$798	$1,009	$743	$1,100	$1,190

This indicates the average salary levels are exceeding this year's plan. If we look further to the probable estimate of $366,000 there appears to be an unexplained amount. If we take the average staff count of 16.8 as of September 30, it seems unlikely the 18.0 probable estimate is a valid number. In order to achieve it there would have to be several staff additions during the last three months. The constraint is on 19.0 staff equivalent for December, however. The total staff equivalency given an average of 18.0 is calculated by multiplying $18.0 \times 12 = 216.0$ gross total. The gross total for the 16.8 average would be 201.6 (16.8×12). The staff equivalency to be achieved in the last three months is thus 14.4 ($216.00 - 201.6 = 14.4$). Dividing this by 3 gives an additional staff count of 4.8 for each of the last three months. This seems unlikely, since the December staff average is 19.0.

As previously mentioned the salaries appear to be overstated. Some of this could be explained by year-end merit increases and by staff additions. This should be explicitly accounted for however. The most likely occurrence is the addition of 2.2 staff equivalencies for the three months ($19.0 - 16.8 = 2.2$).

Let's try to determine the amount to be explained. We know that the 16.8 staff equivalent can be multiplied by $18,492 in order to project this year's average. Also the 2.2 staff additions can be multiplied by the average monthly salary of $1,541 for each of the three months. This of course would be modified if the real salaries were known. The calculation is

$$\$18,492 \times 16.8 = \$310,665$$
$$2.2 \times \$1,541 \times 3 = \underline{\quad 10,171}$$
$$\text{Total} \qquad \$320,836$$

Compare this to the probable estimate of $366,000.

$366,000	Probable estimate
– $320,836	Explainable
$ 45,164	To be explained

There is potential inflation in the $45,164. Sometimes exceptional one-time-only occurrences at year end distort the numbers. In any case an explanation should be sought. Also with these numbers it appears regular salaries will be exceeding this year's approved plan by $60,000 ($366,000 – $306,000).

Let's now look at the other operating expenses. Marketing, consulting, and depreciation are all flat from the YTD actual to the full-year probable estimate. In the depreciation category there should be some experience between September 30 and December 31. This is unless some assets are being removed from the depreciation list. Also for the next year the depreciation is flat. Again, explanations would have to be sought.

Miscellaneous as a category is inadequate if significant expenses are listed there. In the example there is a relatively high amount of expenses for this category. There also appear to be heavy expenses anticipated for the last quarter. Explanation should be sought for these categories.

The actuals YTD in comparison to plan already show some unfavorable variances. Marketing and travel expenses have already exceeded plan. There are further anticipated expenses for travel. It is anticipated that entertainment will exceed plan. These are indicators of the need for explanation and/or justification.

These brief examples point out the need for expense control in planning. This can be achieved through a systematic review procedure and participation in the planning exercise by management.

ANALYTICAL APPROACHES TO PLAN REVIEWS

Staffing

Calculating staff equivalencies is an important part of analyzing the impact of staffing changes in an organization. The example that follows has been designed so as to emphasize how these calculations assist in determining the effects of staff changes.

Assume the schedule in table 13-6 represents next year's total plan of a small financial institution.

In this example the probable estimate for the current year was increased significantly in the last quarter. The staff equivalency count went from 90.0 at the end of September to 100.0 in December. This example was placed here to emphasize how some departments may inflate their last quarter's estimate in order to make the next year's changes not appear as significant. In this example the staff equivalency for next year is planned at 100.0 for each of the months, hence no change from December of this year. The analyst needs to be aware of such changes in the last quarter, which have a tendency to distort the plan for next year.

TABLE 13-6 A Simple Staffing Plan

	This Year's Plan	This Year's Probable Estimate	Next Year's Plan
Jan	78.0	78.1	100.0
Feb	80.0	81.0	100.0
Mar	81.0	83.4	100.0
Apr	82.0	87.7	100.0
May	85.0	90.0	100.0
Jun	84.0	90.0	100.0
Jul	85.0	90.0	100.0
Aug	90.0	90.0	100.0
Sept	90.0	90.0	100.0
Oct	90.0	92.0	100.0
Nov	90.0	92.5	100.0
Dec	90.0	100.0	100.0
Total	1,025.0	1,064.7	1,200.0
Average	85.4	88.7	100.0

$(1,025 \div 12 = 85.4)$ $(1,064.7 \div 12 = 88.7)$ $(1,200.0 \div 12 = 100.0)$

A way of smoothing out these changes and thereby assessing their impact on this year versus next year is to work with average staff equivalencies. The full-time equivalent (FTE) staff average for this year was planned at 85.4. However, the probable estimate shows the average to be 88.7. The organization, therefore, is averaging an unfavorable staff variance of 3.3 FTE for the whole year. The increase of next year's plan over this year's probable is 11.3 FTE $(100.0 - 88.7 = 11.3)$. This is the real impact of planned changes of next year over this year, given this year's probable estimate.

Some of the 11.3 FTE impact could be attributable to turnover and delayed hiring that occurred in the current year. The analyst would most likely focus on obtaining more details on the increases in November and December of the current year. It would probably be worthwhile to determine the staff increases over plan in the current year that occurred in the months of January through September.

The regular staff may be considered as those who are either full-time or part-time but are on a permanent basis. Temporary staff is excluded from this count.

FTE staff factors are based on an hourly buildup. Assume for example there are 2,020 scheduled staff work hours in a given year. This excludes any vacation allowances. This buildup may occur as follows:

Jan	21 workdays × 8 hours =	168
Feb	20 workdays × 8 hours =	160
Mar	21.5 workdays × 8 hours =	172
Apr	21 workdays × 8 hours =	168
May	22 workdays × 8 hours =	176
Jun	21 workdays × 8 hours =	168
Jul	21 workdays × 8 hours =	168
Aug	23 workdays × 8 hours =	184
Sep	19 workdays × 8 hours =	152
Oct	23 workdays × 8 hours =	184
Nov	21 workdays × 8 hours =	168
Dec	20 workdays × 8 hours =	160
F*	<1> workday × 8 hours =	<8>
Total		2,020

*Floating holiday.

This, of course, changes every year. Therefore, the scheduled hours in each month will be different from year to year.

For example, assume a staff member has worked 500 hours in a year and has no vacation entitlement or sick leave; the full time equivalency is 0.25 (500 ÷ 2,020 = 0.25).

To help you better understand staff equivalency factors, table 13-7 has been prepared. This "impact guide" will help you evaluate the impact of staff changes in an organization. Its use can be explained by taking an example of an organization that is increasing its staff by 10 persons on June 1 of a current year. This equates to an impact of 5.8 equivalent staff for the current year. This is derived by calculating the number of months remaining in the year, dividing it by 12, and then multiplying by the number of staff. In this example the calculation is thus

$$\frac{\text{Number of months remaining in the year}}{\text{Number of months in the year}} = \text{Resultant impact factor.}$$

$$\frac{7}{12} = 0.583.$$

0.583	×	10	=	5.8
Resultant		Net staff		Full-Time
impact		changes		Staff
factor		for the		Equivalency
		month		Impact

The reciprocal of this is 4.2 (10.0 − 5.8 = 4.2). This becomes the impact of the current year's changes upon next year. Thus, the change in June of this year will impact next year with an FTE of 4.2 persons. The reciprocal helps determine what portion of the increase in next year's salaries is caused by additions to staff in the present year. The impact on next year's salaries is a full year's salary.

The factors in the staff equivalency impact guide (table 13-7) represent changes that occur on the first of the month only. Any changes that occur during the month would have to be accounted for by interpolating from one month to the next.

For example, if a change occurs on May 15, one would need to interpolate between the May and June factors. The factor for May is 0.667 and for June 0.583. The difference between the two factors is 0.084. If we divide this by 31, which represents 31 days for May, we have a daily factor of 0.0027096. We then take this factor and multiply it by the number of days in the month not affected by the change. In this example it is 14 days (May 1 through May 14). Thus the calculation is 14 × 0.0027096 = 0.037934. We then subtract the amount from the factor for May. Thus 0.667 − 0.037934 = 0.62906. Hence 0.62906 is the impact factor to be used for a staff change that occurs beginning on May 15.

TABLE 13-7 Staff Equivalency Impact Guide

Month of Change	Current Year Impact (Assumes change occurs on 1st day of month)	Reciprocal Impact on Next Year (Staff Equivalency)
Jan	1.000	0.000
Feb	0.917	0.083
Mar	0.833	0.167
Apr	0.750	0.250
May	0.667	0.333
Jun	0.583	0.417
Jul	0.500	0.500
Aug	0.417	0.583
Sep	0.333	0.667
Oct	0.250	0.750
Nov	0.167	0.833
Dec	0.083	0.917

Another way of calculating this factor is to take the number of days in May affected by this change and add the daily factors to the month of June's factor. The calculation would thus be 17 × 0.0027096 = 0.046063. (0.583 + 0.046063 = 0.62906.)

In addition to using this guide for staff equivalency impact calculations, it can also be used for calculating the impact of salary. Take for example the hiring of one additional staff member on September 1 of the current year. Assume the person's annual salary is $21,000. The impact factor for September is 0.333. This is multiplied against the $21,000 salary. The calculation results in a salary impact of $6,993 (0.333 × $21,000 = $6,993). This means the impact on the current year is $6,993 if one adds a staff member on September 30 at an annual salary of $21,000. The impact of this staff addition on next year is 0.667. You will notice that 0.333 + 0.667 = 1.0. The salary for this staff addition for next year is thus $14,007 (0.667 × $21,000 = $14,007). We have essentially accounted for this person's salary impact for the two calendar years ($6,993 + $14,007 = $21,000).

Aggregate Compensation Increases

In analyzing the expense plan for an organization it is important to have visibility on average increases both in absolute dollars and in percentages. The average salary calculations shown in table 13-8 are a method of gaining visibility on salary level changes. Assume the probable estimate for this year is an average staff of 88.7

TABLE 13-8 Average Salary Calculations

	Probable Estimate Current Year		Next Year's Plan		Change from Current Year
Salaries	$1,698,281		$2,107,562		$409,281
Total salary					
percentage change	$409,281	÷	$1,698,281	=	24.1%
Staff(FTE)	88.7		100.0		11.3
FTE Staff					
Percentage Change	11.3	÷	88.7	=	12.7%
	This year		Next year		
Average salary	$1,698,281		$2,107,562		
per FTE staff	÷ 88.7		÷ 100.0		
	= $19,146.35		= $21,075.62		
Average salary	Next year		This year		Average increase
increase per	$21,075.62	−	$19,146.35	=	$ 1,929.27
FTE staff	$ 1,929.27	÷	$19,146.35	=	10.08%
calculation					
Average Salary Increase			Amount	$1,929.27	
Per FTE Staff			Percent	10.08%	
Salary impact	Average salary		FTE Staff		
of staff additions[1]	next year	×	increase		
FTE	$21,075.62	×	11.3	=	$238,154.50

[1]Assuming the staff increases were at salary levels within the average range.

FTE with an aggregate salary of $1,698,281. Also assume the plan for next year is an average staff of 100.0 FTE with an aggregate salary $2,107,562. Some of the questions to be raised would be: What is the aggregate staff FTE and salary change? What is the impact of FTE changes? What is the percentage increase in salaries?

Assuming the staff additions all have proposed salaries within the average range these questions can be readily answered. Table 13-8 shows the calculations that answer each of these questions.

From these calculations management is informed on the impact of next year's salary plan and the specifics of what goes behind the numbers.

The explanation of the $409,281 in salary change is now explainable as follows:

Salary increases (existing staff)		
$ 1,929.27 × 88.7 =	$171,126	
Staff Additions		
$21,075.62 × 11.3 =	$238,155	
Total	$409,281	

Analyzing Other Operating Expenses

In reviewing other operating expenses, the items that appear as obvious changes are those with high percentage and dollar changes. The underlying reasons should be sought. For example, volume changes could be driving certain expenses in a given direction.

In certain organizations expenses are inflated in the probable estimate for the last months of the current year in order to make the next year's increases not look so high. There is a formula that can be applied against such estimates so as to enable the analyst to uncover the possible inflation. One must be cautioned that what appears as inflation to a cost analyst may appear to be a legitimate and explainable expense to the manager. The formula appears as follows:

Current year's probable estimate expense reality formula:
1. Actual expenses year-to-date (YTD)
2. +/− Exceptional items YTD
3. = YTD normalized trend
4. × 12 ÷ number of months YTD
5. = Full year normal trend
6. +/− Anticipated exceptional items remainder of current year; Add back in +/− exceptional items from Number 2.
7. = Current year's probable estimate as calculated
8. − Current year's probable estimate as submitted
9. = Gross variance (possible inflation)

1. The *actual expenses year-to-date* (YTD) represent the total of all expenses through a specified month. An example of this would be the YTD expenses as of September. Assuming a calendar year, this would include all expenses from January through September, a total of 9 months.

2. *Exceptional items* include one-time-only expenses. This would be things that are not expected to be repeated again. This category could also represent a lack of expenses—that is, expenses that should have occurred but did not.

3. The YTD *normalized* trend is calculated by taking the year-to-date expenses and subtracting or adding any of the exceptional items.

4. This fraction provides an annualized (12 month) indication of what the expenses would be given no exceptional items and a steady state. The year-to-date portion represents the actual expenses to date. If, for example, the YTD is through September, the calculation would be expressed $12/9 \times$ YTD normalized trend. An alternative to this is the YTD normalized trend divided by 9 and then multiplied by 12.

5. The *full year normalized trend* is the result of calculations in line 4.

6. All *anticipated exceptional items* for the remainder of the year and from item 2 are added back in or subtracted out as appropriate.

7. The resultant current year outlook as calculated is provided as the *current year's probable estimate as calculated.*

8. The *probable estimate as submitted* by the organization is subtracted from the current year's outlook as it appears on line 7 of this formula.

9. The resultant *gross variance* appearing on this line reveals items for possible explanation by the organization that submitted its probable estimate. A negative figure on this line would indicate a possible understatement of planned expenses.

The Comparative Three

The following are additional formulas for plan analysis. They provide the analyst with additional quantitative tools. As a matter of note if an organization experiences an expense level that is significantly below plan, it probably means they have not done a good job at planning. Unless there are operational factors that changed their expenses level they probably inflated their expense levels during the previous planning exercise.

The three comparisons to focus on are as follows:

1. Current year probable estimate
   – current year's plan
   = unfavorable/favorable variance from plan.

2. Current year's probable estimate
   – last year's plan
   = unfavorable/favorable change from last year.

3. Next year's plan
   – current year's probable estimate
   = unfavorable/favorable change from current year

These three formulas should prove helpful in isolating variances for further analysis. The idea is to identify variances so they can be researched further.

14

Product Management
and Pricing

The activities of cost analysis are valuable to many organizations within a financial institution. Some organizations and committees rely heavily on the data and guidance provided by the cost analysts. The data is most useful in making decisions concerning organizational and product continuance or change. Committees such as a pricing committee depend upon data in making pricing decisions.

Those performing cost analysis may find themselves in a consultative role as they advise the various patrons of cost analysis data on interpretation, application, and decisions arising out of the use of cost analysis data. Often the recipients need to know the potential impact of a future course of action. In this chapter we will cover the interface of cost analysis with such organizations as product management or marketing, line organizations, and key committees.

PRODUCT MANAGEMENT

As financial institutions have faced a more diverse and competitive marketplace, some have found they need a formal product management function. Product management is the systematic development, delivery, and maintenance of products to enhance their quality and profitability. A product manager monitors a product's development, production, marketing, and delivery.

Product managers are accountable for

- Ideas for product improvements and new products

- Development of new products

- Strategies for products

- Coordination between the processing areas and customers

- Cognizance of legal, regulatory, and other environmental considerations pertaining to specific products

- Coordination of a marketing program that is consistent with a product's strategy

- Development of a consistent and systematic pricing policy

Essentially a product manager is held accountable for knowing the intricacies of a product from the processing areas to the marketplace.

Financial institutions with no system of product managers may have a marketing department or a committee that oversees all the necessities in managing a product. If such is the case, then a careful monitoring for consistent and systematic product evaluation is necessary.

In recent years the marketing area in financial institutions has become more narrowly defined as an advertising function. This is especially true in institutions that offer a diversity of products. The management of products both in sales and delivery has been given over to a product management function in many financial institutions. Product managers are accountable for the conceptual, developmental, and logistical aspects of products. They must interface with marketing, line groups, and their sales staff. They are the ones who bring things together for financial institution's products as those products are being offered to customers.

Product management focuses on consistency in every aspect of product sales and delivery. As the driving force behind quality of service, these managers look to cost analysis for support in preparing for reviews by the pricing committee and senior management reviews.

The Pricing Committee

Whether a financial institution is small or large it is likely to realize beneficial results from having a pricing committee. There are a number of advantages to having such a committee organized for the purpose of product pricing. The following are items to consider relative to the functioning of a pricing committee.

The committee usually reviews fee-based products of a noncredit nature. Credit-related products, such as loans, are usually reviewed by another committee, such as an asset/liability management committee.

All products should be reviewed for costing updates on a specific cycle, say every 12 months. The committee may defer this review to the cost analysis manager. Therefore, it is discretionary whether the pricing committee should be reviewing the frequency of product costings and giving direction.

It is most important, however, to have a specific review cycle for product pricing purposes. The secretary of the pricing committee, in conjunction with the cost analysis manager or product management, may keep records and a suspense file on product pricing review schedules. Product management should evaluate each product for strategic pricing, depending upon cost analysis to produce analyses of profit and loss for proposed pricing changes. If sufficient coordination and lead time have occurred, then new cost data should be available with the pricing review.

Products should be reviewed on a regular cycle for strategic pricing purposes, annually for example. There are occasions when tactical pricing is necessary. These may arise at a moment's notice.

The pricing committee membership should reflect a good cross section of the bank's senior managers. Ideally, the membership should consist of no more than seven persons. In small banks it may be prudent to have a smaller committee, say three persons. The members should represent functions that have a vested interest in the pricing of products. The following are suggested functions from which to draw representatives:

Product management or marketing

Income-producing groups (line groups)

Operations

Chief financial officer or controller

Cost analysis manager

The committee should have a chairperson, secretary, and alternates. Rules on what constitutes a quorum and proxy voting should be clearly stated in the committee's charter.

Given that financial institutions are centers of much activity, it may be difficult to get everyone together at one time. Hence it is a good idea to have a stated time, date, and place of meeting well in advance. Proposed agenda and supporting data should be included with the meeting announcement package.

TABLE 14-1 Pricing Review Sheet

Name of Product: _Commercial deposits_   Product Description: _____

Current Price: _$1.50_   Merchant deposits at a teller window

Date of Last Price Change: _2/1/x_   _____

Unit Cost: _$1.42 Rounded_   _____

Amount and % of last Price Change:

_$.25_   / _20%_

Proposed Price : _$2.00_   Effective date : _2/1/x_

Amount and % of Proposed Change:

_$.50_   / _33%_

Product Strategy: _Labor intensive. Plan to offer an incentive to those merchants who have their deposits_

_more organized._____

_____

_____

Impact or Price change

1. Profits this year: _$2,150_   Next Year: _$3,700_

2. Customer reaction: _No drop offs are expected_

3. Regulatory/Government considerations: _None_

4. Operational considerations: _None_

5. Competition: _The Main Street Bank charges $1.00 per deposit._

Product Management/Marketing Approval: _____

Cost Analysis Approval: _____

During the meeting, product management of marketing generally outlines and explains any proposed pricing changes and the underlying strategies and tactics. The cost analysis manager explains the financial reports—that is, the profit-and-loss impact statement and any relevant cost data.

It is the chairperson's job to ensure the major issues are adequately covered and that concerns are raised and discussed. The chairperson also keeps the meeting moving in a positive and productive direction toward making pricing decisions.

The secretary takes notes on the proposals, relevant discussion, and decisions. Minutes are later produced and distributed to attendees and departments affected.

TABLE 14-2 Profit-and-Loss Impact of Price Changes

	This Year			Next Year		
	Without Change	With Change	Net Difference	Without Change	With Change	Net Difference
Revenue	$10,050	12,200	2,150	11,100	14,800	3,700
Costs	9,500	9,500	0	11,000	11,000	0
Net income before tax	550	2,700	2,150	100	3,800	3,700

```
   6700   deposits anticipated this year    7,400 deposits anticipated next year.
-   600   already occurred in January
   ----
   6100   remaining in the year             It is anticipated the current unit cost of $1.42 will
× $ 2.00                                    increase next year.
   -----
 $12,200
```

No drop-offs anticipated

The secretary also works closely with product management or marketing to ensure any fee changes are properly communicated to the institution's customers.

The functioning of a pricing committee should not be perfunctory and mundane. The members should have insights and knowledge that will add much to the purpose of the committee. Positive contributors should be encouraged to participate in the committee's activities.

As part of the review agenda there are three suggested forms to include for each product being priced. They are pricing review sheet (table 14-1); the profit-and-loss impact sheet (table 14-2); and the competition information sheet (table 14-3). The suggested review sheet has blank lines to be filled in with name of product, a brief product description and characteristics, current price, date of last price change, amount and percentage of last price change, proposed price, effective date of proposed price change, amount and percentage of proposed price change, and a brief description of the product's strategy. The review sheet also has a section labeled "Impact of price change."

The profit-and-loss impact sheet (table 14-2) lists revenue, costs, and net income before tax for the following: this year without and with change, net impact of the change, next year without and with change, and the impact of the changes on next year. An addendum to this form would be needed for unit cost updates. Any changes in costs attributable to updating must be discernible from the impact of pricing changes.

TABLE 14-3 Analysis of Competition

Product: Commercial Deposits

	Name of Institution	Current Price	Estimation of Quality and Direction of Products
1.	First Bank	$1.25	Plans for price increase to $1.35 have been shown in recent mailing.
2.	Dry Gulch Bank	—	No charge. They use this as a loss leader. However merchants complain about their quality of service.
3.	Main Street Bank	1.00	They only charge $1.00. Their service is considered superior. No indication of a price increase.
4.			
5.			
6.			
7.			

The analysis of competition (table 14-3) is a listing of the competition by institution name, their products' prices, and an assessment of their products' quality. Also any knowledge of the competition's intended direction (strategy) for the product is helpful. Some products are not comparable in pricing structure from one institution to another. This should not be a hindrance to listing the pricing structure, however.

PRICING CONSIDERATIONS

In reviewing a product for pricing the committee and product management or marketing may take into consideration the following:

- Profitability
- Product marketplace strategy

- Competition

- Perceived quality (the perceived value of the service to the customer)

- Regulatory/governmental considerations

- Community impact

- Customer base

- Potential cross impact to other products

- Opportunities for potential cost reduction

The profitability consideration is one of answering how much is the institution willing to lose or profit on the product being repriced. Some products are inherently unprofitable. Therefore, a view must be taken as to how much should be absorbed in losses on such a product. Sometimes a financial institution must offer a service at an inherent loss as part of a larger package of services. This practice is giving way to "unbundling" services and letting them stand alone. Profitability is usually the goal. In reviewing the mix of fees for a product, management should seek to optimize the profitability without deteriorating the customer base. This is where reliable market research and sensitivity analyses are useful. Also this may indicate a need to reduce costs rather than increase the price.

Product strategy centers around establishing a goal for a given product. The goal may be to provide a high-quality service that is exclusive to a particular customer base. Or it may be planned obsolescence, or discouraging unprofitable customers.

It is a good idea to find out what the competition is charging for a similar product. Two things are to be considered though. First, the competition may be about to reprice their product, and, second, the quality of their product may be different from what your institution is offering. Obviously the product management or marketing people of one financial institution cannot phone the product management of another bank to discuss these matters. It takes a more subtle approach to determine what the competition is doing. Sometimes the competition has a different product bundling and pricing structure than does your institution. This makes price comparisons difficult.

A product's perceived quality in the marketplace will determine how well you can sell a price increase. If the quality is not unique, specialized, and indispensable, then the product may suffer a loss of patronage. Quality is the bottom line of success for a product. In the long run the success of a product is a function of its perceived quality in the marketplace.

The regulatory or governmental considerations center around legal ramifications, if any, of a proposed change. Any limitations or prohibitions should be properly researched and discussed prior to any decision on pricing.

The impact of price changes on the community must be considered. A substantial increase in fees for a particular product could adversely affect a disadvantaged segment of the community. Hence, the profit motive may become a social issue within this context.

The expected customer reaction to price changes should be quantified. Sometimes the loss of customers given a certain level of increase can be predicted fairly accurately. Not only do changes in customer levels affect profitability, but they also affect the processing and support areas. Based on the foregoing, it is prudent to assess the impact of customer level changes on the institution.

The change in price of one product may have an impact on another product. Any possible cross impacts such as this should be explored in advance of pricing decisions. The idea is to ensure the overall marketplace strategy is being conformed to as pricing decisions are made.

Pricing Strategies

An overall goal in setting a pricing strategy may be the maximization of profits within the context of providing a high-quality service to customers at a reasonable price. Pricing to achieve this goal requires great skill. Pricing decisions must be well planned and executed. Sufficient analysis of relevant information is important.

In setting pricing strategies some financial institutions have emerged as leaders. They have a reputation for boldly stepping out with pricing changes and structures that are different from what presently exists. But a word of caution. Those who take the lead must have a through knowledge of the risks of their decisions. Offering free checking accounts with no minimum balance is not going to bring in profits to a financial institution. It may do the opposite by bringing in more customers and concomitantly higher operating costs. In order to step out as a leader, a financial institution must have a market knowledge that makes them aware of the market's potential. If they raise the prices to the highest level possible, they are counting on the perceived quality and reputation of their product to carry them through the initial reaction in the marketplace. If customers can discern a quality that is above the competition, then a price change may not drive them to a competitor.

One of the reasons for having cost information available during pricing reviews is to have visibility on potential profit levels given certain pricing scenarios. But what if a financial institution's costs are at the same level as the fees or even higher? Should the institution raise fees to cover inefficiencies? Or are the fees to low? What is the competition's price for this same service? These questions suggest a product knowledge that extends to knowing how efficient the production for a given product is. They also suggest a knowledge of what is being offered by the competition. Should there be low productivity in conjunction with the delivery of a specific product, then higher fees will only mask the problem in the short run.

On the wholesale side where there is bulk processing, the business is more price sensitive. Customers will unbundle their relationship with a financial institution when they can receive a major processing service at a lower price elsewhere. This, of course, assumes the quality of delivery is perceived as being equal.

Financial institutions can realize a substantial increase in fees by charging for services rendered. For example, some financial institutions charge for all transactions conducted on behalf of customers and for advice, research, and assistance in putting together third-party deals. Some institutions have become aware of many opportunities for fee income by having their account officers charge for putting deals together that may have been done gratis by the institution in previous years. Time is money. The financial institution is essentially selling its services to its customers.

When a financial institution raises prices it risks a decline in volume. This is why sensitivity analyses are so important. The impact of an increase in price should be greater than the impact of decreased volume (business). For some services the demand is relatively inelastic. That is, the demand is still there regardless of the pricing level. It is necessary service with no alternative choices available. Maybe your institution is the only one in the area that offers a particular service. The tolerance level is high for price increases in noncompetitive service offerings. Where the same service is offered by several banks in an area, then the quality must be discernible and the service be competitively priced given that quality. Responses to pricing are usually elastic when alternatives are available to the customers. That is, they may change financial institutions for a service offering that is available elsewhere at a lower price. Pricing in a competitive environment entails comparing one's financial institution to the other financial institutions. At the same time maintaining profitability is an important goal.

The following is a simple example of a pricing sensitivity analysis. Assume the institution offers a service at $1.00 per transaction, such as money orders. The present volume is 12,000 transactions per year. This results in $12,000 ($1.00 × 12,000 = $12,000) revenue for a given year. Assume there has been a proposal to raise the fee to $1.25. This is a $0.25 or 25 percent increase. Also assume that it is estimated some 15 percent of the customers will take their business elsewhere as a result of the price increase. The analysis is as follows:

Revenue at existing price	*Revenue with proposed price increase*	*Net increase/ (decrease) in revenue*
$1.00 × 12,000 =	$1.25 × 10,200 =	
$12,000	$12,750	$750
	(100% − 15% = 85%)	($12,750 − $12,000 = $750)
	.85 × 12,000 = 10,200	

The sensitivity analysis indicates the price increase may result in a net revenue increase of $750. This is in spite of a 15 percent decrease in business.

The frequency of reviews for pricing should be once or twice a year for a product group or product line. It should not be any sooner or confusion will result. It is also costly to produce new price lists. If all the services of a product group or product line are reviewed for repricing at the same time, an integration of strategy can be realized. The logistics will also be easier than if the pricing were on a piecemeal basis. Exceptions to this are repricings for tactical purposes. In any event, these kinds of repricings need to be in concert with the overall established strategy.

The following are points to consider in developing an overall pricing strategy:

- An active stance in looking for opportunities to charge for services rendered will enhance the revenue of a financial institution.

- Pricing can be used as a means to encourage customers toward use of automated services in lieu of labor-intensive services of the same kind.

- Revenue can be increased by raising prices, increasing customers, and eliminating discounts.

- Discounts, such as those for volume or bulk business and off-hours processing should be given close scrutiny in terms of profit contribution.

- Customers are willing to pay for something if they think they can afford it and the value being received is worth the price being paid.

Tactical Maneuvers in Product Pricing

There are times when pricing decisions must be made quickly and are not part of the normal schedule or agenda. The perceived need for this kind of pricing usually occurs when the marketplace has changed. Marketplace changes such as regulatory decisions, a competitor's actions, and the business environment in general all prompt change. Sometimes these come without warning—hence the need for a tactical response.

Financial institutions should be aware that a homogeneous appearance of all financial institutions to the marketplace is eroding. Customers are looking for a difference between the financial institution on one corner from the financial institution on the other corner. To be sure, customers seek out financial institutions for convenience, quality, competence, and overall image. They also look for that special attention of service that caters to their special needs. Customers seek out financial institutions that will help them to optimize their financial position. They look for financial institution staff who have product knowledge. These characteristics must be kept in mind as a financial institution positions itself for response to the marketplace.

Too often tactical pricing decisions are a passive reaction to an event that has occurred elsewhere. But tactical pricing should be active. This is a new trend possible as the forces of deregulation allow financial institutions to enter into areas that were previously not available. In any case tactical pricing is short term. It is a pricing arrangement to position a financial institution in the marketplace immediately yet in conformance with an overall strategy. Tactical pricing must be consistent with strategic pricing.

The following points may be helpful in making tactical pricing decisions:

- Some opportunities are lost through inaction.

- Decisions made in haste may have to be rescinded later.

- Prince cuts are generally counterproductive.

- One must not wait for cost updates when they are not forthcoming in the near future and fees are clearly below market. This is especially true if a product is due for repricing anyway.

- A financial institution cannot expect to optimize its profitability if it offers services at a loss.

"Me too" pricing can lead a financial institution away from profitability. For example, if a competitor financial institution offers free checking accounts with no balance minimums, does that mean one's institution should respond with the same offering? Not necessarily. To begin with, the competitor is obviously losing money on the low balance accounts that this pricing level will attract. Checking accounts are expensive to maintain. Second, customer loyalty will cause some customers to stay with a financial institution in spite of price differences. This is where differentiation of one institution's image from another's is important in meeting one's competition in the marketplace. The customers who change their account in response to an offer for a free account are probably those with low average balances. Those who have balances above pricing minimums would be insulated from the motivation of a free checking account since they essentially already have one. The institution that offers free checking accounts to all is in effect doing a favor to the other financial institutions in the area as they are absorbing cost attracting customers.

Pricing should be viewed as a vehicle for profit improvement through fee revenue optimization.

15

Designing, Building, and Implementing a New Cost Accounting System

Some organizations grow, others consolidate and therefore reduce in size. Along with these two typical responses to the ever changing business environment, we see changes in management personnel and philosophy. Sometimes new directions are necessary. In the financial services market, change is inevitable. In response to change, both internal and external, new courses of action are being taken, current thinking is being revised, and approaches are being modified.

As a financial institution changes so does its management's needs. Cost analysis is affected by these changes because of its mandate to provide information to management. Obvious changes such as organizational realignments and new-product offerings are visible to those in cost analysis. But changes in strategy and philosophy are not always as apparent.

Another type of change is growth. A certain level of growth can render a cost information system useless. Hence the cost manager must be aware of inadequacies—both current and future. Future inadequacies are to be anticipated given present trends. What is to be avoided is having the quality of one's cost data diminish because of rigidity.

This chapter is intended as a catalyst for reviewing the adequacy of one's cost information system. Some of the subject mentioned as candidates for change are data delivery, calculation techniques, and costing approaches. A checklist for evaluating an existing system and determining the need for consultants is included.

PLANNING FOR CHANGE

One of the first steps in planning for change is to assess your institution's present cost system. A list of shortcomings and areas in need of improvement should be made. Some of the symptoms of an ineffective and perhaps obsolete system are as follows:

- A basic lack of understanding by most analysts of the conceptual framework of and procedural sequences in the system (indicating an overly complex system)

- A plethora of detail, activity, and paper in order to produce the needed results

- Overall lack of confidence in the numbers produced by the system

- Unexplainable variances

- Lack of reconcilability to the general ledger

- Cost ineffectiveness, the value of the data being insufficient to support the cost of effort to produce it

- Transfer pricing that tends to cause large variances from plan

- A long list of qualifiers and conditional assumptions preceding the data presentation

- Slowness or infrequency of output

- High overhead (G&A) rates (indicating a lack of specific information that would normally lead to direct assignments or allocations)

Any or all of these deficiencies can impair a financial institution's success. The more of these weaknesses that exist in an institution's cost system, the more propensity there should be toward change.

Take the deficiencies as the starting point in planning for change. Concentrate on these areas in redesigning your cost system.

The next step is to identify present and future needs. All financial institutions need cost/benefit information that will allow measurement of profitability and performance as well as control of costs. They also need information that will facilitate decision making such as determining pricing levels for products. These are the basics.

A survey of line, product, or marketing, and other managers may produce a lengthy list of things they would like to have available from a cost system. Some may be necessary. Others may be discretionary. For example, product management or marketing may need information relative to product profitability on an actual and a pro forma basis. This would facilitate decision making on the introduction, modification, or discontinuance of existing products. They may indicate they would like to have information on fixed and variable costs. But is the additional request cost justified? Will it provide useful information? This needs to be answered before the request can be seriously considered for inclusion in system redesign.

In the marketing area there may be a need for information relative to product profitability, market share, and market segmentation. Financial institutions need to know what they are selling and to whom. They also need information that allows them the opportunity to cross-sell and strategically price to the market place. Sensitivity analysis given different pricing levels may be needed.

On the cost control side there is a need for information that will flag cost-containment or cost-reduction opportunities. There is also a need for information that indicates or prescribes staffing levels.

These are just a few of the needs that may presently exist. But what of the future? Where is the institution going? Is it expanding its product lines? Where will the institution be in the next 5 to 10 years? Will its structure and direction change? One must imagine the future paths the institution may take. The needs and objectives of the organization must be taken into consideration. The assessment of present circumstances and needs lays the groundwork for future planning. The aim is to be open and aware that change is ultimately necessary, as time passes.

Flexibility Is Key

If a system is designed with flexibility then it should be adaptable to changes in the institution's management style and to organizational growth. As the chain of command changes so does the philosophy of what is needed for decision making. An integrative thinker at the top may enjoy receiving volumes of detailed information. However, at the opposite pole is the decisive manager who only wants to see data summarized at its highest level. Most challenging of all is a management structure that has both styles of managers. The costing system should be flexible enough to accommodate either style with minimal change. It should be a matter of being able to call out some reports and to suppress certain other reports.

In institutions where there is a decisive style at the top, the input of primary data that is detailed may be considered superfluous. Therefore, the ability to modify for different types of input in the future may be necessary within these kinds of structures.

As an institution grows so does its organizational structure. There is a tendency toward departmental expansion during times of growth. When a department's hierarchy changes, management information reporting must change. It may be a matter of adding, deleting, or changing numerical designators, literal descriptions, and information needs. There should be enough room for growth in the table structure for the numerical codes and enough flexibility to be able to make changes in cost routing techniques.

In the event that growth exceeds expectations, the system should be designed with enough flexibility to accommodate future growth. The system must be designed so as to accommodate that which doesn't exist today but may exist in the future.

Considerations in Building a New System

In the early stages of planning for a new or redesigned cost information system there are many decisions to be made. Among them is the scope and parameters of the new system. Is it just going to track costs? Is it going to be a transfer system as well? Will it report profitability by organization, product, and customer? How will it account for overhead and residuals recoupment? Is funds accounting going to be included? If so, what are the proposed techniques? What are the proposed levels of reporting? How frequent will the reports be produced? From this comes a clear definition statement on what the system will and won't do. Intention, reasoning, and logic should be part of the statement. It is essential to have a clear understanding among the participants as to the intended direction of the project.

No doubt there are many factors providing impetus for establishing or improving one's cost information system. The following is a list of factors that cause financial institutions to realize they need to have a firm grasp of what it is costing them to do business:

- Profit margins are being squeezed tighter and tighter.

- Compensation is too costly.

- The impact of operating expenses on functional activities and products needs to be known.

- Decisions on product lines must be made.

- Inefficiencies and extravagances need uncovering.

These are just a few of the important reasons why some form of systematic cost analysis is necessary for each financial institution. This need is true of all financial institutions, regardless of size.

The uses for cost/profitability data are many. It is important to review the intended use of the data as one designs the conceptual framework of the system. The major applications are cost/profitability reporting for organizations, products, and customers; cost control; cost transfers; cost analysis; funds accounting; and pricing.

Make a list of these objectives before establishing or revising any system. Objectives should include flexibility; ease and economy of use and maintenance; as usefulness and a management tool. The system should include or be reconcilable to total organizational, product, and customer reporting, and address pricing issues decisions needs. The system should permit formatting of data for different decision applications and be compatible and consistent with other systems, particularly feeder systems.

Once these basic conceptual and policy issues have been resolved, a feasibility study is in order. A certain amount of simulation may be conducted by using flowcharts to trace how data will be derived to suit report formats.

Pitfalls

An ideal or perfect system will take a long time to design and implement. It may well become obsolete before it is fully in use. Don't expect perfection on the first pass. But it something doesn't fit because of faulty design, don't try to force it. Doing so will tarnish the quality of the system.

A system without a map will produce aimless results, so spend as much time as you need preparing documentation.

Don't try to force the system on other organizations in the institution. Try to sell them on the idea by showing them how they will benefit.

Don't cross the implementation bridge until design testing has proved the system is workable, usable, and therefore useful. The numbers must be credible from the start. Revising your deadline in order to achieve quality may be better than a timely implementation that is plagued with problems.

Keep people informed. Capture their attention. Let them know what is happening. Direct their attention, interest, and commitment toward getting the job done.

Don't try to do everything at once. Build on success achieved bit by bit.

Finally, don't promise to cure all ills. Instead, focus on the potential benefits of the proposed output from the system.

In order to justify a cost information system one must be able to sell the concept and the expected results to senior management. Their interest may lie in receiving more timely, accurate, and detailed information. These are the attributes of an effective system.

Systems that are vastly integrated and automated can become costly. They also may be difficult to cost-justify. The worth of the beneficial data must be weighed by management as they consider the cost and benefits of automating versus some other alternative. Often a system's concept can be sold on the merits of the decision-making information that it will make available to management.

There is a need for bottom-up integrity of information. That is, the data must come together in a well-defined and logical order at the lowest levels. There must be an audit trail that allows tracing of the process from one hierarchy to the next. The accuracy of the numbers should be verifiable at each level. A careful construct will add to the acceptability of the system. It will also allow for analysis of what is occurring throughout the institution at various levels.

Another item to consider is the information data base. Understanding how the information is captured and stored is important. If it is highly complex and unexplainable, then there will be doubt cast on the accuracy of what is being reported. However, if it is simple and easy to understand, it will be more acceptable.

Selection of Methodology

As mentioned earlier in this book there are basically two costing methodologies: standard and nonstandard. Either methodology could be based on current/actual data or budgeted (plan) data. There are advantages and disadvantages to each methodology.

Keeping in mind that standard costing utilizes the development of prescribed costs let's look at the standard approach again. The advantages are:

1. Volume variances can be sorted out from spending variances.

2. Inefficiencies can be isolated and quantified.

3. Excess capacity becomes known and can be financially quantified.

4. The costs are relatively stable from one reporting period to the next.

The basic disadvantages of standard costing are as follows:

1. The system may be complex and therefore costly to maintain.

2. Unless there is a total capturing and relocation of the costs from residual pools, the true item costs are not known.

In nonstandard costing, the basic approach is *average item costing* (AIC). The total costs are divided by the total volume to arrive at a total per item cost. Some refer to it as the "actual costing" approach.

The advantages of AIC are as follows:

1. The methodology is relatively simple to work with and explain.

2. The true item costs are known.

The disadvantages are:

1. The item costs have a tendency to fluctuate with volume, and are therefore relatively unstable.

2. Volume and spending variances are often difficult to discern.

3. Inefficiencies are unknown.

A standard costing system is more costly to develop, implement, and maintain than is a nonstandard system. It requires a higher maintenance cost than the nonstandard approach because time standards must be kept. As a project, a standard costing system takes longer, from design through implementation, than does a nonstandard system. Even if an institution elects to use standard costs, it is unlikely that this technique would be used across the board in all situations and in all areas. Standard costs would probably be used in high-volume, high-cost areas. Some form of average costs would probably be used in areas of relatively insignificant volume and cost.

All of these factors must be weighed against the benefits of having a system that prescribes what the costs *should* be. This really goes back to the philosophy and commitment of senior management. The advantages, disadvantages, cost, and commitment of each methodology must be weighed against this backdrop.

Whichever of these two methodologies is selected, occasional special applications and designs will be needed. And because each institution is unique, certain approaches may require modification in order to facilitate the selected methodology.

THE USE OF OUTSIDE CONSULTANTS

Consultants can play a vital role in assisting an institution as it faces the challenges of implementing or changing its cost system. As outside assistants, consultants can objectively review the strength's and weaknesses of the cost/profitability data being produced and reported to management. They can assess where the needs are, both in the systematization of reporting and in its content. They can also see blindspots that may not be apparent to incumbent staff. The role of consultants is to augment or supplement management. Consultants assist by helping with ideation. They can serve as a partner in dialogue and provide feedback. This process can be most helpful to an institution.

Consultants can function in a range of capacities, from "on-call advisor" to "project coordinator." The frequency and intensity of their use depends upon the resident resources of the institution. If the institution has adequate staff to execute the project and feels they are competent in cost analysis design, then they may wish to have a consultant review their project plan for consistency, viability, and conceptual integrity. If an institution lacks the internal resources and knowledge to put together a costing system, it may need the dedicated resources of an outside consultant to help with the project all the way from conceptualization through implementation. In this case consultants would serve as project coordinators as a supplement to management.

One of the advantages of utilizing consultants in "scoping" a project in its earliest stages is the benefit of their experience in installations of cost systems in other financial institutions.

Outside consultants can help in organizing and getting a project going. They can also serve as educators to the institution staff on costing methodologies, techniques, and systems. In the event of an organizational deadlock consultants can be used to get the project moving. Their role is to help management in whatever aspect of the project is deemed needful. In this context, consultants can advise and suggest a course of direction.

In using consultants it is best to obtain an understanding of what they will do and what they won't do. Agreed to hours and billing rates are essential. Accountability needs to be established early on. The institution's management should have a consultant project log with stated objectives, target dates, and estimated hours when the consultants are on-site. At a minimum there should be weekly progress reviews.

In selecting consultants, one should focus on their sensitivity to assisting, given the specialized needs of the institution, as opposed to a canned approach, which may or may not work. The larger a project is, the higher the cost will be. For large projects it is prudent to have more than one consulting firm review the proposed project and bid on it. Usually consultants are selected based on the overall impression the institution's management forms of the consultant's ability to conduct the project according to the bank's needs and budget constraints.

BUILDING A PROJECT TEAM

The institution with sufficient internal resources may wish to assemble a project team. One of the issues to be resolved is whether to create a project organization with full-time dedicated staff or to create a matrix organization with part-time resources being dedicated to the projects.

If a full-time dedicated staff is put on to the project, how many cost analysts, industrial engineers, and systems analysts should there be? Consultants can help assess project staffing needs. The existing cost analysis staff should become part of the team, even if only part-time. It is essential they be kept abreast of the project and its technology. If the project manager is separate from the cost analysis manager, there respective authority over the future system needs to be resolved early on.

If the project is matrix managed, then a clear commitment to objectives needs to be set forth to assure that other priorities that encroach upon the project from time to time will not hinder or delay it. The project manager should assume control of the project and give it direction, tracking the costs from the start.

Project Management

Project management is the process of administering all aspects of a working project. It involves the traditional management functions of planning, organizing, directing, controlling, and communicating.

Some of the things the project manager will get involved in during the early phases of the project include

- Seeking approval on procuring consultants

- Managing the consultants engagement

- Deciding the methodology (standard versus nonstandard) and recommending it for approval

- Organizing the project approach including the formulation of tasks and dependencies

- Determining resources needed

- Obtaining the resources needed

- Writing a project statement that sets forth the scope, parameters, perceived benefits, needed resources, and estimated cost of the project

- Ensuring that a detailed design is prepared for approval

- Preparing an impact analysis on other systems, projects, and organizations throughout the bank

- Evaluating the intended direction of the project as it pertains to the corporate goals

The process of managing a project is dynamic. As the environment is temporary, things are subject to change. A project manager must foster a high level of energy among the project team members. The manager must keep track of many things at the same time. With this as a backdrop there are three things a project manager must be aware of that can cause a project to fail. They are schedule slippages, cost over-runs, and performance deficiencies. One or all of these can jeopardize the effectiveness of a project. This is important to keep in mind as one contemplates a major project.

Let's look at some of the factors that can hinder the effectiveness of a project.

Lack of coordination of staff accountabilities.   An example of this would be several people going in different directions without purpose. The cure for this is to realign the accountabilities toward a focus on the common goal.

Lack of dedicated time. This is indicative of insufficient resource commitment. Part-time team members who don't have the time to devote to the project should be replaced.

Lack of proper planning. If this occurs the project is in jeopardy of aimless direction. It should be put into a holding pattern until its direction is planned. "Who is to do it?" and "When and how is it to be done?" need to be resolved.

Smokescreening of progress by the team members or manager. This can either be in the form of saying the project is progressing well when it isn't or by finding a scapegoat to blame when things go wrong. Weekly meetings and in-depth progress checks against plan are necessary in preventing this. Communication is essential.

Lack of monitoring the critical path. Essential dependencies need to be pinpointed and closely managed.

A change in project direction without a full integrative impact analysis. Afterthoughts that translate into appendixes and deletions can have a profound effect on the workability of a new system. What may seem as a simple change could become complex to the system. Be aware of the potential impact and test any changes against the original system design.

A lack of proper documentation. A procedure for documenting should be a priority.

A lack of project definition. The project must have a statement clearly describing what the system will do, won't do, and how it will do it. This should include estimates of both development and ongoing maintenance costs. How the project will be managed must be clearly stated.

There must be a way to measure progress and achievement against a plan. This is necessary for project control. Project control involves checking the target dates against schedule and the quality of the work and the costs incurred against plan. Project management essentially involves preparing a good project plan and a timetable for the project and then following them.

A good project plan includes

- A summary statement of the project's objectives

- A project schedule listing names, who is to do the tasks; dates with progress reviews, time for each task, and dependencies, and separate attachments describing each task in more detail

- Flowcharts

- A financial plan and analysis that details the total anticipated costs of the project.

Organizing the Cost Analysis Function

The need for cost analysis no matter the size of the institution has already been well established in this book. Given this need there are certain things to consider in setting up or reorganizing this function in order to meet a financial institution's needs.

This chapter offers helpful suggestions on staffing, writing a charter, communicating, and establishing a viable organization. With proper planning and organizational contact, the function will have a much better chance of success.

Smaller financial institutions that are just beginning this function have a unique opportunity to construct an overall framework that is integrative and flexible from the start.

The two major selling points for establishing a cost analysis and control function are that it allows definition of what it is costing to offer a particular service and consequent cost containment.

THE EFFECTIVE ORGANIZATION

For a cost analysis function to be effective it must serve the needs of the organization(s) it serves. This implies the need for feedback and continuous dialogue between cost analysis and user (client) base. If the manager considers his or her staff as internal consultants who are serving the needs of the institution, then the first hurdle of justifying their existence has been overcome.

It is not easy to manage a group of professionals, balance the needs of financial management with that of the client base, and continue monitoring the changes that are occurring throughout an institution. But these are all important maintenance factors that can add to the success of a cost analysis function.

The expectations of the user base must be served. These expectations change with time. They are a function of current management thinking and tenure, the institution's profitability status, its business plans, recent external development, the institution's goals, the institution's anticipatory posture, technology, and the competitive position in the marketplace.

"We've always done it this way" is a phrase that should never be uttered in a changing environment. As technology and the institution change, so must the cost analysis function.

The effective cost analysis organization is one that is

Alert and responsive to changes within the institution

Communicative

Innovative

Responsive to requests

Flexible and open

Clear in its charter and direction

Available

Supportive

Friendly

Accurate

Credible

In organizing and staffing a cost analysis function there are many things to consider. The size of the institution, its management style, centralization versus decentralization, and the mandate for the function are just a few of the things to be considered. Generally the larger the institution, the more specialized the cost analysis function will be. Conversely the smaller the institution the more integrated the function will be with that of similar functions. In smaller institutions cost analysis may be the mainstay of an overall analytical support function that generates management information both in studies and on a regular reporting basis.

The functions that are closely aligned to cost analysis in smaller institutions are financial analysis; work measurement; functional, organizational, and customer reporting and analysis; financial planning; and asset/liability management.

Since the duties of a staff member are manifold in a smaller institution, the staff must be flexible in their ability to switch project assignments many times during a brief period.

As an institution grows in size each of these functions usually matures and becomes a separate organization. It is during this maturation process that staffing becomes a challenge.

From the standpoint of a startup operation it becomes a matter of deciding what is to be done and evolving from there. This requires input from senior management. The more quantitatively oriented they are, the more focus there will be on the cost analysis function. This emphasis on quantitative data will obviously determine the direction of the function. A quantitative emphasis will call for reporting and analysis of special and unstructured projects in addition to routine and repetitive assignments. In institutions where there is little emphasis on quantitative analysis, the cost analysis function is usually given to a structured reporting mode. This presents little challenge to those who may be analytically oriented. Fewer institutions than ever are still in this mind-set however. With the increased challenges of financial services, senior management sees the ever increasing need for active decision information.

In some of the large institutions there is a question regarding centralization versus decentralization for the cost analysis function. In a centralized function usually one or both of the following occurs: headquarters cost analysis becomes a central policy-making function or it is a complete function that serves the whole institution and is organizationally and usually geographically integrated. If it is only a centralized policy-making function then there are probably decentralized costing efforts residing elsewhere in the institution.

In a decentralized environment the cost analysis function is usually divided up among the various income-producing organizations. The function then becomes specialized along the lines of the organization it serves. In this decentralized mode it usually becomes a financial control function for the organization, encompassing activities such as planning.

There are advantages and disadvantages to each type of organization. In a highly centralized cost analysis function, management has a high degree of control over policy and the priorities of support activity. In the centralized concept there is more coordinative control from a larger organizational standpoint. The staff is usually engaged in a breadth of specialized cost analysis activity. They become professional cost analysts as opposed to financial generalists. A centralized function lends itself more to a centralized and integrated cost accounting system. Staff is drawn from a pool of analysts for high-priority assignments.

In a decentralized function there tends to be an emphasis on specialized organizational support as opposed to the narrower scope of cost analysis activity. Decentralized cost analysis functions may experience varying degrees of autonomy depending upon their mandate from senior management. They may find themselves reporting to the central financial department on a dotted line basis. In this case it is a matter of either adhering to a set of policies and procedures or apprising the central department of their activities.

The advantages of having a decentralized function are an organizationally dedicated and oriented staff, more autonomy, a clearer mission, and less reporting layers for review. The disadvantages are a possible loss of perspective of the institution as a whole, variations in policy and procedures, and the possible loss of coordination in establishing information delivery systems.

Regardless of what is decided on the organizational composition of a cost analysis function, there is clearly a need for a charter. The charter needs to be established early in the formation of a new cost analysis function. The expectations of management should be clearly stated. This will probably involve polling the management of several departments as to their expectations. A clear distinction should be made between needs and wants. The charter should list the client organizations and what is to be done for them. In order to accomplish this, the journalistic "five W's" should be answered—who, what, when, where, why—and how.

Who is to do the cost analyses and for what departments?

What is the content and context of the function? That is, what activities shall the function perform? What are the circumstances under which these functions would be performed?

When shall key costings and reports be due? Or more appropriately, what is the frequency of costing, report generation, and major projects?

Where should the limits of this function be established organizationally, functionally, and geographically?

Why is this function being established? Are there specific needs in the organization that prompted its formation?

How is the function to be organized and staffed? What is the required staffing complement?

Organizing

The formal organization chart is a function of the character and the size of the institution. A smaller institution would find it advantageous to have a small pool of analysts with specific assignments rather than a segmented and departmentalized structure. The larger institution may find it best to structure and departmentalize their staff according to products or organizational functions.

ACCOUNTING VERSUS ANALYSIS

The core of cost analysis as a function is its cost accounting system. The system may not necessarily be a computer system. It may just be a formal procedure for the collection of cost data in the institution. Those performing cost analysis rely heavily on this system, whatever it is.

It is most important to have some formalized and comprehensive procedure for the gathering and processing of cost data. Cost accounting in financial institutions, however, is quite different from its counterpart in manufacturing (as explained in chapter 1). The costs in financial institutions are mostly period costs.

Whatever the cost accounting system is, it must tie or reconcile to the general ledger of the institution. It is wise to subordinate the cost accounting system to the general ledger system. Cost accounting should therefore be subordinate to and somewhat remote from the financial accounting system that is used for external reporting.

The issue of defining cost accounting as being in a management information system environment needs to be resolved early in the establishment of a conceptual framework for a cost accounting system. If it isn't, then there is room for much confusion and misunderstanding. However, this does not preclude establishment of a general ledger system with codes that prepare the data for cost accounting applications. What is being said here is the data should be fed to a second system, "cost accounting," for analysis and management reporting purposes. This allows for allocations and movement of data without any impairments to the integrity of the general ledger data.

Clearly, cost accounting data needs to be held in an environment that allows for subjective allocations and assignment of the data. Flexibility is needed whenever the elements of analysis are present. Cost accounting data exists for management decision-making purposes. Hence the need for the ability to juxtapose data at management's request. An institution's management is in need of the information that will allow them to properly evaluate the profitability of certain entities.

It cost accounting is a new function in an institution, it is best to start with a simple and easy to understand system. With time and experience, the system can be improved and expanded. Obviously the ideal system would be one that is automated; has organizational, product, and customer profitability ties; and is capable of showing the costs and profitability of every activity or product in the institution. Such systems are complex, costly. and time consuming to maintain, however.

A worthy alternative is a modular approach, building each module of a new system toward an integrated complement. The cost analyst can realize, and be recognized for, small successes along the way when a modular approach is taken.

Staffing

Staffing should be accomplished with the thought of providing growth and development opportunities. The complement a manager should seek is one that provides optimal utilization of resources. A manager may hire less experienced staff in whom growth potential is evident. But if anticipating organizational growth, the manager may be wise to hire experienced staff. Applicants attracted to analysis are usually looking for growth opportunities and challenges; the manager needs to provide these while getting the job done.

A particular challenge for the manager pertains to retention of staff. Turnover is costly and disruptive. Hence staff retention is an important consideration. Turnover is usually due to the high visibility of cost analysts. God analysts are in high demand by managers elsewhere in the institution. Hence an element of competition.

First let's look at the qualities that are imperative. There are three qualities to look for in hiring staff: analytical skills, communicative skills (oral and written), and human relations skills. The absence of any one of these may cause the analyst difficulty in interfacing with other organizations and consequently in completing projects. The use of these criteria should result in a higher success rate on hiring capable and productive staff.

Experienced candidates should have an analytical background in their work experience. Sometimes a person's mix of work experience and academic background will show if he or she has been progressing in the analytical realm.

The level and nature of the assignments needs to be made clear at this juncture. Is the work you are offering going to be routine and repetitive? Or is it unstructured? Is it simple or complex? A proper fit of the person to the job results in a more balanced organization.

Sometimes it is difficult to find candidates who have costing experience within a financial institution. A search for new staff may involve finding people from other industries. The common denominators should be an analytical orientation and possession of quantitative skills. In a multiple staff setting the manager may realize the benefits of a hybrid team. This would provide a capability of responding to a breadth of projects.

Once the staff member is hired, it is suggested the manger map out a career strategy with him or her. Show a genuine interest in the staff member's career progression and personal development. A person who is made to feel important will find it easier to identify with an organization and its goals.

Hiring Checklist

Look for the following qualities in the candidate for a cost analyst position.

Independence. Self-starter with little need for supervision and guidance.

Ability to grasp and assume control of situations that are inherently unclear, to sort out and arrange facts and discern the relevant details.

Analytical orientation. Original thinking, mental synthesis; synergism with others; mental organization; good judgment.

Good human relations. Sensitivity and empathy with others, trustworthiness; professionalism.

Communication skill in speech and writing.

WRITING THE CHARTER

The purpose and scope of the cost analysis function is made clearer through the development of a charter. In determining the purpose and charter for cost analysis the following may prove useful.

Try to determine senior management's perspective regarding the usefulness of cost data. The following basic questions should be answered at a minimum.

Is senior management numbers oriented?
(That is, do they have an orientation toward detailed quantitative data?)

Where is their current focus?
(Where are they concentrating their resources?)

What are their needs in terms of information for decision making?

Prepare a list of desired results for the cost analysis function from these surveys. This list should be compiled in such a way that those items mentioned most frequently will be taken as priority. Survey all other potential users of cost data. Determine their needs.

Based on the organization of the institution, income center, and cost center reporting accountabilities are to be established. It is important to define those organizations for whom you will be analyzing and reporting data.

Survey the present information systems. Determine if the information systems are adequate and in line with the cost analysis charter. Determine volume or unit measurement availability. Do they readily align to product descriptions? Are there any information limitations to costing the various products and services? If so, make a wish list and let it be known. Enlist the help of those who are supportive and are in a position to influence change.

If you don't have a pricing committee try to get one organized and functioning (see chapter 14).

Communication Is Key

It is very important to establish a mutual dialogue with those who have an impact on the cost analysis function. In a positive sense specific needs should be communicated to those who will be providing information and support to cost analysis. On the user side a list of expectations is drawn up after discussions with them. These initial contacts are to set the stage for future working relationships.

In as short a time as possible try to cost-justify your function's existence. This can be accomplished by developing and producing meaningful management information. This may have to be on a summary level at first with the proviso that you will supply more detailed analyses at a later date. Focus on areas that have never been quantified before but listed as a priority by senior management. Be prepared, however, for some contention. Some organizations simply refuse to allow "outsiders" into their area for study. A skilled manager will attempt to defuse this by conveying the benefits of management information to the departmental management. For smaller institutions this is not necessarily a problem.

Align your product costings with the schedule of fees. This will allow visibility on the profitability of individual products and convey a sense of profit accountability.

Establishing Credibility

Credibility is established with a good communication process as a backdrop. The most obvious basis for credibility is the numbers themselves. Accurate quantitative research and presentation is of paramount importance.

This whole process requires review and feedback. It also requires openness and flexibility to accept suggestions. If the process of research and presentation is well thought out and presented according to expectations, then credibility will follow naturally. If, however, management has doubts about research, presentation, and consistency, then devote some effort to rethinking the process and making adjustments as necessary. Often questions by users indicate their need for some explanation of the methodologies of cost analysis. If this is the case then by all means present an explanation of methodologies and approach.

Potential Roadblocks

As in any organizational startup there are going to be roadblocks. Some can be prevented by establishing clear lines of authority and work accountabilities. As a new organization begins, others may view it as diminishing their own authority and accountabilities. This possible encroachment view no doubt gives cause for concern to some. Some institutions have two or three different sets of numbers quantifying the same function or products. Clearly this is inefficient. One organization needs to be sanctioned as having numerical authority for cost data. Often it is the cost analysts. They are generally the ones who research, develop, and present the cost data. This may also hold true for profitability reporting for major organizations, product lines, and customers.

Clarifications like these need to be resolved at higher levels. The pros and cons need to be discussed. There should be no gray areas lest confusion exist. The bottom line is to have a working relationship of exchanging information with other departments within the institution, one that is complementary and complimentary. This can occur if issues are resolved to attain higher purposes and clout is given less emphasis.

The Expectations of Operating Management

In measuring tasks for product costing the analyst finds an interesting paradox. Operating management has a vested interest in allowing sufficient time for each task. But those who market and manage the products are interested in seeing that each product is delivered at the lowest possible cost without deterioration of quality.

Operating management expects their activities to be properly measured and reported. This requires much discussion, research, and review with the assigned cost analyst.

The operating departments would also like to see as little disruption as possible during the research phase of the costing effort. This requires courtesy. The idea is to realize the benefits of collaboration. The analyst thereby may receive the best available information in the most effective and efficient manner.

The Expectations of Product Management

This function is new to many banks. It is centered around the concept of having a person assigned as manager of a specific product. The product manager, as this person is called, then sees to it that all operational, marketing, and pricing tasks on behalf of a product are running smoothly and are in conformance with an overall strategy.

Product managers have several information needs. They need to know the revenue, expense, and activity of each product for which they are accountable. They look to cost analysis for reports that would contain this information.

It is essential to develop an understanding and appreciation for product management's own mandate. At the same time, cost analysis as an organization must be accurate, consistent, and objective in reporting data on products. Product management relies heavily on cost analysis for decision information. Often cost analysis is called upon to explain product management's financial statements to the pricing committee and senior management. In light of this fact product management or marketing is probably one of the heaviest users of cost analysis data.

The Expectations of Senior Management

Cost analysis plays a part in providing senior management with decision information. The degree of provision depends upon the size and organizational structure of the bank. In the smaller financial institutions there tends to be a very direct line of access between senior management and the analyst.

Senior management has a need for information that is accurate and representative enough so as to place them into receiving the proper knowledge. To the extent that potential decisions can be quantified, such information should be made available to them.

The high level of visibility that cost analysis data receives makes it essential that it be readily explainable, logical, and easy to understand.

Setting Up a New Function

Many smaller financial institutions, as they experience growth, eventually face the challenges of establishing some sort of cost analysis function. The formalization usually comes about when the controller finds he or she has no more time to devote to special studies and is getting behind on internal profitability reporting by responsibility center.

At this juncture the controller may simple delegate monthly worksheets, schedules, and reports to the nearest able body. But as a financial institution grows and continues to face the pressures of the marketplace, it becomes essential to have a cost analysis function.

In the beginning it may be only a person devoting part of his or her time toward this kind of work. The idea is to start somewhere. It is just as important for a small institution to know how much it is costing them to do business in a certain area as it is for a large institution.

The cost analysis function in a medium-sized institution may well a carryover from the earlier days when the institution was much smaller. If this is the case then management should consider the merits of upgrading the function to face the increased complexity and meet its challenges.

The process of establishing cost analysis as a formal function involves a number of considerations. Many of them have already been mentioned in this chapter. However, the following is a checklist of what to do and how to set up a cost analysis function in a smaller to medium-sized institution.

- Decide what is to be done. Outline a charter and get it approved.

- Given the charter, determine the staffing level needed. Also determine the skills desired in positions to be filled.

- Decide on the methodology to be employed, such as standard or actual. No matter how basic it is, a "system" needs to be established. This does not necessarily mean it should be computerized or automated. What is does mean is it should be consistent and systematic in approach.

- Start a pricing committee if none exists (see chapter 14).

- Design cost and profitability reports.

- Determine who is to receive the output from cost analysis.

These are the imperatives to consider in starting up a cost analysis function. The process entails much thought and discussion in addition to action.

17

Summary of Cost Analysis

Cost analysis is an important function to have in a financial institution. It is a central core for the gathering and distribution of meaningful management information. It also helps management discover and act upon opportunities for profit.

This final chapter is intended to provide an overall summary and wrap-up of the concepts presented in this textbook. The intent of presenting this material was to provide tools to those performing cost studies. One must be flexible in adapting these tools to his or her own environment—there is no one best way of performing cost analyses. The approach selected depends on management philosophy, the information systems in place, and the desired outcome.

REVIEW OF MAJOR CONCEPTS AND IDEAS

Cost Analysis in Financial Institutions

Many of the concepts and processes of the manufacturing environment are applicable to costing in the service environment. There are differences however. Manufacturing costing has reached a high level of sophistication and standardization. By necessity manufacturers must have a viable cost system. Their external reporting requires it. By contrast financial institutions use cost data for internal management information purposes only.

In recent years financial institutions have come to realize how important it is to have a cost analysis function. At the same time they have recognized that manufacturing costing concepts and procedures can go only so far in application to financial institution costing. For example, financial institutions do not have an inventory to carry as do manufacturers. Financial institutions, therefore, are essentially working with period costs. Their inventory is almost instantaneous. Cost analysis in financial institutions tends to be more analytical than the cost accounting of manufacturing. It is perhaps because it is more challenging (and more satisfying) to work on the conceptual level that cost analysis in financial institutions has risen to the status of a profession in recent years.

Costing Concepts

There are basically two kinds of concepts or methodologies used in cost analysis. They are actual (average item) costing; and standard costing. All others are essentially variations of these two.

Actual (average item) costing is used when no standard data is available. It is easier to develop and maintain than standard costing is. Unit costs are determined by dividing the total cost by the associated volume.

Standard costing is prescriptive, relying on benchmark data to determine what the cost *should* be.

Remember that there is no one best way to structure costs. What is good for one institution may not be appropriate for another. Therefore, the concepts and procedures are adapted to fit the needs of an individual institution.

Work Measurement Techniques

Work is measured in estimating how long a task takes to perform or how long it should take. The method most often used is called *time ladders* because it breaks a worker's day into work segments (ladders). The intent is to capture time allocations related to specific tasks. The tasks are then built into activities for costing purposes, which are folded into the costing of products.

There are predetermined, more precise methods that rely on basic body movements for time allocation purposes. These methods require training and experience in order to accurately use and apply them. They take more time to work with than time ladders. But in certain situations they are more accurate. They are only useful in measuring routine and repetitive tasks.

Data Processing Costing

A financial institution's data processing center provides a number of services to the entire organization. Many institutions try to control their expenses by developing unit costs for the services provided. They in turn develop a transfer pricing procedure that charges the users for their share of the services utilized.

Capacity levels for costing are often hard to set in DP costing. Transfer pricing can either be set at cost or at time level other than cost. The idea is to provide services to the users at a reasonable cost while at the same time recouping a significant portion of the data processing center's costs.

Allocation Concepts and Systems

An important aspect in costing is the use of allocation procedures. Allocations are used on applying overhead and other indirect expenses. They are also used in allocating indirect or shared revenue. They are developed by the use of bases or concepts.

Commonly used bases for allocating expenses include staff count, square footage occupied, percentage of total expenses, and percentage of total revenue. Commonly used bases for allocating revenue include time spent, balances, and previous percentage of total revenue.

Allocating expenses for development of an institutionwide general and administrative overhead rate provides some interesting challenges. The first challenge is to make the basis of allocation understandable to the users. The second challenge is integrity and accuracy of data. The third is the data's relevancy. These are three distinct and definitive hurdles to overcome in developing an expense allocation system.

Organizational Profitability Reporting

This is the first element of the triad of organizational, product, and customer profitability reporting, which should tie or be reconcilable to one another at the bottom line. Few financial institutions have been able to achieve this. Small financial institutions have a distinct advantage in being able to design their reporting systems from the ground up with the aim of achieving this reconciliation. For medium to large financial institutions, it is an expensive proposition.

In organizational profitability reporting the profitability of each revenue-generating organization is reported. The items to report include revenue, expense, applicable balances, and activity.

Product Profitability Reporting

As costs are aligned to products, revenue must also be aligned to products. This tells management which products are profitable. They can use this information to form an overall strategy for the marketplace and to set prices.

Customer Profitability Reporting

Commercial customer reporting is more prevalent than is consumer customer reporting, perhaps because it is important to be able to review the total relationship these large customers have with the institution. The institution needs to know which accounts are profitable and which aren't.

Customer information profiles provide useful data for selling more services to the same customers. As the financial services industry becomes more deregulated, it will have more products to offer consumer customers. With marketing profiles of customers, a bank can target products.

The Essentials of Decision Information

The complexity and unstructured nature of cost analysis becomes apparent as the analyst compiles and arranges information for decision making on a proposed project. Assumptions need to be made and tested. "What it?" kinds of analyses need to occur. The risks of a proposed project have to be quantified. The cash flow and ultimate return to the bank should be determined. The analyst is challenged to make the data meaningful.

The Cost Study Process

There are several things that occur in conducting a costing project. The relevant information on revenue, expense, balances, and activity is gathered and arranged into a logical format. Usually the first step involves aligning expenses on an organizational basis. Following this the information is arranged according to functions. Last, the information is arranged as a subset of the functions. This information is aligned to activities or products. The final result should be meaningful and valid information that accurately reflects the cost and profitability of the organizations, products, and customers being studied.

Cost Control and Expense Planning

Staff compensation is a significant area of cost for most financial institutions. Controlling compensation requires a budget system that allows for plans to be compared to actual occurrences. Equivalencies and impacts should be taken into consideration. They are important in determining what is affecting the compensation changes in an institution. Cost control of other operating expenses sometimes is a matter of requiring approval and a check against what is wanted versus what is needed.

Product Management and Pricing

As some financial institutions grow and expand products, they find it necessary to have some form of consistent pricing and management of their products. For small financial institutions it may be an ad hoc committee of senior management. For the larger financial institutions it may be a formal organization.

Pricing is the financial institution's strategy for positioning each of its product offerings in the marketplace. The presence of such strategies could result in more revenue and realized opportunities in the marketplace.

Designing, Building, and Implementing a New Cost Accounting System

As financial institutions grow and as they change in areas of emphasis there are times when change in management reporting is needed. The change may be the start up of a cost analysis function, or it may be a major overhaul of an existing system when new or different information is needed. A system is antiquated when it can no longer serve the needs of the major recipients of the information.

Among the most important considerations whether starting up a cost analysis function or revamping an obsolete one is whether the cost of producing the new information is justified.

It is advisable to proceed with caution when it comes to the complexity of a system. It may be better to start out with a basic system that has much flexibility for change and growth than to try to do everything at once.

Organizing the Cost Analysis Function

Banks that are starting a cost analysis function will find it best to write a charter outlining what the function will do. The function needs to be clearly defined and staff levels and experience decided, and goals set.

Some aspects of costing are complex and unstructured; others are routine and structured. It is important to match the person to the task in this respect. Cost analysis assignments require three basic individual skills: oral and written communicative, analytical, and human relations.

Summary

The role of cost analysis in financial institutions is integral to the process of effective management. The information produced and analyzed provides an institution's management with valuable decision information. Cost and profitability information on the triad of organizational, product, and customers is essential to mapping the direction of an institution and its marketing efforts.

Cost analysis has emerged as a profession out of necessity. This new profession faces welcome challenges in the changing, more competitive financial services environment.

Glossary

Absorption costing — The process of accounting for both direct and indirect expenses in conducting a costing project, also includes accounting for overhead as a cost component.

Account analysis — The accumulation of information on a customer's account, includes activity, charges, balances, and surplus funds credits.

Activity — The lowest level of processing at which a standard unit cost is developed.

Activity based costing (ABC) — A cost system that establishes cost pool related to individual cost drivers.

Actual cost — The capturing of all relevant costs associated with an entity being costed, usually on a full-absorption basis (based on a given volume level).

Actual hours — The total staff hours consumed in completion of a task.

Allocation — Apportionment of revenue, costs, or balances to organizations, product lines, or customers for management reporting purposes, based on logical concepts.

Allowance — A factor, either time or percentage, added to the normal time to complete a task to account for personal, fatigue, and delay time.

Approved price — A price set or established by management or a pricing committee.

Average item cost — Total relevant costs divided by a specified volume.

Average item costing (AIC) — The process of putting actual costs on a per item basis.

Balance deficiency — The absence of sufficient balances from a customer to compensate for the price associated with the use of a service provided to the customer by the financial institution.

Budget — A quantified and predetermined course of action in the form of a financial plan.

Capacity costs — The costs necessary in order to provide processing capability above a given level, viewed by some as a fixed cost.

CIF — Customer information file.

Clean time — Time estimates used for relative value factor development.

COF — Cost of funds, interest expense based on a specified rate, time, and amount.

COM — Computer output microform, either microfiche or microfilm.

Compensating balance — A specific balance level maintained as part of a loan agreement or as payment for services used.

Computer program — A set of instructions ordered sequentially directing a computer to perform a specific set of tasks.

Contribution margin — A point at which profits are measured above the line from overhead, usually referenced as the contribution to overhead and profit.

Controllable cost — An expenditure that can be incurred or denied by a bank's management.

Cost accounting (or cost analysis) — The quantification of cost data for organizational product and customer reporting.

Cost accounting (or cost analysis) system — A management information system that provides cost and profitability data useful for making decisions on organizational evaluation, product innovation, pricing, planning, cost control, transfers, allocations, and customer relationship management.

Cost center (responsibility center) — The lowest organizational level for which costs are tracked.

Cost control — The process of cost containment through review and approval procedures. A systematic approach to cost containment through analysis of both planned and incurred expenditures.

Cost object — The result of aggregating expenses toward an activity or product with a value.

Cost driver — The causal relationship between the incurence of cost and activities.

CPU — Central (data) processing unit, directs and performs the basic functions of the computer.

Cross-selling — Selling additional products to customers.

DASD — Direct access storage device, provides direct access to data in computer.

Data base — Information stored systematically and accessibly by a computer system.

Deposit credit — An allowance for funds on deposit, a memo of credit given rather than interest paid; based on a specified rate, time, and principal.

Direct costs — Costs integral to the process being measured, tracked directly (not allocated).

Disk — A magnetic storage medium that allows for random access of information.

Disk drive — A mechanical device that spins a disk; uses electronic controls (signals) to copy information onto a disk from the computer, and to retrieve information from the disk into the computer's memory.

DP — Data processing, automated, electronic.

Earning assets (funds using) — The placing of funds on the asset side of a bank's balance sheet. (Examples include business loans—domestic and international; consumer loans—direct and indirect, secured and unsecured; real estate loans—conventional, FHA, VA; securities—investment and trading accounts; and lease financing—leverage and financing.)

Economic value added — The determination as to whether an activity is adding value to the production process.

EDP — Electronic data processing. See DP.

Effectiveness — Achieving the desired results.

Efficiency — Ratio of actual performance to prescribed performance.

Estimated actual — Use of year-to-date historical or actual data for a portion of a year as a means of forecasting for the remainder of the year, similar to annualizing actual data.

EXCP — Execute command program.

Fee waiver — A concession of not charging the stated price for a service rendered.

File — Information stored on a computer's magnetic disk.

Financial Management For Data Processing — A professional organization devoted to expanding knowledge of Financial Management in the Data Processing environment.

Fixed cost — A cost category for which total costs are at the same level regardless of volume increase or decreases.

Flowchart — A graphic depiction of a flow of work or data.

Float — An uncollected balance, e.g., checks and other instruments in transit or in the process of collection; the difference between the ledger balance and the collected balance for the same item.

Frequency analysis — The process of adding quantitative weights to time factors or volumes for an equitable distribution of a task's time consumption, often a ratio of a dependency factor (task) to a determinant factor (major task).

Full absorption — A cost that contains all relevant and conceivable direct and indirect expenses, includes overhead allocations.

Functional reporting — Classifying revenue, costs, or balances according to a predetermined organizational function such as wholesale or retail banking.

Funds pool — A common pool of internal funds available for redistribution elsewhere in the bank.

G&A — General and administrative expense, usually a reference to overhead burden.

Hard dollar costs — Costs incurred on an invoice basis; out-of-pocket costs resulting in a cash flow.

Hard dollar revenue — Revenue that is accrued or accounted for on the general ledger.

Hardware — The mechanical components of a computer system, includes central circuitry and peripheral equipment such as modems, printers, and monitors.

Historical averaging — The process of comparing relationships of previously recorded data in order to draw inferences on the measurement of tasks.

HVA factor — Holidays, vacations, and absences factor, used only in costing projects that are of an individual nature rather than a whole processing center, applied against gross paid hours as opposed to net available hours.

Imputed cost — A cost that is not presently accounted for on an explicit basis, but can exist on a implied basis.

Incremental approach — The difference between two alternative values on a comparative basis; also the additional value of one course of action over another.

Incremental cost — The net difference in cost between two alternatives; costs that occur as a result of additional activity.

Incremental revenue — The net difference in revenue between two alternatives; revenue that occurs as a result of additional activity.

Indirect cost — Costs that are not of a direct nature in the production of a service or activity but are supportive.

Indirect non-specific costs — Indirect costs that cannot be specifically identified with a product or activity.

Indirect specific costs — Indirect costs that can be specifically identified with a product or activity.

Interface — The linking of two systems together for the purpose of data transfer.

I/O — Input/output.

LIBOR — London interbank offered rate.

Line function — A revenue-producing organization.

Managed costs — Costs that are within the authority of a manager to incur or deny; discretionary costs.

MAP — Marketing action plan, a strategic and integrative approach to marketing a product on a pro-active basis.

Marginal cost — The cost of producing additional units of volume in a processing or operational area.

Marginal income — The net income derived from additional units of a service (product); revenue minus cost.

Market segmentation — A systematic analysis of the marketplace whereby demographics and industry and customer profiles are used to target products.

Memory — The storage capacity of a computer.

MICR — Magnetic identification code recognition.

Microfiche — A microfilm of a document.

Mixed cost — A cost that contains both fixed and variable components.

Modem — Modulate/demodulate device, converts signals from a computer for use on phone lines and also from phone lines to a computer.

Monitor — A television screen for displaying computer data, a cathode ray tube (CRT).

MVS — Multiple virtual storage, an extension of an operating system (IBM).

NABCA — *(A.K.A. National Association for Bank Cost and Management Accounting)*; an association of professional practitioners of cost analysis and management accounting in financial institutions.

Natural value unit(NVU) — A unit of volume measurement that is compatible with a process being measured.

Negative spread — The result of a cost-of-funds rate exceeding a revenue yield rate.

Noncontrollable costs — Assigned or allocated costs such as overhead.

Normal (average) capacity — The level of processing or production that will satisfy the average demand over time, includes allowance factors for seasonal fluctuations.

Normal time — The amount of time it should take an experienced or trained person to complete a specific task. (See also *Standard time.*)

Operating system — The software that allows for operations to commence in a computer system; input/output, accounting, storage assignment, scheduling, debugging, and data management.

Organization chart — A schematic representation of reporting relationships and functional accountabilities.

Out-of-pocket costs — Costs that represent a necessary outflow of cash in order to compensate for an associated resource utilization.

Overhead — Costs that are remote from the production of a service, usually administrative and institutional expenses.

Overrecovery of costs — The excess amount of cost recouped in applying rates for recovery; the difference between the amount recovered and amount incurred.

PCI — Program-controlled interruption.

Peripheral — Any device that is connected to a computer; e.g., modems, printers, and disk drives.

Planning — The process of determining a course of action prior to its consummation.

Practical capacity — The maximum level at which a processing area or hardware configuration can realistically operate.

Price concession — Any deviation from the approved price, includes fee waivers and discounts.

Product — The lowest level at which revenues are reported.

Product cost — The per unit cost of a product as it is delivered to customer.

Productivity — In work measurement, the ratio of output to input, an indicator of efficiency; the measurement of performance against a standard; standard hours ÷ actual hours; effective and optimal use and output of all factors of production, especially the human factor.

Product group — A group of related product lines; the highest level of reporting.

Product line — A group of products.

Product management — A function that oversees a product's operational, marketing, and pricing tasks.

Price concession — Any deviation from the approved price, includes fee waivers and discounts.

Profitability reporting — The reporting of revenue, costs, and other relevant data on organizations, products, and customers.

Pro forma — A quantitive forecast, projection, or restatement of a business plan.

Quantity variance — (See *Volume variance*).

Rate variance — The difference between actual costs incurred and standard or planned costs.

Relative values — A work analysis technique that relies on the use of relative weights for work or processing performed; used for tasks, activities, and products compared with the unit lowest in processing time, which has a value of 1.0.

Relevant cost — Costs that apply to the project, product, or entity being studied.

Relevant range — A band of measurement that is closely aligned to the data being studied.

Residual cost — The difference between a predetermined cost and an actual cost.

Responsibility accounting — A management information system that tracks and reports revenue, costs, and other relevant data on an organizational basis.

Resources (funds, sources) — On the liability land equity side of a financial institution's balance sheet. (Examples include demand deposits—business and personal checking; savings deposits—interest-bearing savings accounts; time deposits—CD's; borrowed money-placements from other banks; capital and equity).

Self-logging — A work analysis technique that relies on the employee to indicate his or her time devoted to each task of accountability during a specified time span.

Sequential closeout — Allocation or transfer-out of expenses by allocating departments in a sequence to other departments as they close out their expenses.

SIC — Standard Industrial Classification.

Simultaneous closeout — Allocation or transfer-out of expenses by all providing departments (service departments) as they all close out their expenses at the same time.

Soft dollar costs — Allocated costs of an indirect nature such as overhead.

Soft dollar revenue — Opportunity revenue, which is not accrued or collected as cash.

Software — Computer programs.

Spending variance — The difference between the amount budgeted and the amount incurred.

Spread — The difference between the revenue yield and the cost of funds related to a specific balance; expressed as a percentage.

Standard cost — A prescriptive or predetermined cost initially expressed on a per unit basis.

Standard time — A measured, predetermined unit of time that prescribes how long it should take in order to complete a specific task; includes allowance factors.

Strategy — A definitive, comprehensive, and long-range approach to the conceptualization and resolution of a goal.

Support areas — Organizational entities that provide indirect participation in the production of a product or activity.

SUT — Standard unit time. (See *Standard time.*)

Tactical — A short-term approach to the conceptualization and resolution of a goal.

Task — The level at which a standard unit time is developed.

Task list — A work measurement identifier that documents and describes the tasks in a particular function.

Theoretical capacity — The absolute limits of processing capability for an operation area or for equipment with no allowances for downtime.

Time allowance — A decimal factor added to the normal time to complete a job; contingency for personal needs, fatigue, and unavoidable delay.

Time ladders — A work measurement process that accounts for a worker's time by time segments. (See *Self-logging*.)

Transfer price — The price charged by one providing organization to its internal client or user base.

Unbundling — The separation of products and services from one another for pricing purposes.

Underrecovery — The shortfall in cost recoupment in applying rates for recovery.

Unit cost — The total cost related to a defined unit of output.

Variable cost — A cost accumulation that varies as a function of volume or activity.

VM — Virtual machine, a time share application that allows for multiple use from remote terminals.

Volume variance — Variance from anticipated, prescribed, or planned level of volume.

Bibliography

BOOKS

Belasco, Kent S., *Analyzing Bank Staffing Levels,* Chicago: Probus Publishing Co., 1991.

Belasco, Kent S., *Earnings Enhancement Handbook for Financial Institutions,* Chicago: Probus Publishing Co., 1991.

Belasco, Kent S., *Bank Productivity,* Chicago: Probus Publishing Co., 1990.

Cole, Leonard P., *Management Accounting for Financial Institutions,* Chicago: Probus Publishing Co., 1994.

Jannott, Paul F., *Improving Bank Profits,* Chicago: Probus Publishing Co., 1993.

Johnson, Hazel J., *Strategic Capital Budgeting,* Chicago: Probus Publishing Co., 1994.

Koeb, Gary W., *Retail Fee Income Opportunities,* Chicago: Probus Publishing Co., 1993.

Nolan, Richard L., *Management Accounting & Control of Data Processing,* Institute of Management Accounting, Montvale, N.J., 1990.

Nowesnich, Mary, *Relationship Marketing,* Chicago: Probus Publishing Co., 1993.

Quinlan, Terence A., *EDP Cost Accounting,* New York: Wiley, 1989.

Sachs, William S. and Frank Elston, *The Information Technology Revolution in Financial Services*, 300 pp, (1-55737-385-5), Chicago: Probus Publishing Co., 1994.

Santoro, Nicholas J., *Bank Operations Management*, Chicago: Probus Publishing Co., 1992.

Smith, Robert F., *A Purchasing Policy Manual for Banks*, Chicago: Probus Publishing Co., 1989.

Swords, Williams E., *Managing Float in the Banking Industry*, Chicago: Probus Publishing Co., 1991.

PERIODICALS

Anonymous. Some Ways to Generate Noninterest Income. *ABA Banking Journal* 82, no. 6 (June 1990): 18, 20.

Bream, Robert W. Cut Expenses Before You Add or Raise Fees. *Credit Union Executive* 30, no. 2 (Summer 1990): 36-39.

Britt, Phil. Building fee income. *Savings & Community Banker* 2, no. 3 (March 1993): 22-29.

Canner, Glenn B.; Varvel, Walter A. Revitalizing the Fed's Functional Cost Analysis. *Bank Management* 67, no. 2 (February 1991): 46-47.

Cates, David C. Measuring Fee Income Profitability. *Bank Management* 66, no. 12 (December 1990): 48-50.

Dyche, David B., Jr. A Road Map for Increased Profitability. *Bankers Magazine* 175, no. 5 (September/October 1992): 47-51.

Foster, Bill. Fees Modify Behavior. *Credit Union Magazine* 57, no. 10 (October 1991): 64-65.

Goodison, Nicholas. Banking services and their cost to customers. *Banking World* 11, no. 5 (May 1993): 25.

Harrington, Joseph. Boosting Fee Income Adds Up in Dollars—And Sense. *Savings Institututions* 112, no. 1 (January 1991): 26-27.

Holland, Kelley. Banking on fees. *Business Week* no. 3301 (January 18, 1993): 72-73.

March, Robert T. Weighing the Options of Bank Compensation—Fees vs. Balances. *Corporate Controller* 4, no. 6 (July/August 1992): 20-24.

Masonson, Leslie N. Bank pricing study provides useful yardstick. *Healthcare Financial Management* 47, no. 5 (May 1993): 146-148.

Samel, Ben R.; Henthorne, Tony L.; Warren, Trudy C. A process for determining an ATM pricing strategy. *Journal of Retail Banking* 15, no. 2 (Summer 1993): 25-29.

Svare, J. Christopher. Focus on Fees, Cost Controls Should Keep Bank Profit Steady. *Bank Management* 68, no. 9 (September 1992): 44-48.

Symons, Paula. Fee vs. Free. *Credit Union Management* 14, no. 2 (February 1991): 22-24, 35.

van der Velde, Marjolijn. Profitability Analysis. *Bank Management* 66, no. 12 (December 1990): 64-65.

White, Phillip D. Five Cornerstones for Increasing Fee Income in the 1990s. *Bottomline* 7, no. 3 (March 1990): 29-31.

Wheatley, Edward W. The CFO's Perspective on Commercial Bank Service Charges Implications for Relationship Management. *Journal of Professional Services Marketing* 6, no. 1 (1990): 109-118.

Index

A

ABC system, 40
Activity-based costing, 40
Activity burden rate, 95
Activity points, 49
Actual costs, 9
Actual hours, 42
Administration, average item costing of, 76-77
Advertising, 283
AIC. *See* Average item costing
Allocation(s), 145-66, 331
  determination of bases or concepts, 153
  expense, 152-53
  funding, 146-50
  general and administrative expense
    rates (overhead), 159-62
  general issues of, 162-63
  and general ledger, 145
  issues, 162-63
  revenue, 150-52
Amortization, 30, 136
Analysis charges, 2
Automation, 242
Automobiles, 278
Average item costing, 11-12, 57-88, 314
  administrative function example, 76-77
  checklist for, 73-74

complete product example, 78-79
concept of, 57
consistency in costing and tracking, 11-12
cost-volume relations in, 79-83
data types, 74-76
for data processing, 125
nonstandard techniques, 84-88, 314
practical levels in, 75-76
processing area example, 58-73
pros and cons, 88
sequences and steps in, 58

B

Budgeted data, 75

C

Capacity planning, 116
Capital purchases/leasing, 276-79
Cash flow, of hard dollars, 26
Central processing unit, 117, 124
Chargeback systems, 141
Charitable contributions, 276, 284
Clean times, 49
Collection, 285
Commercial (corporate) banking and
  services, 3-4

checklist for, 108
concept of, 89-92
current data in, 109
disadvantages of, 114
elements of, 91-92
estimated actual data in, 109
frequency analysis in, 90-91
planned or budgeted data in, 110
processing area example, 93-109
standard times in, 90
variance analysis in, 110-12
volume counts in, 112
work measurement and, 41
Standard costs, 9
Standard Industrial Code, 204
Standard time, 42
    activity-aligned, 90
Standard unit time, 97
Stationery and supplies, 282
Steady state, 112
Stopwatch methods, 42-43, 53-55
Subscriptions, 285
Subsidiary companies, 4

T

Telecommunications, 282
Time allowances, 42, 92
Time ladders, 43, 44, 330
Time measurement units, 56
Total costs, 29, 70
Transfer pricing, 119, 137-41
Travel authorization form, 283
Travel expenses, 284
Tuition reimbursement, 285

U

Unit cost identification, 29
Unit point dollar value, 50

V

Variable costs, 29
Variance analysis, 110-12
Volume measurements, 24, 122
Volume variances, 144

W

Workload definitions, 133
Work measurement, 41-56, 330
    historical averaging, 42
    methods time measurement, 56
    predetermined time standards, 55-56
    relative values, 44, 46-51
    self-logging or time ladders, 44-45
    stopwatch, 53-55
    work sampling, 52-53
Work sampling, 43, 52-53

Z

Zero-based budgeting, 287-90

About the Author

Lenoard P. Cole, a consultant to financial institutions, lives near San Diego, California. He specializes in performance measurement, executive information and control reporting, profit improvement, cost and profitability reporting, and management accounting issues.

As senior manager for Price Waterhouse, Mr. Cole was the management accounting national product manager for their financial services product group. He directed cost accounting, profitability measurement and management information reporting projects.

Before becoming a consultant, Mr. Cole was a vice president of a large West Coast bank where he managed several financial administration functions including cost analysis, financial analysis, and international planning and reporting. He also served as a senior staff member in asset/liability management.

A frequent speaker, Mr. Cole has spoken at several conferences, including the Council on International Banking (CIB), Bank Administration Institute (BAI), the National Commercial Finance Association (NCFA), and the National Association for Bank Cost and Management Accounting (aka NABCA).

He is a faculty member at the University of Southern California, the University of Phoenix and California State University at San Marcos. He holds B.S. and M.B.A. degrees from the University of Southern California. He is also the author of *Management Accounting for Financial Institutions*.